# FABIAN ESSAYS IN SOCIALISM

# FABIAN ESSAYS IN SOCIALISM

*by* G. Bernard Shaw    Sidney Webb

William Clarke    Sydney Olivier

Graham Wallas    Annie Besant

Hubert Bland

Edited by

G. BERNARD SHAW

GLOUCESTER, MASS.

PETER SMITH

1967

# PREFACE

The essays in this volume were prepared last year as a course of lectures for delivery before mixed audiences in London and the provinces. They have been revised for publication, but not recast. The matter is put, not as an author would put it to a student, but as a speaker with only an hour at his disposal has to put it to an audience. Country readers may accept the book as a sample of the propaganda carried on by volunteer lecturers in the workmen's clubs and political associations of London.[1] Metropolitan readers will have the advantage of making themselves independent of the press critic by getting face to face with the writers, stripping the veil of print from their personality, cross-examining, criticising, calling them to account amid surroundings which inspire no awe, and before the most patient of audiences. For any Sunday paper which contains a lecture list will shew where some, if not all, of the seven essayists may be heard for nothing; and on all such occasions questions and discussion form part of the procedure.

The projection and co-ordination of these lectures is not the work of any individual. The nominal editor is only the member told off to arrange for the publication

[1] In the year ending April 1889, the number of lectures delivered by members of the Fabian Society alone was upwards of 700.

of the papers, and see them through the press with whatever editorial ceremony might be necessary. Everything that is usually implied by the authorship and editing of a book has in this case been done by the seven essayists, associated as the Executive Council of the Fabian Society; and not one of the essays could be what it is had the writer been a stranger to his six colleagues and to the Society. But there has been no sacrifice of individuality—no attempt to cut out every phrase and opinion the responsibility for which would not be accepted by every one of the seven. Had the sections been differently allotted, they would have been differently treated, though the net result would probably have been the same. The writers are all Social Democrats, with a common conviction of the necessity of vesting the organization of industry and the material of production in a State identified with the whole people by complete Democracy. But that conviction is peculiar to no individual bias: it is a Capitol to which all roads lead; and at least seven of them are represented in these Fabian Essays; so that the reader need not fear oppression here, any more than in the socialized State of the future, by the ascendancy of one particular cast of mind.

There are at present no authoritative teachers of Socialism. The essayists make no claim to be more than communicative learners.

LONDON
*December 1889*

# CONTENTS

## THE BASIS OF SOCIALISM

1. ECONOMIC                         *By G. Bernard Shaw*

RENT   The Cultivation and Population of the Earth—Economic Origin of the County Family—Economic Rent of Land and Ability—Tenant Right—The Advent of the Proletarian      *Page*   17

VALUE   Mechanism of Exchange—Price and Utility—Effects of Supply—Law of Indifference—Total and Final Utility—Relation of Value to Cost of Production      *Page*   26

WAGES   The Proletariat—Sale of Labor—Subsistence Wage—Capitalism—Increase of Riches and Decrease of Wealth—Divorce of Exchange Value from Social Utility      *Page*   33

CONCLUSION   Apparent Discrepancies between History and Theory—Socialism—Pessimism and Private Property—Economic Soundness of Meliorism      *Page*   39

2. HISTORIC
                *By Sidney Webb, LL.B., Barrister at Law,*
                        *Lecturer on Political Economy*
                        *at the City of London College*

THE DEVELOPMENT OF THE DEMOCRATIC IDEAL
Ancestry of English Socialism—The Utopians—Introduction of the Conception of Evolution—The Lesson of Democracy      *Page*   46

THE DISINTEGRATION OF THE OLD SYNTHESIS
The Decay of Medievalism—The Industrial Revolution—The French Revolution—The Progress
of Democracy                                Page 52

THE PERIOD OF ANARCHY  Individualism—Philosophic Radicalism and Laisser-faire—The Utilitarian Analysis                             Page 58

THE INTELLECTUAL AND MORAL REVOLT; AND
ITS POLITICAL OUTCOME  The Poets, Commu-
nists, Philosophers, Christian Socialists, and Evo-
lutionists—The Extension of State Activity—
Existing State Registration, Inspection and Direct Organization of Labor—The Radical Programme                                      Page 64

THE NEW SYNTHESIS  Evolution and the Social
Organism—Liberty and Equality—Social Health
                                            Page 77

3.  INDUSTRIAL
                    By William Clarke, M.A., Cambridge

THE SUPERSESSION OF INDIVIDUALIST PRODUC-
TION  The Cottage Industry—The Mechanical
Inventions—The Factory System              Page 84

THE GROWTH OF THE GREAT INDUSTRY  The
Expansion of Lancashire—The White Slavery—
State Interference                          Page 95

THE DEVELOPMENT OF THE WORLD-COMMERCE
The Triumph of Free Trade—The Fight for New
Markets—The Carriers of the World          Page 102

THE DIFFERENTIATION OF MANAGER AND CAPI-
TALIST  The Rise of Co-operation and the Joint
Stock Company—The "Ring" and the "Trust"—
The Despotism of Capitalist Communism  Page 109

4. MORAL        *By Sydney Olivier, B.A., Oxford*

THE EVOLUTION OF MORALITY   The Common
End—The Conditions of Freedom—The Indi-
vidual and the Race—The Growth of Social
Consciousness—Convention and Law        Page 131

PROPERTY AND MORALS   The Reaction of Prop-
erty-Forms on Moral Ideas—Class Morality—
Negation of the Conditions of Freedom—Social
Dissolution                                Page 145

THE RE-INTEGRATION OF SOCIETY   The Order-
ing of the Primary Conditions—The Idea of the
Poor Law—Secondary Conditions—Morality and
Reason—The Idea of the School            Page 155


THE ORGANIZATION OF SOCIETY

5. PROPERTY UNDER SOCIALISM
                *By Graham Wallas, M.A., Oxford*

VISIBLE   WEALTH   Consumers'   Capital—Producers' Capital                            Page 165

DEBTS AND SERVICES   Deferred and Anticipated
Consumption—Interest                       Page 173

IDEAS   Copyright   and   Patent   Right—Education                                       Page 182

6. INDUSTRY UNDER SOCIALISM
                            *By Annie Besant*

THE ORGANIZATION OF LABOR   Rural—Urban—
International                               Page 187

THE DISTRIBUTION OF THE PRODUCT   The Individual—The Municipality—The State      Page 200

SOCIAL SAFEGUARDS  The Stimulus to Labor—
The Provision for Initiative—The Reward of
Excellence    *Page 205*


*THE TRANSITION TO SOCIAL DEMOCRACY*

7. TRANSITION    *By G. Bernard Shaw*

MEDIEVALISM TO CAPITALISM  The Old Order
—Merchant Adventurer, Pirate, Slave-Trader,
Capitalist—The Old Order burst by the New
Growth—Chaos    *Page 213*

ANARCHY TO STATE INTERFERENCE  Political
Economy—Hegelian Conception of the Perfect
State—Socialism: its Practical Difficulties—Im-
practicability of Catastrophic Change—Democracy the antidote to Bureaucracy—The State
interferes    *Page 216*

STATE INTERFERENCE TO STATE ORGANIZATION
Hard Times—Revival of Revolutionary Social-
ism—Remaining Steps to the Consummation of
Democracy—Machinery of Socialism—Social
Pressure—Urban Rents—The New Taxation—
State Organization of Labor its indispensable
complement—The Unemployed—Solution of the
Compensation difficulty—Economic Reactions of
the Progress of Municipal Socialism—Militant
Socialism abandoned but not dishonored  *Page 228*

8. THE OUTLOOK    *By Hubert Bland*

THE CONDITION OF ENGLISH PARTIES  The Lines
of Progress—The Rate of Progress in Thought
and Industry compared with that in Politics—
Alleged Disappearance of the Whig    *Page 247*

THE SOCIALIZING OF POLITICS    Political Myopia
—Sham Socialism—Red Herrings—Dreams of
Permeating the Liberal Party—Disillusionment—
The New Departure                        Page 254

THE DUTIES OF THE HOUR    The True Line of
Cleavage—Hopes and Fears—The Solidarity of
the Workers                              Page 265

INDEX                                    Page 269

# THE BASIS OF SOCIALISM

# 1. ECONOMIC

## By G. Bernard Shaw

All economic analyses begin with the cultivation of the earth. To the mind's eye of the astronomer the earth is a ball spinning in space without ulterior motives. To the bodily eye of the primitive cultivator it is a vast green plain, from which, by sticking a spade into it, wheat and other edible matters can be made to spring. To the eye of the sophisticated city man this vast green plain appears rather as a great gaming table, your chances in the game depending chiefly on the place where you deposit your stakes. To the economist, again, the green plain is a sort of burial place of hidden treasure, where all the forethought and industry of man are set at naught by the caprice of the power which hid the treasure. The wise and patient workman strikes his spade in here, and with heavy toil can discover nothing but a poor quality of barley, some potatoes, and plentiful nettles, with a few dock leaves to cure his stings. The foolish spendthrift on the other side of the hedge, gazing idly at the sand glittering in the sun, suddenly realizes that the earth is offering him gold—is dancing it before his listless eyes lest it should escape him. Another man, searching for some more of this tempting gold, comes upon a great hoard of coal, or taps a jet of petroleum. Thus is Man mocked by Earth his step-mother, and never knows as he tugs at her closed hand whether it contains diamonds or flints, good red wheat or a few clayey and blighted

cabbages. Thus too he becomes a gambler, and scoffs
at the theorists who prate of industry and honesty and
equality. Yet against this fate he eternally rebels. For
since in gambling the many must lose in order that the
few may win; since dishonesty is mere shadowgrasping
where everyone is dishonest; and since inequality is
better to all except the highest, and miserably lonely
for him, men come greatly to desire that these capricious gifts of Nature might be intercepted by some
agency having the power and the goodwill to distribute
them justly according to the labor done by each in the
collective search for them. This desire is Socialism; and,
as a means to its fulfilment, Socialists have devised
communes, kingdoms, principalities, churches, manors,
and finally, when all these had succumbed to the old
gambling spirit, the Social Democratic State, which
yet remains to be tried. As against Socialism, the
gambling spirit urges man to allow no rival to come
between his private individual powers and Step-
mother Earth, but rather to secure some acres of her
and take his chance of getting diamonds instead of
cabbages. This is Private Property or Unsocialism.
Our own choice is shewn by our continual aspiration
to possess property, our common hailing of it as sacred,
our setting apart of the word Respectable for those
who have attained it, our ascription of pre-eminent
religiousness to commandments forbidding its violation, and our identification of law and order among
men with its protection. Therefore is it vital to a living
knowledge of our society that Private Property should
be known in every step of its progress from its sources
in cupidity to its end in confusion.

Let us, in the manner of the Political Economist,
trace the effects of settling a country by private property with undisturbed law and order. Figure to your-
self the vast green plain of a country virgin to the
spade, awaiting the advent of man. Imagine then the
arrival of the first colonist, the original Adam, devel-

oped by centuries of civilization into an Adam Smith,
prospecting for a suitable patch of Private Property.
Adam is, as Political Economy fundamentally assumes
him to be, "on the make": therefore he drives his spade
into, and sets up his stockade around, the most fertile
and favorably situated patch he can find. When he has
tilled it, Political Economy, inspired to prophesy by the
spectacle, metaphorically exhibits Adam's little patch
of cultivation as a pool that will yet rise and submerge
the whole land. Let us not forget this trope: it is the
key to the ever-recurring phrase "margin of cultivation," in which as may now be perceived, there lurks
a little unsuspected poetry. And truly the pool soon
spreads. Other Adams come, all on the make, and
therefore all sure to pre-empt patches as near as may be
to the first Adam's, partly because he has chosen the
best situation, partly for the pleasure of his society and
conversation, and partly because where two men are
assembled together there is a two-man power that is far
more than double one-man power, being indeed in
some instances a quite new force, totally destructive of
the idiotic general hypothesis that society is no more
than the sum of the units which compose it. These
Adams, too, bring their Cains and Abels, who do not
murder one another, but merely pre-empt adjacent
patches. And so the pool rises, and the margin spreads
more and more remote from the centre, until the pool
becomes a lake, and the lake an inland sea.

## RENT

But in the course of this inundation the caprices of
Nature begin to operate. That specially fertile region
upon which Adam pitched is sooner or later all pre-
empted; and there is nothing for the new comer to pre-
empt save soil of the second quality. Again, division of
labor sets in among Adam's neighbors; and with it, of

course, comes the establishment of a market for the exchange of the products of their divided labor. Now it is not well to be far afield from that market, because distance from it involves extra cost for roads, beasts of burden, time consumed in travelling thither and back again. All this will be saved to Adam at the centre of cultivation, and incurred by the new comer at the margin of cultivation. Let us estimate the annual value of Adam's produce at £1,000, and the annual produce of the new comer's land on the margin of cultivation at £500, assuming that Adam and the new comer are equally industrious. Here is a clear advantage of £500 a year to the first comer. This £500 is economic rent. It matters not at all that it is merely a difference of income and not an overt payment from a tenant to a landlord. The two men labor equally; and yet one gets £500 a year more than the other through the superior fertility of his land and convenience of its situation. The excess due to that fertility is rent; and before long we shall find it recognized as such and paid in the fashion with which we are familiar. For why should not Adam let his patch to the new comer at a rent of £500 a year? Since the produce will be £1,000, the new comer will have £500 left for himself, or as much as he could obtain by cultivating a patch of his own at the margin; and it is pleasanter, besides, to be in the centre of society than on the outskirts of it. The new comer will himself propose the arrangement; and Adam may retire as an idle landlord with a perpetual pension of £500 rent. The excess of fertility in Adam's land is thenceforth recognized as rent and paid, as it is to-day, regularly by a worker to a drone. A few samples of the way in which this simple and intelligible transaction is stated by our economists may now, I hope, be quoted without any danger of their proving so difficult as they appear in the text books from which I have copied them.

Stuart Mill[1] says that "the rent of land consists of the excess of its return above the return to the worst land in cultivation". Fawcett[2] says that "the rent of land represents the pecuniary value of the advantages which such land possesses over the worst land in cultivation". Professor Marshall[3] says that "the rent of a piece of land is the excess of its produce over the produce of an adjacent piece of land which would not be cultivated at all if rent were paid for it". Professor Sidgwick[4] cautiously puts it that "the normal rent *per acre* of any piece" [of land] "is the surplus of the value of its produce over the value of the net produce per acre of the least advantageous land that it is profitable to cultivate". General Walker[5] declares that "specifically, the rent of any piece of land is determined by the difference between its annual yield and that of the least productive land actually cultivated for the supply of the same market, it being assumed that the quality of the land as a productive agent is, in neither case, impaired or improved by such cultivation". All these definitions are offered by the authors as elaborations of that given by their master Ricardo,[6] who says, "Rent is that portion of the produce of the earth which is paid to the landlord for the use of the original and indestructible powers of the soil."

[1] "Principles of Political Economy," Vol. I., Index to chap. xvi. (1865).
[2] "Manual of Political Economy," Book II., chap. iii., p. 116 (1876).
[3] "Economics of Industry," Book II., chap. iii., sec. 3, p. 84 (1879).
[4] "Principles of Political Economy," Book II., chap. vii., p. 301 (1883).
[5] "Brief Text Book of Political Economy," chap. ii., sec. 216, p. 173 (1885).
[6] "Principles of Political Economy and Taxation," chap. ii., p. 34 (1817).

### THE COUNTY FAMILY

Let us return to our ideal country. Adam is retiring from productive industry on £500 a year; and his neighbors are hastening to imitate him as fresh tenants present themselves. The first result is the beginning of a tradition that the oldest families in the country enjoy a superior position to the rest, and that the main advantage of their superior position is that they enjoy incomes without working. Nevertheless, since they still depend on their tenants' labor for their subsistence, they continue to pay Labor, with a capital L, a certain meed of mouth honor; and the resultant association of prosperity with idleness, and praise with industry, practically destroys morality by setting up that incompatibility between conduct and principle which is the secret of the ingrained cynicism of our own time, and which produces the curious Ricardian phenomenon of the man of business who goes on Sunday to the church with the regularity of the village blacksmith, there to renounce and abjure before his God the line of conduct which he intends to pursue with all his might during the following week.

According to our hypothesis, the inland sea of cultivation has now spread into the wilderness so far that at its margin the return to a man's labor for a year is only £500. But as there is always a flood tide in that sea, caused by the incessant increase of population, the margin will not stop there: it will at last encroach upon every acre of cultivable land, rising to the snow line on the mountains and falling to the coast of the actual salt water sea, but always reaching the barrenest places last of all, because the cultivators are still, as ever, on the make, and will not break bad land when better is to be had. But suppose that now, at last, the uttermost belt of free land is reached, and that upon it the yield to a man's year's labor is only £100. Clearly

now the rent of Adam's primeval patch has risen to
£900, since that is the excess of its produce over what
is by this time all that is to be had rent free. But Adam
has yielded up his land for £500 a year to the tenant.
It is this tenant accordingly who now lets Adam's patch
for £900 a year to the new comer, who of course loses
nothing by the bargain, since it leaves him the £100 a
year with which he must be content anyhow. Accordingly he labors on Adam's land; raises £1,000 a year
from it; keeps £100 and pays £900 to Adam's tenant,
who pays £500 to Adam, keeping £400 for himself, and
thus also becoming an idle gentleman, though with a
somewhat smaller income than the man of older family. It has, in fact, come to this, that the private property in Adam's land is divided between three men, the
first doing none of the work and getting half the produce; the second doing none of the work and getting
two fifths of the produce; and the third doing all the
work and getting only one tenth of the produce. Incidentally also, the moralist who is sure to have been
prating somewhere about private property leading
to the encouragement of industry, the establishment of
a healthy incentive, and the distribution of wealth
according to exertion, is exposed as a futile purblind
person, starting *a priori* from blank ignorance, and proceeding deductively to mere contradiction and patent
folly.

All this, however, is a mere trifle compared to the
sequel. When the inland sea has risen to its confines—
when there is nothing but a strip of sand round the
coast between the furrow and the wave—when the very
waves themselves are cultivated by fisherfolk—when
the pastures and timber forests have touched the snow
line—when, in short, the land is all private property,
yet every man is a proprietor, though it may be only
of a tenant right. He enjoys fixity of tenure at what is
called a fair rent: that is, he fares as well as he could
on land wholly his own. All the rent is economic rent:

the landlord cannot raise it nor the tenant lower it: it is fixed naturally by the difference between the fertility of the land for which it is paid and that of the worst land in the country. Compared with the world as we know it, such a state of things is freedom and happiness.

### THE PROLETARIAT

But at this point there appears in the land a man in a strange plight—one who wanders from snow line to sea coast in search of land, and finds none that is not the property of some one else. Private Property had forgotten this man. On the roads he is a vagrant: off them he is a trespasser: he is the first disinherited son of Adam, the first Proletarian, one in whose seed all the generations of the earth shall yet be blest, but who is himself for the present foodless, homeless, shiftless, superfluous, and everything that turns a man into a tramp or a thrall. Yet he is still a man with brain and muscle, able to devise and execute, able to deal puissantly with land if only he could get access to it. But how to get that access! Necessity is the mother of Invention. It may be that this second Adam, the first father of the great Proletariat, has one of those scarce brains which are not the least of Nature's capricious gifts. If the fertile field yields rent, why not the fertile brain? Here is the first Adam's patch still yielding its £1,000 a year to the labor of the tenant who, as we have seen, has to pay £900 away in rent. How if the Proletarian were boldly to bid £1,000 a year to that man for the property? Apparently the result would be the starvation of the Proletarian, since he would have to part with all the produce. But what if the Proletarian can contrive—invent—anticipate a new want—turn the land to some hitherto undreamt-of use—wrest £1,500 a year from the soil and site that only yielded

£1,000 before? If he can do this, he can pay the full £1,000 rent, and have an income of £500 left for himself. This is his profit—the rent of his ability—the excess of its produce over that of ordinary stupidity. Here then is the opportunity of the cunning Proletarian, the hero of that modern Plutarch, Mr. Samuel Smiles. Truly, as Napoleon said, the career is open to the talented. But alas! the social question is no more a question of the fate of the talented than of the idiotic. In due replenishment of the earth there comes another Proletarian who is no cleverer than other men, and can do as much, but not more than they. For him there is no rent of ability. How then is he to get a tenant right? Let us see. It is certain that by this time not only will the new devices of the renter of ability have been copied by people incapable of inventing them; but division of labor, the use of tools and money, and the economies of civilization will have greatly increased man's power of extracting wealth from Nature. All this increase will be so much gain to the holder of a tenant right, since his rent is a fixed payment out of the produce of his holding, and the balance is his own. Therefore an addition to the produce not foreseen by the landlord enriches the tenant. So that it may well be that the produce of land on the margin of cultivation, which, as we have seen, fixes the produce left to the cultivators throughout the whole area, may rise considerably. Suppose the yield to have doubled; then our old friends who paid £900 rent and kept £100 for themselves, have now, though they still pay £900 rent, £1,100 for themselves, the total produce having risen to £2,000. Now here is an opportunity for our Proletarian who is not clever. He can very well offer to cultivate the land subject to a payment of, for instance, £1,600 a year, leaving himself £400 a year. This will enable the last holder of the tenant right to retire as an idle gentleman receiving a net income of £700 a year, and a gross income of £1,600, out of which he pays £900

a year rent to a landlord who again pays to the head
landlord £500. But it is to be marked that this £700 a
year net is not economic rent. It is not the difference
between the best and the worst land. It has nothing to
do with the margin of cultivation. It is a payment for
the privilege of using land at all—for access to that
which is now a close monopoly; and its amount is regulated, not by what the purchaser could do for himself
on land of his own at the margin, but simply by the
landholder's eagerness to be idle on the one hand, and
the proletarian's need of subsistence on the other. In
current economic terms the price is regulated by supply
and demand. As the demand for land intensifies by the
advent of fresh proletarians, the price goes up; and the
bargains are made more stringent. Tenants' rights, instead of being granted in perpetuity, and so securing
for ever to the tenant the increase due to unforeseen
improvements in production, are granted on leases for
finite terms, at the expiration of which the landlord
can revise the terms or eject the tenant. The payments
rise until the original head rents and quit rents appear
insignificant in comparison with the incomes reaped
by the intermediate tenant holders or middlemen.
Sooner or later the price of tenant right will rise so high
that the actual cultivator will get no more of the
produce than suffices him for subsistence. At that point
there is an end of sub-letting tenant rights. The land's
absorption of the proletarians as tenants paying more
than the economic rent stops.

And now, what is the next proletarian to do? For all
his forerunners we have found a way of escape: for
him there seems none. The board is at the door, in-
scribed "Only standing room left"; and it might well
bear the more poetic legend, *Lasciate ogni speranza,
voi ch' entrate.* This man, born a proletarian, must die
a proletarian, and leaves his destitution as an only
inheritance to his son. It is not yet clear that there is
ten days life in him; for whence is his subsistence to

come if he cannot get at the land? Food he must have,
and clothing; and both promptly. There is food in the
market, and clothing also; but not for nothing: hard
money must be paid for it, and paid on the nail too;
for he who has no property gets no credit. Money then
is a necessity of life; and money can only be procured
by selling commodities. This presents no difficulty to
the cultivators of the land, who can raise commodities
by their labor; but the proletarian, being landless, has
neither commodities nor means of producing them. Sell
something he must. Yet he has nothing to sell—except
himself. The idea seems a desperate one; but it proves
quite easy to carry out. The tenant cultivators of the
land have not strength enough or time enough to
exhaust the productive capacity of their holdings. If
they could buy men in the market for less than these
men's labor would add to the produce, then the purchase of such men would be a sheer gain. It would
indeed be only a purchase in form: the men would
literally cost nothing, since they would produce their
own price, with a surplus for the buyer. Never in the
history of buying and selling was there so splendid a
bargain for buyers as this. Aladdin's uncle's offer of
new lamps for old ones was in comparison a catch-
penny. Accordingly, the proletarian no sooner offers
himself for sale than he finds a rush of bidders for him,
each striving to get the better of the others by offering
to give him more and more of the produce of his labor,
and to content themselves with less and less surplus.
But even the highest bidder must have some surplus,
or he will not buy. The proletarian, in accepting the
highest bid, sells himself openly into bondage. He is
not the first man who has done so; for it is evident that
his forerunners, the purchasers of tenant right, had
been enslaved by the proprietors who lived on the rents
paid by them. But now all the disguise falls off: the
proletarian renounces not only the fruit of his labor,
but also his right to think for himself and to direct his

industry as he pleases. The economic change is merely
formal: the moral change is enormous. Soon the new
direct traffic in men overspreads the whole market, and
takes the place formerly held by the traffic in tenant
rights. In order to understand the consequences, it is
necessary to undertake an analysis of the exchange of
commodities in general, since labor power is now in
the market on the same footing as any other ware
exposed there for sale.

### EXCHANGE VALUE

It is evident that the custom of exchanging will arise
in the first instance as soon as men give up providing
each for his own needs by his own labor. A man who
makes his own tables and chairs, his own poker and
kettle, his own bread and butter, and his own house
and clothes, is jack of all trades and master of none.
He finds that he would get on much faster if he stuck
to making tables and chairs, and exchanged them with
the smith for a poker and kettle, with bakers and dairy-
men for bread and butter, and with builders and tailors
for a house and clothes. In doing this, he finds that his
tables and chairs are worth so much—that they have
an exchange value, as it is called. As a matter of general convenience, some suitable commodity is set up
to measure this value. We set up gold, which, in this
particular use of it, is called money. The chairmaker
finds how much money his chairs are worth, and exchanges them for it. The blacksmith finds out how
much money his pokers are worth, and exchanges them
for it. Thus, by employing money as a go-between,
chairmakers can get pokers in exchange for their chairs,
and blacksmiths chairs for their pokers. This is the
mechanism of exchange; and once the values of the
commodities are ascertained it works simply enough.
But it is a mere mechanism, and does not fix the values

or explain them. And the attempt to discover what does fix them is beset with apparent contradictions which block up the right path, and with seductive coincidences which make the wrong seem the more promising.

The apparent contradictions soon shew themselves. It is evident that the exchange value of anything depends on its utility, since no mortal exertion can make a useless thing exchangeable. And yet fresh air and sunlight, which are so useful as to be quite indispensable, have no exchange value; whilst a meteoric stone, shot free of charge from the firmament into the back garden, has a considerable exchange value, although it is an eminently dispensable curiosity. We soon find that this some-how depends on the fact that fresh air is plenty and meteoric stones scarce. If by any means the supply of fresh air could be steadily diminished, and the supply of meteoric stones, by celestial cannonade or otherwise, steadily increased, the fresh air would presently acquire an exchange value which would gradually rise, whilst the exchange value of meteoric stones would gradually fall, until at last fresh air would be supplied through a meter and charged for like gas, and meteoric stones would be as unsaleable as ordinary pebbles. The exchange value, in fact, decreases with the supply. This is due to the fact that the supply decreases in utility as it goes on, because when people have had some of a commodity, they are partly satisfied, and do not value the rest so much. The usefulness of a pound of bread to a man depends on whether he has already eaten some. Every man wants a certain number of pounds of bread per week: no man wants much more; and if more is offered he will not give much for it—perhaps not anything. One umbrella is very useful: a second umbrella is a luxury: a third is mere lumber. Similarly, the curators of our museums want a moderate collection of meteoric stones; but they do not want a cartload apiece of them. Now the exchange value is fixed by the utility, not of the most use-

ful, but of the least useful part of the stock. Why this
is so can readily be made obvious by an illustration.
If the stock of umbrellas in the market were sufficiently
large to provide two for each umbrella carrier in the
community, then, since a second umbrella is not so
useful as the first, the doctrinaire course would be to
ticket half the umbrella at, say, fifteen shillings, and
the other half at eight and sixpence. Unfortunately,
no man will give fifteen shillings for an article which
he can get for eight and sixpence; and when the public
came to buy, they would buy up all the eight and sixpenny umbrellas. Each person being thus supplied
with an umbrella, the remainder of the stock, though
marked fifteen shillings, would be in the position of
second umbrellas, only worth eight and sixpence. This
is how the exchange value of the least useful part of
the supply fixes the exchange value of all the rest.
Technically, it occurs by "the law of indifference".
And since the least useful unit of the supply is generally that which it last produced, its utility is called
the final utility of the commodity. The utility of the
first or most useful unit is called the total utility of the
commodity. If there were but one umbrella in the
world, the exchange value of its total utility would be
what the most delicate person would pay for it on a
very wet day sooner than go without it. But practically,
thanks to the law of indifference, the most delicate
person pays no more than the most robust: that is,
both pay alike the exchange value of the utility of the
last umbrella produced—or of the final utility of the
whole stock of umbrellas. These terms—laws of indif-
ferences, total utility, and final utility—though ad-
mirably expressive and intelligible when you know
beforehand exactly what they mean, are, taken by
themselves, failures in point of lucidity and suggestive-
ness. Some economists, transferring from cultivation to
utility our old metaphor of the spreading pool, call
final utility "marginal utility". Either will serve our

present purpose, as I do not intend to use the terms
again. The main point to be grasped is, that however
useful any commodity may be, its exchange value can
be run down to nothing by increasing the supply until
there is more of it than is wanted. The excess being
useless and valueless, is to be had for nothing; and
nobody will pay anything for a commodity as long as
plenty of it is to be had for nothing. This is why air
and other indispensable things have no exchange value,
whilst scarce gewgaws fetch immense prices.

These, then, are the conditions which confront man
as a producer and exchanger. If he produces a useless
thing, his labor will be wholly in vain: he will get
nothing for it. If he produces a useful thing, the price
he will get for it will depend on how much of it there
is for sale already. If he increases the supply by producing more than is sufficient to replace the current
consumption, he inevitably lowers the value of the
whole. It therefore behoves him to be wary in choosing
his occupation as well as industrious in pursuing it.
His choice will naturally fall on the production of those
commodities whose value stands highest relatively to
the labor required to produce them—which fetch the
highest price in proportion to their cost, in fact. Suppose, for example, that a maker of musical instruments
found that it cost him exactly as much to make a harp
as to make a pianoforte, but that harps were going out
of fashion and pianofortes coming in. Soon there
would be more harps than were wanted, and fewer
pianofortes: consequently the value of harps would
fall, and that of pianofortes rise. Since the labor cost
of both would be the same, he would immediately de-
vote all his labor to pianoforte making; and other manufacturers would do the same, until the increase of
supply brought down the value of pianofortes to the
value of harps. Possibly fashion then might veer from
pianofortes to American organs, in which case he
would make less pianofortes and more American or-

gans. When these, too, had increased sufficiently, the exertions of the Salvation Army might create such a demand for tambourines as to make them worth four times their cost of production, whereupon there would instantly be a furious concentration of the instrument-making energy on the manufacture of tambourines; and this concentration would last until the supply had brought down the profit[7] to less than might be gained by gratifying the public craving for trombones. At last, as pianofortes were cheapened until they were no more profitable than harps; then American organs until they were no more profitable than pianos; and then tambourines until they were level with American organs; so eventually trombones will pay no better than tambourines; and a general level of profit will be attained, indicating the proportion in which the instruments are wanted by the public. But to skim off even this level of profit, more of the instruments may be produced in the ascertained proportion until their prices fall to their costs of production, when there will be no profit. Here the production will be decisively checked, since a further supply would cause only a loss; and men can lose money, without the trouble of producing commodities, by the simple process of throwing it out of window.

What occurred with the musical instruments in this illustration occurs in practice with the whole mass of manufactured commodities. Those which are scarce, and therefore relatively high in value, tempt us to produce them until the increase of the supply reduces their value to a point at which there is no more profit to be made out of them than out of other commodities. The general level of profit thus attained is further exploited until the general increase brings down the price of all commodities to their cost of production,

[7] Profit is here used colloquially to denote the excess of the value of an article over its cost.

the equivalent of which is sometimes called their normal value. And here a glance back to our analysis of the spread of cultivation, and its result in the phenomenon of rent, suggests the question: What does the cost of production of a commodity mean? We have seen that, owing to the differences in fertility and advantage of situation between one piece of land and another, cost of production varies from district to district, being highest at the margin of cultivation. But we have also seen how the landlord skims off as economic rent all the advantage gained by the cultivators of superior soils and sites. Consequently, the addition of the landlord's rent to the expenses of production brings them up even on the best land to the level of those incurred on the worst. Cost of production, then, means cost of production on the margin of cultivation, and is equalized to all producers, since what they may save in labor per commodity is counterbalanced by the greater mass of commodities they must produce in order to bring in the rent. It is only by a thorough grasp of this levelling-down action that we can detect the trick by which the ordinary economist tries to cheat us into accepting the private property system as practically just. He first shews that economic rent does not enter into cost of production on the margin of cultivation. Then he shews that the cost of production on the margin of cultivation determines the price of a commodity. Therefore, he argues, first, that rent does not enter into price; and second, that the value of commodities is fixed by their cost of production, the implication being that the landlords cost the community nothing, and that commodities exchange in exact proportion to the labor they cost. This trivially ingenious way of being disingenuous is officially taught as political economy in our schools to this day. It will be seen at once that it is mere thimblerig. So far from commodities exchanging, or tending to exchange, according to the labor expended in their production, commodities produced well within the margin of cultivation will fetch as high a price as commodities produced at the margin with much greater labor. So far from the landlord costing nothing, he costs all the difference between the two.

This, however, is not the goal of our analysis of value. We now see how Man's control over the value of commodities consists solely in his power of regulating their supply. Individuals are constantly trying to decrease supply for their own advantage. Gigantic conspiracies have been entered into to forestall the world's wheat and cotton harvests, so as to force their value to the highest possible point. Cargoes of East Indian spices have been destroyed by the Dutch as cargoes of fish are now destroyed in the Thames, to maintain prices by limiting supply. All rings, trusts, corners, combinations, monopolies, and trade secrets have the same object. Production and the development of the social instincts are alike hindered by each man's consciousness that the more he stints the community the more he benefits himself, the justification, of course, being that when every man has benefited himself at the expense of the community, the community will benefit by every man in it being benefited. From one thing the community is safe. There will be no permanent conspiracies to reduce values by increasing supply. All men will cease producing when the value of their product falls below its cost of production, whether in labor or in labor *plus* rent. No man will keep on producing bread until it will fetch nothing, like the sunlight, or until it becomes a nuisance, like the rain in the summer of 1888. So far, our minds are at ease as to the excessive increase of commodities voluntarily produced by the labor of man.

## WAGES

I now ask you to pick up the dropped subject of the spread of cultivation. We had got as far as the appearance in the market of a new commodity—of the proletarian man compelled to live by the sale of himself! In order to realize at once the latent horror of this, you have only to apply our investigation of value, with its inevitable law that only by restricting the supply of a commodity can its value be kept from descending finally to zero. The commodity which the proletarian sells is one over the production of which he has practically no control. He is himself driven to produce it by an irresistible impulse. It was the increase of population that spread cultivation and civilization from the centre to the snowline, and at last forced men to sell themselves to the lords of the soil: it is the same force that continues to multiply men so that their exchange value falls slowly and surely until it disappears altogether—until even black chattel slaves are released as not worth keeping in a land where men of all colors are to be had for nothing. This is the condition of our English laborers to-day: they are no longer even dirt cheap: they are valueless, and can be had for nothing. The proof is the existence of the unemployed, who can find no purchaser. By the law of indifference, nobody will buy men at a price when he can obtain equally serviceable men for nothing. What then is the explanation of the wages given to those who are in employment, and who certainly do not work for nothing? The matter is deplorably simple. Suppose that horses multiplied in England in such quantities that they were to be had for the asking, like kittens condemned to the bucket. You would still have to feed your horse—feed him and lodge him well if you used him as a smart hunter—feed him and lodge him wretchedly if you used him only as a drudge. But the cost of keeping would not mean that the horse had an exchange value. If you got him for nothing in the first instance—if no one would give you anything for him when you were done with him, he would be worth nothing, in spite of the cost of his keep. That is just the case of every member of the proletariat who could be replaced by one of the unemployed to-day. Their wage is not the price of themselves: for they are worth nothing: it is only their keep. For bare subsistence wages you can get as much common labor as you want, and do what you please with it within the limits of a criminal code which is sure to be interpreted by a proprietary-class judge in your favor. If you have to give your footman a better allowance than your wretched hewer of match-wood, it is for the same reason that you have to give your hunter beans and a clean stall instead of chopped straw and a sty.[8]

## CAPITALISM

At this stage the acquisition of labor becomes a mere question of provender. If a railway is required, all that is necessary is to provide subsistence for a sufficient number of laborers to construct it. If, for example, the railway requires the labor of a thousand men for five years, the cost to the proprietors of the site is the subsistence of a thousand men for five years. This subsistence is technically called capital. It is provided for by the proprietors not consuming the whole excess over wages of the produce of the labor of their

[8] When one of the conditions of earning a wage is the keeping up of a certain state, subsistence wages may reach a figure to which the term seems ludicrously inappropriate. For example, a fashionable physician in London cannot save out of £1,000 a year; and the post of Lord Lieutenant of Ireland can only be filled by a man who brings considerable private means to the aid of his official salary of £20,000.

other wage workers, but setting aside enough for the
subsistence of the railway makers. In this way capital
can claim to be the result of saving, or, as one ingenious apologist neatly put it, the reward of abstinence,
a gleam of humor which still enlivens treatises on
capital. The savers, it need hardly be said, are those
who have more money than they want to spend: the
abstainers are those who have less. At the end of the
five years, the completed railway is the property of the
capitalists; and the railway makers fall back into the
labor market as helpless as they were before. Sometimes
the proprietors call the completed railway their capital;
but, strictly, this is only a figure of speech. Capital is
simply spare subsistence. Its market value, indicated by
the current rate of interest, falls with the increase of
population, whereas the market value of established
stock rises with it.[9] If Mr. Goschen, encouraged by his
success in reducing Consols, were to ask the proprietors of the London and North Western Railway to
accept as full compensation for their complete expropriation capital just sufficient to make the railway
anew, their amazement at his audacity would at once
make him feel the difference between a railway and
capital. Colloquially, one property with a farm on it is
said to be land yielding rent; whilst another, with a
railway on it, is called capital yielding interest. But
economically there is no distinction between them
when they once become sources of revenue. This would
be quite clearly seen if costly enterprises like railways
could be undertaken by a single landlord on his own
land out of his own surplus wealth. It is the necessity
of combining a number of possessors of surplus wealth,

[9] The current rate must, under present conditions, eventually fall to zero, and even become "negative." By that
time shares which now bring in a dividend of 100 per
cent., may very possibly bring in 200 or more. Yet the fall
of the rate has been mistaken for a tendency of interest to
disappear. It really indicates a tendency of interest to
increase.

and devising a financial machinery for apportioning their shares in the produce to their shares in the capital contributed, that modifies the terminology and external aspect of the exploitation. But the modification is not an alteration: shareholder and landlord live alike on the produce extracted from their property by the labor of the proletariat.

"OVER POPULATION"

The introduction of the capitalistic system is a sign that the exploitation of the laborer toiling for a bare subsistence wage has become one of the chief arts of life among the holders of tenant rights. It also produces a delusive promise of endless employment which blinds the proletariat to those disastrous consequences of rapid multiplication which are obvious to the small cultivator and peasant proprietor. But indeed the more you degrade the workers, robbing them of all artistic enjoyment, and all chance of respect and admiration from their fellows, the more you throw them back, reckless, on the one pleasure and the one human tie left to them—the gratification of their instinct for producing fresh supplies of men. You will applaud this instinct as divine until at last the excessive supply becomes a nuisance: there comes a plague of men; and you suddenly discover that the instinct is diabolic, and set up a cry of "over population". But your slaves are beyond caring for your cries: they breed like rabbits; and their poverty breeds filth, ugliness, dishonesty, disease, obscenity, drunkenness, and murder. In the midst of the riches which their labor piles up for you, their misery rises up too and stifles you. You withdraw in disgust to the other end of the town from them; you appoint special carriages on your railways and special seats in your churches and theatres for them; you set your life apart from theirs by every class barrier you can devise; and yet they swarm about you still: your face gets stamped with your habitual loathing and suspicion of them: your ears get so filled with the language of the vilest of them that you break into it when you lose your self-control: they poison your life as remorselessly as you have sacrificed theirs heartlessly. You begin to believe intensely in the devil. Then comes the terror of their revolting; the drilling and arming of bodies of them to keep down the rest; the prison, the hospital, paroxysms of frantic coercion, followed by paroxysms of frantic charity. And in the meantime, the population continues to increase!

## "ILLTH"

It is sometimes said that during this grotesquely hideous march of civilization from bad to worse, wealth is increasing side by side with misery. Such a thing is eternally impossible: wealth is steadily decreasing with the spread of poverty. But riches are increasing, which is quite another thing. The total of the exchange values produced in the country annually is mounting perhaps by leaps and bounds. But the accumulation of riches, and consequently of an excessive purchasing power, in the hands of a class, soon satiates that class with socially useful wealth, and sets them offering a price for luxuries. The moment a price is to be had for a luxury, it acquires exchange value, and labor is employed to produce it. A New York lady, for instance, having a nature of exquisite sensibility, orders an elegant rosewood and silver coffin, upholstered in pink satin, for her dead dog. It is made: and meanwhile a live child is prowling barefooted and hunger-stunted in the frozen gutter outside. The exchange-value of the coffin is counted as part of the national wealth; but a nation which cannot afford food and clothing for its children cannot be allowed to pass as wealthy because it has provided a pretty coffin for a dead dog. Exchange value itself, in fact, has become bedevilled like everything else, and represents no longer utility, but the cravings of lust, folly, vanity, gluttony, and madness, technically described by genteel economists as "effective demand". Luxuries are not social wealth: the machinery for producing them is not social wealth: labor skilled only to manufacture them is not socially useful labor: the men, women, and children who make a living by producing them are no more self-supporting than the idle rich for whose amusement they are kept at work. It is the habit of counting as wealth the exchange values involved in these transactions that makes us fancy that the poor are starving in the midst of plenty. They are starving in the midst of plenty of jewels, velvets, laces, equipages, and racehorses; but not in the midst of plenty of food. In the things that are wanted for the welfare of the people we are abjectly poor; and England's social policy to-day may be likened to the domestic policy of those adventuresses who leave their children half-clothed and half-fed in order to keep a carriage and deal with a fashionable dressmaker. But it is quite true that whilst wealth and welfare are decreasing, productive power is increasing; and nothing but the perversion of this power to the production of socially useless commodities prevents the apparent wealth from becoming real. The purchasing power that commands luxuries in the hands of the rich, would command true wealth in the hands of all. Yet private property must still heap the purchasing power upon the few rich and withdraw it from the many poor. So that, in the end, the subject of the one boast that private property can make—the great accumulation of so-called "wealth" which it points so proudly to as the result of its power to scourge men and women daily to prolonged and intense toil, turns out to be a simulacrum. With all its energy, its Smilesian "self-help", its merchant-princely enterprise, its ferocious sweating and slave-driving, its prodigality of blood, sweat and tears, what has it heaped up, over and above the pittance of its slaves? Only a monstrous pile of frippery, some tainted class literature and class art, and not a little poison and mischief.

This, then, is the economic analysis which convicts Private Property of being unjust even from the beginning, and utterly impossible as a final solution of even the individualist aspect of the problem of adjusting the share of the worker in the distribution of wealth to the labor incurred by him in its production. All attempts yet made to construct true societies upon it have failed: the nearest things to societies so achieved have been civilizations, which have rotted into centres of vice and luxury, and eventually been swept away by uncivilized races. That our own civilization is already in an advanced stage of rottenness may be taken as statistically proved. That further decay instead of improvement must ensue if the institution of private property be maintained, is economically certain. Fortunately, private property in its integrity is not now practicable. Although the safety valve of emigration has been furiously at work during this century, yet the pressure of population has forced us to begin the restitution to the people of the sums taken from them for the ground landlords, holders of tenant right, and capitalists, by the imposition of an income tax, and by compelling them to establish out of their revenues a national system of education, besides imposing restrictions—as yet only of the forcible-feeble sort—on their terrible power of abusing the wage contract. These, however, are dealt with by Mr. Sidney Webb in the historic essay which follows. It should not touch upon them at all, were it not that experience has lately convinced all economists that no exercise in abstract economics, however closely deduced, is to be trusted unless it can be experimentally verified by tracing its expression in history. It is true that the process which I have presented as a direct development of private property between free exchangers had to work itself out in the Old World indirectly and tortuously through a struggle with political and religious institutions and survivals quite antagonistic to it. It is true that cultivation did not begin in Western Europe with the solitary emigrant pre-empting his private property, but with the tribal communes in which arose subsequently the assertion of the right of the individual to private judgment and private action against the tyranny of primitive society. It is true that cultivation has not proceeded by logical steps from good land to less good; from less good to bad; and from bad to worse: the exploration of new countries and new regions, and the discovery of new uses for old products, has often made the margin of cultivation more fruitful than the centre, and, for the moment (whilst the centre was shifting to the margin), turned the whole movement of rent and wages directly counter to the economic theory. Nor is it true that, taking the world as one country, cultivation has yet spread from the snowline to the water's edge. There is free land still for the poorest East End match-box maker if she could get there, reclaim the wilderness there, speak the language there, stand the climate there, and be fed, clothed, and housed there whilst she cleared her farm; learned how to cultivate it; and waited for the harvest. Economists have been ingenious enough to prove that this alternative really secures her independence; but I shall not waste time in dealing with that. Practically, if there is no free land in England, the economic analysis holds good of England, in spite of Siberia, Central Africa, and the Wild West. Again, it is not immediately true that men are governed in production solely by a determination to realize the maximum·of exchange value. The impulse to production often takes specific direction in the first instance; and a man will insist on producing

pictures or plays although he might gain more money
by producing boots or bonnets. But, his specific impulse once gratified, he will make as much money as he
can. He will sell his picture or play for a hundred
pounds rather than for fifty. In short, though there is
no such person as the celebrated "economic man", man
being wilful rather than rational, yet when the wilful
man has had his way he will take what else he can get;
and so he always does appear, finally if not primarily,
as the economic man. On the whole, history, even in
the Old World, goes the way traced by the economist.
In the New World the correspondence is exact. The
United States and the Colonies have been peopled by
fugitives from the full-blown individualism of Western
Europe, pre-empting private property precisely as assumed in this investigation of the conditions of cultivation. The economic relations of these cultivators
have not since put on any of the old political disguises.
Yet among them, in confirmation of the validity of our
analysis, we see all the evils of our old civilizations
growing up; and though with them the end is not yet,
still it is from them to us that the great recent revival
of the cry for nationalization of the land has come,
articulated by a man who had seen the whole tragedy
of private property hurried through its acts with unprecedented speed in the mushroom cities of America.

On Socialism the analysis of the economic action of
Individualism bears as a discovery, in the private appropriation of land, of the source of those unjust privileges against which Socialism is aimed. It is practically
a demonstration that public property in land is the
basic economic condition of Socialism. But this does
not involve at present a literal restoration of the land
to the people. The land is at present in the hands of
the people: its proprietors are for the most part absen-
tees. The modern form of private property is simply a
legal claim to take a share of the produce of the
national industry year by year without working for it.

It refers to no special part or form of that produce; and in process of consumption its revenue cannot be distinguished from earnings, so that the majority of persons, accustomed to call the commodities which form the income of the proprietor his private property, and seeing no difference between them and the commodities which form the income of a worker, extend the term private property to the worker's subsistence also, and can only conceive an attack on private property as an attempt to empower everybody to rob everybody else all round. But the income of a private proprietor can be distinguished by the fact that he obtains it unconditionally and gratuitously by private right against the public weal, which is incompatible with the existence of consumers who do not produce. Socialism involves discontinuance of the payment of these incomes, and addition of the wealth so saved to incomes derived from labor. As we have seen, incomes derived from private property consist partly of economic rent; partly of pensions; also called rent, obtained by the subletting of tenant rights; and partly of a form of rent called interest, obtained by special adaptations of land to production by the application of capital: all these being finally paid out of the difference between the produce of the worker's labor and the price of that labor sold in the open market for wages, salary, fees, or profits.[10] The whole, except economic rent, can be added directly to the incomes of the workers by simply discontinuing its exaction from them. Economic rent, arising as it does from variations of fertility or advantages of situation, must always be held as common or social wealth, and used, as the revenues raised by taxation are now used, for public purposes, among which Socialism would make national insurance and the provision of capital matters of the first importance.

[10] This excess of the product of labor over its price is treated as a single category with impressive effect by Karl Marx, who called it "surplus value" (*mehrwerth*).

The economic problem of Socialism is thus solved; and the political question of how the economic solution is to be practically applied does not come within the scope of this essay. But if we have got as far as an intellectual conviction that the source of our social misery is no eternal well-spring of confusion and evil, but only an artificial system susceptible of almost infinite modification and readjustment—nay, of practical demolition and substitution at the will of Man, then a terrible weight will be lifted from the minds of all except those who are, whether avowedly to themselves or not, clinging to the present state of things from base motives. We have had in this century a stern series of lessons on the folly of believing anything for no better reason than that it is pleasant to believe it. It was pleasant to look round with a consciousness of possessing a thousand a year, and say, with Browning's David, "All's love; and all's law". It was pleasant to believe that the chance we were too lazy to take in this world would come back to us in another. It was pleasant to believe that a benevolent hand was guiding the steps of society; overruling all evil appearances for good; and making poverty here the earnest of a great blessedness and reward hereafter. It was pleasant to lose the sense of worldly inequality in the contemplation of our equality before God. But utilitarian questioning and scientific answering turned all this tranquil optimism into the blackest pessimism. Nature was shewn to us as "red in tooth and claw": if the guiding hand were indeed benevolent, then it could not be omnipotent; so that our trust in it was broken: if it were omnipotent, it could not be benevolent; so that our love of it turned to fear and hatred. We had never admitted that the other world, which was to compensate for the sorrows of this, was open to horses and apes (though we had not on that account been any the more merciful to our horses); and now came Science to shew us the corner of the pointed ear of the horse on our own heads, and present the ape to us as our blood relation. No proof came of the existence of that other world and that benevolent power to which we had left the remedy of the atrocious wrongs of the poor: proof after proof came that what we called Nature knew and cared no more about our pains and pleasures than we know or care about the tiny creatures we crush underfoot as we walk through the fields. Instead of at once perceiving that this meant no more than that Nature was unmoral and indifferent, we relapsed into a gross form of devil worship, and conceived Nature as a remorselessly malignant power. This was no better than the old optimism, and infinitely gloomier. It kept our eyes still shut to the truth and that there is no cruelty and selfishness outside Man himself; and that his own active benevolence can combat and vanquish both. When the Socialist came forward as a meliorist on these lines, the old school of political economists, who could see no alternative to private property, put forward in proof of the powerlessness of benevolent action to arrest the deadly automatic production of poverty by the increase of population, the very analysis I have just presented. Their conclusions exactly fitted in with the new ideas. It was Nature at it again—the struggle for existence— the remorseless extirpation of the weak—the survival of the fittest—in short, natural selection at work. Socialism seemed too good to be true: it was passed by as merely the old optimism foolishly running its head against the stone wall of modern science. But Socialism now challenges individualism, scepticism, pessimism, worship of Nature personified as a devil, on their own ground of science. The science of the production and distribution of wealth is Political Economy. Socialism appeals to that science, and, turning on Individualism its own guns, routs it in incurable disaster. Henceforth the bitter cynic who still finds the world an eternal and unimprovable doghole, with the

placid person of means who repeats the familiar misquotation, "the poor ye shall have always with you",
lose their usurped place among the cultured, and pass
over to the ranks of the ignorant, the shallow, and the
superstitious. As for the rest of us, since we were taught
to revere proprietary respectability in our unfortunate
childhood, and since we found our childish hearts so
hard and unregenerate that they secretly hated and
rebelled against respectability in spite of that teaching,
it is impossible to express the relief with which we
discover that our hearts were all along right, and that
the current respectability of today is nothing but a
huge inversion of righteous and scientific social order
weltering in dishonesty, uselessness, selfishness, wan-
ton misery, and idiotic waste of magnificent oppor-
tunities for noble and happy living. It was terrible to
feel this, and yet to fear that it could not be helped—
that the poor must starve and make you ashamed of
your dinner—that they must shiver and make you
ashamed of your warm overcoat. It is to economic science—once the Dismal, now the Hopeful—that we are
indebted for the discovery that though the evil is enormously worse than we knew, yet it is not eternal—not
even very long lived, if we only bestir ourselves to
make an end of it.

# 2. HISTORIC

## By Sidney Webb

THE DEVELOPMENT OF THE DEMOCRATIC IDEAL

In discussing the historic groundwork of Socialism, it is worth remembering that no special claim is
made for Socialism in the assertion that it possesses a
basis in history. Just as every human being has an
ancestry, unknown to him though it may be; so every
idea, every incident, every movement has in the past
its own long chain of causes, without which it could
not have been. Formerly we were glad to let the dead
bury their dead: nowadays we turn lovingly to the
records, whether of persons or things; and we busy
ourselves willingly among origins, even without conscious utilitarian end. We are no longer proud of having ancestors, since everyone has them; but we are
more than ever interested in our ancestors, now that
we find in them the fragments which compose our
very selves. The historic ancestry of the English social
organization during the present century stands witness
to the irresistible momentum of the ideas which Socialism denotes. The record of the century in English
social history begins with the trial and hopeless failure
of an almost complete industrial individualism, in
which, however, unrestrained private ownership of
land and capital was accompanied by subjection to a

political oligarchy. So little element of permanence was there in this individualistic order that, with the progress of political emancipation, private ownership of the means of production has been, in one direction or another, successively regulated, limited and superseded, until it may now fairly be claimed that the Socialist philosophy of to-day is but the conscious and explicit assertion of principles of social organization which have been already in great part unconsciously adopted. The economic history of the century is an almost continuous record of the progress of Socialism.[1]

Socialism, too, has in the record of its internal development a history of its own. Down to the present generation, the aspirant after social regeneration naturally vindicated the practicability of his ideas by offering an elaborate plan with specifications of a new social order from which all contemporary evils were eliminated. Just as Plato had his Republic and Sir Thomas More his Utopia, so Babœuf had his Charter of Equality, Cabet his Icaria, St. Simon his Industrial System, and Fourier his ideal Phalanstery. Robert Owen spent a fortune in pressing upon an unbelieving generation his New Moral World and even Auguste Comte, superior as he was to many of the weaknesses of his time, must needs add a detailed Polity to his Philosophy of Positivism.

The leading feature of all these proposals was what may be called their statical character. The ideal society was represented as in perfectly balanced equilibrium, without need or possibility of future organic alteration. Since their day we have learned that social reconstruction must not be gone at in this fashion. Owing mainly to the efforts of Comte, Darwin, and Herbert Spencer, we can no longer think of the ideal society as an unchanging State. The social ideal from being

[1] See "Socialism in England" (American Economic Association, vol. iv., part 2, May 1889), in which a portion of this essay has been embodied.

static has become dynamic. The necessity of the constant growth and development of the social organism has become axiomatic. No philosopher now looks for anything but the gradual evolution of the new order from the old, without breach of continuity or abrupt change of the entire social tissue at any point during the process. The new becomes itself old, often before it is consciously recognized as new; and history shews us no example of the sudden substitution of Utopian and revolutionary romance.

Though Socialists have learnt this lesson[2] better than most of their opponents, the common criticism of Socialism has not yet noted the change, and still deals mainly with the obsolete Utopias of the pre-evolutionary age. Parodies of the domestic details of an imaginary Phalanstery, and homilies on the failure of Brook Farm or Icaria, may be passed over as belated and irrelevant now that Socialists are only advocating the conscious adoption of a principle of social organization which the world has already found to be the inevitable outcome of Democracy and the Industrial Revolution. For Socialism is by this time a wave surging throughout all Europe; and for want of a grasp of the series of apparently unconnected events by which and with which it has been for two generations rapidly coming upon us—for want, in short, of knowledge of its intellectual history, we in England to-day see our political leaders in a general attitude of astonishment at the changing face of current politics; both great parties drifting vaguely before a nameless undercurrent which

[2] "I am aware that there are some who suppose that our present bourgeois arrangements must be totally destroyed and others substituted almost at a blow. But however successful a revolution might be, it is certain that mankind cannot change its whole nature all at once. Break the old shell, certainly; but never forget the fact that the new forms *must* grow out of the old" (H. M. Hyndman, "Historical Basis of Socialism", 1883, p. 305).

they fail utterly to recognize or understand.[3] With some dim impression that Socialism is one of the Utopian dreams they remember to have heard comfortably disposed of in their academic youth as the impossible ideal of Humanity-intoxicated Frenchmen, they go their ways through the nineteenth century as a countryman blunders through Cheapside. One or two are history fanciers, learned in curious details of the past: the present eludes these no less than the others. They are so near to the individual events that they are blind to the onward sweep of the column. They cannot see the forest for the trees.

History not only gives the clue to the significance of contemporary events; it also enables us to understand those who have not yet found that clue. We learn to class men and ideas in a kind of geological order in time. The Comte de Paris gives us excellent proofs that in absolute monarchy lies the only safety of social order. He is a survival: the type flourished in the sixteenth century; and the splendid fossils of that age can be studied in any historic museum. Lord Bramwell will give cogent reasons for the belief that absolute freedom of contract, subject to the trifling exception of a drastic criminal law, will ensure a perfect State. His lordship is a survival from a nearer epoch: about 1840 this was as far as social science had got; and there are still persons who have learnt nothing of later date. When I see the Hipparion at South Kensington I do not take his unfamiliar points to be those of a horse of a superior kind: I know that he is an obsolete and superseded pattern, from which the horse has developed. Historic fossils are more dangerous; for they are left at large, and are not even excluded from Downing Street or Westminster. But against the stream of tendencies they are ultimately powerless. Though they sometimes appear

[3] See the article on "Socialism in English Politics," by William Clarke in the *Political Science Quarterly,* December 1888.

victorious, each successive struggle takes place further down the current which they believe themselves to be resisting.

The main stream which has borne European society towards Socialism during the past 100 years is the irresistible progress of Democracy. De Tocqueville drove and hammered this truth into the reluctant ears of the Old World two generations ago; and we have all pretended to carry it about as part of our mental furniture ever since. But like most epigrammatic commonplaces, it is not generally realized; and De Tocqueville's book has, in due course, become a classic which everyone quotes and nobody reads. The progress of Democracy is, in fact, often imagined, as by Sir Henry Maine, to be merely the substitution of one kind of political machinery for another; and there are many political Democrats to-day who cannot understand why social or economic matters should be mixed up with politics at all. It was not for this that they broke the power of the aristocracy: they were touched not so much with love of the many as with hatred of the few;[4] and, as has been acutely said—though usually by foolish persons—they are Radicals merely because they are not themselves lords. But it will not long be possible for any man to persist in believing that the political organization of society can be completely altered without corresponding changes in economic and social relations. De Tocqueville expressly pointed out that the progress of Democracy meant nothing less than a complete dissolution of the nexus by which society was held together under the old *régime*. This dissolution is followed by a period of anarchic spiritual isolation of the individual from his fellows, and to that extent by a general denial of the very idea of society. But man is a social animal; and after more or less interval there

[4] Even Bentham said this of James Mill (Bain's Life of J. M., p. 461), of whom it was hardly true.

necessarily comes into existence a new nexus, differing so entirely from the old-fashioned organization that the historic fossil goes about denying that it is a nexus at all, or that any new nexus is possible or desirable. To him, mostly through lack of economics, the progress of Democracy is nothing more than the destruction of old political privileges; and, naturally enough, few can see any beauty in mere dissolution and destruction. Those few are the purely political Radical abhorred of Comte and Carlyle: they are in social matters the empiricist survivals from a pre-scientific age.

The mere Utopians, on the other hand, who wove the baseless fabric of their visions of reconstructed society on their own private looms, equally failed, as a rule, to comprehend the problem of the age. They were, in imagination, resuscitated Joseph the Seconds, benevolent despots who would have poured the old world, had it only been fluid, into their new moulds. Against their crude plans the Statesman, the Radical, and the Political Economist were united; for they took no account of the blind social forces which they could not control, and which went on inexorably working out social salvation in ways unsuspected by the Utopian.

In the present Socialist movement these two streams are united: advocates of social reconstruction have learnt the lesson of Democracy, and know that it is through the slow and gradual turning of the popular mind to new principles that social reorganization bit by bit comes. All students of society who are abreast of their time, Socialists as well as Individualists, realize that important organic changes can only be (1) democratic, and thus acceptable to a majority of the people, and prepared for in the minds of all; (2) gradual, and thus causing no dislocation, however rapid may be the rate of progress; (3) not regarded as immoral by the mass of the people, and thus not subjectively demoralizing to them; and (4) in this country at any rate, constitutional and peaceful. Socialists may therefore be

quite at one with Radicals in their political methods.
Radicals, on the other hand, are perforce realizing that
mere political levelling is insufficient to save a State
from anarchy and despair. Both sections have been
driven to recognize that the root of the difficulty is economic; and there is every day a wider consensus that
the inevitable outcome of Democracy is the control by
the people themselves, not only of their own political
organization, but, through that, also of the main instruments of wealth production; the gradual substitution
of organized co-operation for the anarchy of the competitive struggle; and the consequent recovery, in the
only possible way, of what John Stuart Mill calls "the
enormous share which the possessors of the instruments of industry are able to take from the produce."[5]
The economic side of the democratic ideal is, in fact,
Socialism itself.

### THE DISINTEGRATION OF THE OLD SYNTHESIS

At the middle of the last century Western Europe
was still organized on a system of which the basis was
virtually a surviving feudalism. The nexus between
man and man was essentially a relation of superiority
and inferiority. Social power still rested either with
the monarch, or with the owners of large landed
estates. Some inroads had already been made in the
perfect symmetry of the organization, notably by the
growth of towns, and the rise of the still comparatively
small trading class; but the bulk of the population was
arranged in an hierarchical series of classes, linked to
one another by the bond of Power.

We are apt to think of England as differing in this
respect from continental Europe, and to imagine that
our popular freedom was won in 1688, if not in 1648,

[5] "Principles of Political Economy", last edition, 1865,
p. 477 (quoting from Feugueray).

or even as far back as Magna Charta itself. But as regards the people at large this was, in the main, merely a difference in political form. In England the aristocratic oligarchy had prevailed over the monarch: in France the King had defeated the Fronde. For the mass of the people in either country there was nothing but obedience.

Even in England the whole political administration was divided between the king and the great families; and not one person in 500 possessed so much as a vote. As lately as 1831 one hundred and fifty persons returned a majority of the House of Commons (Molesworth, "History of the Reform Bill" p. 347). The Church, once a universal democratic organization of international fraternity, had become a mere *appanage* of the landed gentry. The administration of justice and of the executive government was entirely in their hands, while Parliament was filled with their leaders as nominees. No avenue of advancement existed for even exceptionally gifted sons of the people; and the masses found themselves born into a position of life-long dependence upon a class of superior birth.

The economic organization was of a similar character. Two-thirds of the population tilled the soil, and dwelt in lonely hamlets scattered about the still sparsely inhabited country. Though possessing the remnants of ancient communal rights, they were practically dependent on the farmers of the parish, who fixed their wages by a constant tacit conspiracy.[6] The farmers themselves were the obedient serfs of the large proprietors, to whom they paid a customary rent. Though nominally free to move, both farmers and laborers were practically fettered to the manor by their ignorance and their poverty[7]; and though the lord had lost

[6] Referred to in a celebrated passage by Adam Smith, "Wealth of Nations", Book I, chap. viii.
[7] Not to mention the restrictions imposed by the law of "Settlement" (13 and 14 Charles II., chap. 12), which

the criminal jurisdiction of his manorial courts, his powers as Justice of the Peace formed a full equivalent. His unrestrained ownership of the land enabled him to take for himself as rent the whole advantage of all but the very worst of the soils in use; and the lingering manorial rights gave him toll even from that worst. Throughout the countryside his word was law and his power irresistible. It was a world whose nexus was might, economic and political, tempered only by custom and lack of stimulus to change. The poor were not necessarily worse off in material matters than they are now: the agricultural laborer, indeed, was apparently better off in 1750 than at any other time between 1450 and 1850.[8] But it was a world still mainly mediæval in political, in economic, and in social relations: a world of status and of permanent social inequalities not differing essentially from the feudalism of the past.

The system had, however, already begun to decay. The rise of the towns by the growth of trade gradually created new centres of independence and new classes who broke the bonds of innate status. The intrusion of the moneyed city classes and the Indian "Nabobs" into the rural districts tended to destroy the feudal idea. The growth of new sects in religion made fresh points of individual resistance, degenerating often into spiritual anarchy or unsocial quietism. The spread of learning built up a small but active disintegrating force of those who had detected the shams around them. But the real Perseus who was to free the people from their political bondage was Newcomen or Watt, Hargreaves or Crompton, Kay or Arkwright, whichever may be considered to have contributed the main stroke towards

---

enabled two justices summarily to send back to his village any migrating labourer.

[8] This was noticed by Malthus, "Principles of Political Economy", p. 225; see also Professor Thorold Rogers, "History of Agriculture and Prices" and "Six Centuries of Work and Wages".

the Industrial Revolution of the last century.[9] From
the inventions of these men came the machine industry with its innumerable secondary results—the Factory
System and the upspringing of the Northern and Mid-
land industrial towns,[10] and the evangelization of the
waste places of the earth by the sale of grey shirtings.
Throughout one-third of England the manor gave way
to the mill or the mine; and the feudal lord had to
slacken his hold of political and social power in order
to give full play to the change which enriched him
with boundless rents and mining royalties. And so
it happened in England that the final collapse of
Mediævalism came, not by the Great Rebellion nor
by the Whig Treason of 1688, nor yet by the rule of
the Great Commoner, but by the Industrial Revolution
of the eighteenth century, which created the England
of to-day. Within a couple of generations the squire
faded away before the millowner: and feudalism lin-
gered thenceforth only in the rapidly diminishing rural
districts, and in the empty remnants of ceremonial
organization. The mediæval arrangement, in fact, could
not survive the fall of the cottage industry; and it is,
fundamentally, the use of new motors which has been
for a generation destroying the individualist conception
of property. The landlord and the capitalist are both
finding that the steam-engine is a Frankenstein which
they had better not have raised; for with it comes inevitably urban Democracy, the study of Political Economy and Socialism.

The event which brought to a head the influences
making for political change was the French Revolution. The fall of the Bastille was hailed by all who had

[9] Further detail will be found in the following essay. See
also Arnold Toynbee's "Industrial Revolution".
[10] Between 1801–45 the population of Manchester grew
109 per cent., Glasgow 108 per cent., Liverpool 100 per
cent., and Leeds 99 per cent. (Report of Commissioners
on State of Health of Large Towns, 1843–5.)

been touched by the new ideas. "How much the greatest event it is that ever happened in the world; and
how much the best!" wrote Charles James Fox.[11] It
shewed, or seemed to shew, to men that a genuine
social reconstruction was not only desirable but possible. The National Assembly, respectable old oligarchy as it was, pointed the way to legislative fields
not even completely worked out.

When the rulers of England perceived that in
France at least Humpty Dumpty was actually down,
the effect at first was to tighten the existing organization. The mildest agitation was put down with a
cruelly strong hand. The Whig party in the House of
Commons sank to half-a-dozen members. Prices were
kept up and wages down, while the heaviest possible
load of taxation was imposed on the suffering people.
Then came the Peace, the Castlereagh's "White Terror", culminating in the "massacre of Peterloo" (1819)
and Lord Sidmouth's infamous "Six Acts". But the old
order was doomed. The suicide of Castlereagh was not
only the end of the man but also the sign of the collapse of the system. With a series of political wrenches
there came the Repeal of the Test and Corporation
Acts (1828), Catholic Emancipation (1829), the beginnings of legal administrative reform, and finally
the great Reform Bill of 1832, by which the reign of
the middle class superseded aristocratic rule. But the
people were no more enfranchised than they had
been before. The Factory had beaten the Manor for the
benefit, not of the factory hand, but of the millowner.
Democracy was at the gates; but it was still on the
wrong side of them. Its entry, however, was only a
matter of time. Since 1832 English political history is
the record of the reluctant enfranchisement of
one class after another, by mere force of the tendencies

[11] W. J. Lecky, "History of the Eighteenth Century",
Vol. V., p. 453.

of the age. None of these enfranchised classes has ever sincerely desired to admit new voters to share the privileges and submerge the power which it had won but each political party in turn has been driven to "shoot Niagara" in order to compete with its opponents. The Whig Bill of 1832 enfranchised the middle-class for Parliament: the Municipal Corporations Act of 1835 gave them the control of the provincial towns. After a generation of agitation, it was ultimately the Tory party which gave the townspeople in 1867 Household Suffrage. Eleven years later a Conservative majority passed Sir Charles Dilke's Act enfranchising the tenement occupier (1878). In 1885 the Liberals, intending permanently to ruin their opponents, gave the vote to the agricultural laborer; and last year (1888) it was the Tories, not to be outdone, who gave him the control of the local administration of the counties, and placed the government of London in the hands of a popularly elected council. Neither party can claim much credit for its reform bills, extorted as they have been, not by belief in Democracy, but by fear of the opposing faction. Even now the citizen is tricked out of his vote by every possible legal and administrative technicality; so that more than one-third of our adult men are unenfranchised,[12] together with the whole of the other sex. Neither the Conservative party nor the self-styled "Party of the Masses" gives proof of any real desire to give the vote to this not inconsiderable remnant; but both sides pay lip-homage to Democracy; and everyone knows that it is merely a waiting race between them as to which shall be driven to take the next step. The virtual completion of the political revolution is already in sight: and no more striking testimony can be given of the momentum of the new ideas which the Fall of the Bastille effectually spread over the world than this

[12] The number of registered electors at the date of the last Election (1886) was 5,707,823, out of an adult male population of over nine millions.

democratic triumph in England, within less than a century, over the political mediævalism of ten centuries
growth.

The full significance of this triumph is as yet unsuspected by the ordinary politician. The industrial revolution has left the laborer a landless stranger in his own
country. The political evolution is rapidly making him
its ruler. Samson is feeling for his grip on the pillars.

### THE PERIOD OF ANARCHY

The result of the industrial revolution, with its dissolution of mediævalism amid an impetuous reaction
against the bureaucratic tyranny of the past, was to
leave all the new elements of society in a state of unrestrained license. Individual liberty, in the sense of
freedom to privately appropriate the means of production, reached its maximum at the commencement of
the century. No sentimental regulations hindered the
free employment of land and capital to the greatest
possible pecuniary gain of the proprietors, however
many lives of men, women and children were used up
in the process. Ignorant or unreflecting capitalists still
speak of that terrible time with exultation. "It was not
five per cent or ten per cent", says one, "but thousands
per cent that made the fortunes of Lancashire".

Mr. Herbert Spencer and those who agree in his
worship of Individualism,[13] apparently desire to bring
back the legal position which made possible the "white
slavery" of which the "sins of legislators" have deprived
us; but no serious attempt has ever been made to get
repealed any one of the Factory Acts. Women working
half naked in the coal mines; young children dragging
trucks all day in the foul atmosphere of the under-

[13] Few, however, of Mr. Spencer's followers appear to
realise that he presupposes Land Nationalization as the
necessary condition of an Individualist community (see
"Social Statics", *passim*).

ground galleries; infants bound to the loom for fifteen hours in the heated air of the cotton mill, and kept awake only by the overlooker's lash; hours of labor for all, young and old, limited only by the utmost capabilities of physical endurance; complete absence of the sanitary provisions necessary to a rapidly growing population: these and other nameless iniquities will be found recorded as the results of freedom of contract and complete *laisser faire* in the impartial pages of successive blue-book reports.[14] But the Liberal mill-owners of the day, aided by some of the political economists, stubbornly resisted every attempt to interfere with their freedom to use "their" capital and "their" hands as they found most profitable, and (like their successors to-day) predicted of each restriction as it arrived that it must inevitably destroy the export trade and deprive them of all profit whatsoever.

But this "acute outbreak of individualism, unchecked by the old restraints, and invested with almost a religious sanction by a certain soulless school of writers,"[15] was inevitable, after the economic blundering of governments in the eighteenth century. Prior to the scientific investigation of economic laws, men had naturally interfered in social arrangements with very unsatisfac-

[14] It is sometimes asserted nowadays that the current descriptions of factory life under the *régime* of freedom of contract are much exaggerated. This is not the case. The horrors revealed in the reports of official enquiries even exceed those commonly quoted. For a full account of the legislation, and the facts on which it was founded, see Von Plener's "English Factory Legislation". The chief official reports are those of the House of Commons Committee of 1815–6, House of Lords Committee, 1819, and Royal Commission, 1840. Marx ("Capital") gives many other references. See also F. Engel's "Condition of the English Working Classes".

[15] Professor H. S. Foxwell (University College, London), p. 249 of Essay in "The Claims of Labor" (Edinburgh: Co-operative Printing Company, 1886).

tory results. A specially extravagant or a specially
thrifty king debased the currency, and then was surprised to find that in spite of stringent prohibitions
prices went up and all good money fled the country.
Wise statesmen, to keep up wages, encouraged the
woollen manufacturers of England by ruining those of
Ireland, and were then astonished to find English
wages cut by Irish pauper immigration. Benevolent
parliaments attempted to raise the worker's income by
poor law allowances, and then found that they had
lowered it. Christian kings eliminated half the skilled
artisans from their kingdoms, and then found that they
had ruined the rest by disabling industry. Government
inspectors ordered how the cloth should be woven,
what patterns should be made, and how broad the
piece should be, until the manufacturers in despair
cried out merely to be let alone.

When the early economists realized how radically
wrong had been even the well-meant attempts to regulate economic relations by legislation, and how generally these attempts multiplied private monopolies,
they leaned in their deductions heavily towards complete individual liberty. The administration of a populous state is such a very difficult matter, and when done
on false principles is so certain to be badly done, that
it was natural to advocate rather no administration at
all than the interference of ignorant and interested
bunglers. Nature, glorified by the worship of a famous
school of French philosophers and English poets, and
as yet unsuspected of the countless crimes of "the
struggle for existence", appeared at least more trustworthy than Castlereagh. Real democratic administration seemed, in the time of the "White Terror", and
even under the milder Whig hypocrisy which succeeded it, hopelessly remote. The best thing to work
and fight for was, apparently, the reduction to impotence and neutrality of all the "Powers that Be." Their
influence being for the moment hostile to the people,

it behoved the people to destroy their influence altogether. And so grew up the doctrine of what Professor
Huxley has since called "Administrative Nihilism." It
was the apotheosis of *Laisser Faire, Laisser Aller.*

Though the economists have since had to bear all the
blame for what nearly everyone now perceives to have
been an economic and social mistake, neither Hume
nor Adam Smith caught the *laisser faire* fever to as
great an extent as their French contemporaries and
imitators. The English industrial position was not the
same as that of France. The "mercantile system" by
which, as by "Fair Trade" to-day, foreign trade was to
be regulated and encouraged according as it tended
to cause the stock of goods, especially coin and bullion,
to increase in the country, was the same on both sides
of the Channel. But our political revolution had already
been partly accomplished; and the more obvious
shackles of feudalism had been long since struck off.
No Englishman was compelled to grind his corn at the
mill of the lord of the manor;[16] to give up unpaid days
to plough the lord's field and cart the lord's hay; or to
spend his nights in beating the waters of the lord's
marsh so that the croaking of the frogs might not dis-
turb the lord's repose. Our labor dues had long before
been commuted for money payments; and these had

[16] This statement, though generally true of England, is
not absolutely so. It needed an Act of Parliament in 1758
(32 George II, c. 61) to free the inhabitants of the
"village" of Manchester from the obligation to grind all
their corn and grain at the manorial watermills (Clifford's
"History of Private Bill Legislation", Vol. II., p. 478).
Even so late as 1809 they had to obtain the consent of Sir
Oswald Mosley, the lord of the manor, before a company
could be incorporated to provide a water supply (*Ibid*,
p. 480). Leeds was theoretically compelled to grind its
corn, grain and malt at the lord's mills down to 1839, and
actually had then to pay £13,000 to extinguish this feudal
"due" (*Ibid*, p. 498).

become light owing to the change in currency values. Our apprenticeship laws and guild regulations were becoming rapidly inoperative. No vexatious excise or gabelle hampered our manufactures.

Tyranny there was, enough and to spare, and economic spoliation; but they did not take the form of personal interferences and indignities. The non-noble Frenchman was bond, and he knew it; the middle-class Englishman to a great extent thought himself free: his economic servitude, though it galled him, was not clearly distinguishable from the niggardliness of nature. The landlord in France was an obvious tyrant: here he certainly caused (by the abstraction of the economic rent) an artificial barrenness of the workers' labor; but the barrenness was so old and had been so constant that it was not seen to be artificial, and was not resented as such. No peasant rebels against the blight. Accordingly, we have, since 1381, never had in England a burning of the *chateaux*; and accordingly, too, Adam Smith is no complete champion of *laisser faire*, though his great work was effective mainly in sweeping away foreign trade restrictions and regulations, and in giving mobility to labor by establishing the laborer's geographical freedom to move and to enter into the wage contract when and where he best could. The English economists, stopping illogically short of the complete freedom preached by Rousseau and Godwin and the scientific Anarchists of to-day, advocated just as much freedom as sufficed to make the fortunes of Lancashire capitalists and to create the modern proletariat. The Utilitarians are approximately coupled with the Political Economists in connexion with this phase of thought. Although Adam Smith did not belong to their school, almost the whole work of developing and popularizing the new science was done by them. It was not until after the Peace—when Bentham and James Mill were in full vigor, and soon to be reinforced by Austin, Villiers, John Stuart Mill, Roebuck, Grote, Ricardo, and others—that Political Economy became a force in England. The motive and enthusiasm for the new science undoubtedly came from the Utilitarian ethics. If the sole masters of man were pleasure and pain, the knowledge of the natural laws expressing the course of social action, and thus regulating pleasure and pain, became of vital importance. If it is God's will, as Paley and Austin asserted, that men should seek for happiness, then the study of how to obtain economic comfort becomes a sacred duty, and has ever been so regarded by such rational divines as Malthus, Chalmers, Maurice, Kingsley, and the young High Church party of to-day. Christianity and the course of modern thought began to join hands; and we may see in Bishop Berkeley and Paley the forerunners of such a development as the Guild of St. Matthew.[17]

The Utilitarian philosophy, besides aiding in the popularization of economic science, strongly influenced its early character. The tendency to *Laisser Faire* inherited from the country and century of upheaval and revolt against authority, was fostered by Bentham's destructive criticism of all the venerable relics of the past. What is the use of it, he asked, of every shred of social institution then existing. What is the net result of its being upon individual happiness? Few of the laws and customs—little, indeed, of the social organization of that time could stand this test. England was covered with rotten survivals from bygone circumstances; the whole administration was an instrument for class domination and parasite nurture; the progress of the industrial revolution was rapidly making obsolete all laws, customs, proverbs, maxims, and nursery tales; and the sudden increase of population was baffling all expectations and disconcerting all

[17] See its organ, the *Church Reformer*. London: 8, Duke Street, Adelphi.

arrangements. At last it came to be carelessly accepted
as the teaching both of philosophy and of experience
that every man must fight for himself; and "devil take
the hindmost" became the accepted social creed of
what was still believed to be a Christian nation. Utili-
tarianism became the Protestantism of Sociology, and
"how to make for self and family the best of both
worlds" was assumed to be the duty, as it certainly was
the aim, of every practical Englishman.

The new creed of "Philosophic Radicalism" did not
have matters all its own way. Its doctrines might suit
millowners and merchant princes, and all who were
able to enjoy the delight of their own strength in the
battle of life. But it was essentially a creed of Murd-
stones and Gradgrinds; and the first revolt came from
the artistic side. The "nest of singing birds" at the
Lakes would have none of it, though De Quincey
worked out its abstract economics in a manner still un-
surpassed. Coleridge did his best to drown it in
German Transcendentalism. Robert Owen and his
following of enthusiastic communistic co-operators
steadfastly held up a loftier ideal. The great mass of
the wage earners never bowed the knee to the principles upon which the current "White Slavery" was
maintained. But the first man who really made a dint
in the individualist shield was Carlyle, who knew how
to compel men to listen to him. Oftener wrong than
right in his particular proposals, he managed to keep
alive the faith in nobler ends than making a fortune
in this world and saving one's soul in the next. Then
came Maurice, Kingsley, Ruskin, and others who
dared to impeach the current middle class cult; until
finally, through Comte and John Stuart Mill, Darwin

and Herbert Spencer, the conception of the Social Organism has at last penetrated to the minds, though not yet to the books, even of our professors of Political Economy.

Meanwhile, caring for none of these things, the practical man had been irresistibly driven in the same direction. In the teeth of the current Political Economy, and in spite of all the efforts of the millowning Liberals, England was compelled to put forth her hand to succour and protect her weaker members. Any number of Local Improvement Acts, Drainage Acts, Truck Acts, Mines Regulation Acts, Factory Acts, Public Health Acts, Adulteration Acts, were passing into law.[18] The liberty of the property owner to oppress the propertyless by the levy of economic tribute of rent and interest began to be circumscribed, pared away, obstructed and forbidden in various directions. Slice after slice has gradually been cut from the profits of capital, and therefore from its selling value, by socially beneficial restrictions on its user's liberty to do

[18] The beginning of factory legislation is to be found in the "Morals and Health Act", 42 Geo. III, c. 73 (1802). Others followed in 1819, 1825, and 1831; but their provisions were almost entirely evaded owing to the absence of inspectors. After the Reform Bill more stringent enactments in 1833, 1844, and 1847, secured some improvement. The Act of 1878 consolidated the law on the subject. The Radical and Socialist proposals for further development in this direction will be found at page 74. Nearly 400 Local Improvement Acts had been passed up to 1845. In the succeeding years various general Acts were passed, which were henceforth incorporated by reference in all local Acts. The first "Public Health Act" was passed in 1848; and successive extensions were given to this restrictive legislation with sanitary ends in 1855, 1858, 1861, and 1866. Consolidating Acts in 1871, and finally in 1875, complete the present sanitary code, which now forms a thick volume of restrictions upon the free use of land and capital.

as he liked with it. Slice after slice has been cut off the
incomes from rent and interest by the gradual shifting
of taxation from consumers to persons enjoying incomes above the average of the kingdom.[19] Step by
step the political power and political organization of
the country have been used for industrial ends, until
to-day the largest employer of labor is one of the ministers of the Crown (the Postmaster-General); and almost every conceivable trade is, somewhere or other,
carried on by parish, municipality, or the National
Government itself without the intervention of any
middleman or capitalist. The theorists who denounce
the taking by the community into its own hands of
the organization of its own labor as a thing economically unclean, repugnant to the sturdy individual independence of Englishmen, and as yet outside the
sphere of practical politics, seldom have the least suspicion of the extent to which it has already been carried.[20] Besides our international relations and the
army, navy, police and the courts of justice, the community now carries on for itself, in some part or another of these islands, the post office, telegraphs,
carriage of small commodities, coinage, surveys, the
regulation of the currency and note issue, the provision
of weights and measures, the making, sweeping, lighting, and repairing of streets, roads, and bridges, life
insurance, the grant of annuities, shipbuilding, stock-
broking, banking, farming, and money-lending. It
provides for many thousands of us from birth to burial
—midwifery, nursery, education, board and lodging,
vaccination, medical attendance, medicine, public worship, amusements, and interment. It furnishes and
maintains its own museums, parks, art galleries, li-

[19] The *minimum* income chargeable to Income Tax (150)
closely corresponds with the *average* family income. See
Fabian Tract, No. 5, "Facts for Socialists".
[20] See "The Progress of Socialism". (London: The Modern Press, 13 Paternoster Row, E.C. Price One Penny.)

braries, concert-halls, roads, streets, bridges, markets, slaughter-houses, fire-engines, lighthouses, pilots, ferries, surfboats, steamtugs, lifeboats, cemeteries, public baths, washhouses, pounds, harbours, piers, wharves, hospitals, dispensaries, gasworks, waterworks, tramways, telegraph cables, allotments, cow meadows, artizans' dwellings, schools, churches, and reading-rooms. It carries on and publishes its own researches in geology, meteorology, statistics, zoology, geography, and even theology. In our Colonies the English Government further allows and encourages the communities to provide for themselves railways, canals, pawnbroking, theatres, forestry, cinchona farms, irrigation, leper villages, casinos, bathing establishments, and immigration, and to deal in ballast, guano, quinine, opium, salt, and what not. Every one of these functions, with those of the army, navy, police, and courts of justice, were at one time left to private enterprise, and were a source of legitimate individual investment of capital. Step by step the community has absorbed them, wholly or partially; and the area of private exploitation has been lessened. Parallel with this progressive nationalization or municipalization of industry, there has gone on the elimination of the purely personal element in business management. The older economists doubted whether anything but banking and insurance could be carried on by joint stock enterprise: now every conceivable industry, down to baking and milk-selling, is successfully managed by the salaried officers of large corporations of idle shareholders. More than one-third of the whole business of England, measured by the capital employed,[21] is now done by joint stock companies, whose shareholders could be expropriated by the community with no more dislocation of the industries carried on by them than is caused by the daily purchase of shares on the Stock Exchange.

[21] See "Capital and Land" (Fabian Tract, No. 7), page 7.

Besides its direct supersession of private enterprise, the State now registers, inspects, and controls nearly all the industrial functions which it has not yet absorbed. In addition to births, marriages, deaths, and electors, the State registers all solicitors, barristers, notaries, patent agents, brokers, newspaper proprietors, playing-card makers, brewers, bankers, seamen, captains, mates, doctors, cabmen, hawkers, pawnbrokers, tobacconists, distillers, plate dealers, game dealers, all insurance companies, friendly societies, endowed schools and charities, limited companies, lands, houses, deeds, bills of sale, compositions, ships, arms, dogs, cabs, omnibuses, books, plays, pamphlets, newspapers, raw cotton movements, trademarks, and patents; lodging-houses, public-houses, refreshment-houses, theatres, music-halls, places of worship, elementary schools, and dancing rooms.

Nor is the registration a mere form. Most of the foregoing are also inspected and criticised, as are all railways, tramways, ships, mines, factories, canal-boats, public conveyances, fisheries, slaughter-houses, dairies, milkshops, bakeries, baby-farms, gasmeters, schools of anatomy, vivisection laboratories, explosive works, Scotch herrings, and common lodging-houses.

The inspection is often detailed and rigidly enforced. The State in most of the larger industrial operations prescribes the age of the worker, the hours of work, the amount of air, light, cubic space, heat, lavatory accommodation, holidays, and mealtimes; where, when, and how wages shall be paid; how machinery, staircases, lift holes, mines, and quarries are to be fenced and guarded; how and when the plant shall be cleaned, repaired, and worked. Even the kind of package in which some articles shall be sold is duly prescribed, so that the individual capitalist shall take no advantage of his position. On every side he is being registered, inspected, controlled, and eventually, superseded by the community; and in the meantime he is compelled to cede for public purposes an ever-increasing share of his rent and interest.

Even in the fields still abandoned to private enterprise, its operations are thus every day more closely limited, in order that the anarchic competition of private greed, which at the beginning of the century was set up as the only infallibly beneficent principle of social action, may not utterly destroy the State. All this has been done by "practical" men, ignorant, that is to say, of any scientific sociology believing Socialism to be the most foolish of dreams, and absolutely ignoring, as they thought, all grandiloquent claims for social reconstruction. Such is the irresistible sweep of social tendencies, that in their every act they worked to bring about the very Socialism they despised; and to destroy the Individualist faith which they still professed. They builded better than they knew.

It must by no means be supposed that these beginnings of social reorganization have been effected, or the proposals for their extension brought to the front, without the conscious efforts of individual reformers. The "Zeitgeist" is potent; but it does not pass Acts of Parliament without legislators, or erect municipal libraries without town councillors. Though our decisions are moulded by the circumstances of the time, and the environment at least roughhews our ends, shape them as we will; yet each generation decides for itself. It still rests with the individual to resist or promote the social evolution, consciously or unconsciously, according to his character and information. The importance of complete consciousness of the social tendencies of the age lies in the fact that its existence and comprehensiveness often determine the expediency of our particular action: we move with less resistance with the stream than against it.

The general failure to realize the extent to which

our unconscious Socialism has already proceeded—a
failure which causes much time and labor to be
wasted in uttering and elaborating on paper the most
ludicrously unpractical antisocialist demonstrations of
the impossibility of matters of daily occurrence—is due
to the fact that few know anything of local administration outside their own town. It is the municipalities
which have done most to "socialize" our industrial life;
and the municipal history of the century is yet unwrit-
ten. A few particulars may here be given as to this
progressive "municipalization" of industry. Most of
us know that the local governments have assumed the
care of the roads, streets and bridges, once entirely
abandoned to individual enterprise, as well as the
lighting and cleansing of all public thoroughfares, and
the provision of sewers, drains, and "storm-water
courses". It is, perhaps, not so generally known that
no less than £7,500,000 is annually expended on these
services in England and Wales alone, being about 5
per cent of the rent of the country. The provision of
markets, fairs, harbors, piers, docks, hospitals, cemeteries and burial grounds, is still shared with private
capitalists; but those in public hands absorb nearly
£2,000,000 annually. Parks, pleasure grounds, libraries,
museums, baths, and washhouses cost the public funds
over half a million sterling. All these are, however,
comparatively unimportant services. It is in the provision of gas, water, and tramways, that local authorities
organize labor on a large scale. Practically half the gas
consumers in the kingdom are supplied by public gas
works, which exist in 168 separate localities, with an
annual expenditure of over three millions.[22] It need
hardly be added that the advantage to the public is
immense, in spite of the enormous price paid for the
works in many instances and that the further munici-

[22] Government Return for 1887-8, see "Board of Trade
Journal", January, 1889, p. 76-8.

palization of the gas industry is proceeding with great rapidity, no fewer than twelve local authorities having obtained loans for the purpose (and one for electric lighting) in a single year (Local Government Board Report, 1887-8, C—5526, pp. 319—367). With equal rapidity is the water supply becoming a matter of commercial organization, the public expenditure already reaching nearly a million sterling annually. Sixty-five local authorities borrowed money for water supply in 1887-8, rural and urban districts being equally represented (C—5550, pp. 319—367). Tramways and ferries are undergoing the same development. About thirty-one towns, including nearly all the larger provincial centres, own some or all of their own tramways. Manchester, Bradford, Birmingham, Oldham, Sunderland, and Greenock lease their undertakings; but among the municipalities Huddersfield has the good sense to work its lines without any "middleman" intervention, with excellent public results. The tramway mileage belonging to local authorities has increased five-fold since 1878, and comprises more than a quarter of the whole (House of Commons Return, 1887-8, No. 347). The last important work completed by the Metropolitan Board of Works was the establishment of a "free steam ferry" on the Thames, charged upon the rates. This is, in some respects, the most significant development of all. The difference between a free steam ferry and a free railway is obviously only one of degree.

A few more cases are worth mentioning. Glasgow builds and maintains seven public "common lodging houses"; Liverpool provides science lectures; Manchester builds and stocks an art gallery; Birmingham runs schools of design; Leeds creates extensive cattle markets; and Bradford supplies water below cost price. There are nearly one hundred free libraries and reading rooms. The minor services now performed by public bodies are innumerable.[23] This "Municipal Socialism" has been rendered possible by the creation of a local debt now reaching over £181,000,000.[24] Nearly £10,000,000 is annually paid as interest and sinking fund on the debt; and to this extent the pecuniary benefit of municipalization is diminished. The full advantages[25] of the public organization of labor remain, besides a considerable pecuniary profit; whilst the objective differentiation of the economic classes (by the separation of the idle *rentier* from the manager or *entrepreneur*) enormously facilitates popular comprehension of the nature of the economic tribute known as interest. To the extent, moreover, that additional charges are thrown upon the rates, the interest paid to the capitalist is levied mainly at the cost of the landlord, and we have a corresponding "nationalization" of so much of the economic rent. The increase in the local rates has been 36 per cent., or nearly £7,000,-000, in eleven years, and is still growing. They now amount to over twenty-six millions sterling in England and Wales alone, or about 17 per cent. of the rental of the country (C—5,550, p. clxxiv.).

Nor is there any apparent prospect of a slackening of the pace of this unconscious abandonment of individualism. No member of Parliament has so much as

[23] It is not generally known that the Corporation of London actually carried on the business of fire insurance from 1681 to 1683, but was compelled to abandon it through the opposition of those interested in private undertakings, who finally obtained a mandamus in the Court of King's Bench to restrain their civic competitor (Walford's Insurance Cyclopædia, Vol. III., pp. 446–455).

[24] C—5,550, p. 436. This, by the way, is just about one year's rental. We pay every year to the landlords for permission to live in England as much as the whole outstanding cost of the magnificent property of the local governing authorities.

[25] See "The Government Organization of Labor", Report by a Committee of the Fabian Society, 1886.

introduced a Bill to give effect to the anarchist principles of Mr. Herbert Spencer's "Man *versus* the State".
The not disinterested efforts of the Liberty and Property Defence League fail to hinder even Conservative
Parliaments from further Socialist legislation. Mr.
Gladstone remarked to a friend in 1886 that the Home
Rule question would turn the Liberal party into a
Radical party. He might have said that it would make
both parties Socialist. Free elementary and public technical education is now practically accepted on both
sides of the House, provided that the so-called "voluntary schools," themselves half maintained from public
funds, are not extinguished. Mr. Chamberlain and
the younger Conservatives openly advocate far reaching projects of social reform through State and municipal agency, as a means of obtaining popular support.
The National Liberal Federation adopts the special
taxation of urban ground values as the main feature
in its domestic programme,[26] notwithstanding that
this proposal is characterized by old-fashioned Liberals
as sheer confiscation of so much of the landlords' property. The London Liberal and Radical Union, which
has Mr. John Morley for its president, even proposes
that the County Council shall have power to rebuild
the London slums at the sole charge of the ground
landlord.[27] It is, therefore, not surprising that the
Trades Union Congress should now twice have declared in favor of "Land Nationalization" by large ma-
jorities, or that the bulk of the London County Council should be returned on an essentially Socialist platform. The whole of the immediately practicable de-

[26] See Report of Annual Meeting at Birmingham, September 1888.
[27] See resolutions adopted by the Council, at the instance
of the Executive and General Committees, February 8th,
1889. (*Daily News,* 9th February.) Professor Stuart,
M.P., has now introduced a Bill embodying these astonishing proposals.

mands of the most exacting Socialist are, indeed, now often embodied in the current Radical programme; and the following exposition of it, from the pages of the *Star* newspaper, 8th August, 1888, may serve as a statement of the current Socialist demands for further legislation.[28]

### REVISION OF TAXATION

*Object*—Complete shifting of burden from the workers, of whatever grade, to the recipients of rent and interest, with a view to the ultimate and gradual extinction of the latter class.

*Means*—1. Abolition of all customs and excise duties, except those on spirits. 2. Increase of income tax, differentiating in favor of earned as against unearned incomes, and graduating cumulatively by system of successive levels of abatement. 3. Equalization and increase of death duties and the use of the proceeds as capital, not income. 4. Shifting of local rates and house duty from occupier to owner, any contract to the contrary notwithstanding. 5. Compulsory redemption of existing land tax and reimposition on all ground rents and increased values. 6. Abolition of fees on licenses for employment. 7. Abolition of police-court fees.

### EXTENSION OF FACTORY ACTS

*Object*—To raise, universally, the standard of comfort by obtaining the general recognition of a minimum wage and a maximum working day.

[28] It is interesting to compare this programme, with its primary insistence on economic and social reform, with the bare political character of the "Five Points" of the Chartists, viz., Manhood Suffrage, Vote by Ballot, Annual Parliaments, Payment of Members relieved from the property qualification, and Equal Electoral Districts.

*Means*—1. Extension of the general provisions of the Factory and Workshops Acts (or the Mines Regulation Acts, as the case may be) to all employers of labor. 2. Compulsory registration of all employers of more than three (?) workers. 3. Largely increased number of inspectors, and these to include women, and to be mainly chosen from the wage-earning class. 4. Immediate reduction of maximum hours to eight per day in all Government and municipal employment, in all mines, and in all licensed monopolies such as railways, tramways, gasworks, waterworks, docks, harbors, etc.; and in any trade in which a majority of the workers desire it. 5. The compulsory insertion of clauses in all contracts for Government or municipal supplies, providing that (*a*) there shall be no sub-contracting, (*b*) that no worker shall be employed more than eight hours per day, and (*c*) that no wages less than a prescribed minimum shall be paid.

## EDUCATIONAL REFORM

*Object*—To enable all, even the poorest, children to obtain not merely some, but the best education they are capable of.

*Means*—1. The immediate abolition of all fees in public elementary schools, Board or voluntary, with a corresponding increase in the Government grant. 2. Creation of a Minister for Education, with control over the whole educational system, from the elementary school to the University, and over all educational endowments. 3. Provision of public technical and secondary schools wherever needed, and creation of abundant public secondary scholarships. 4. Continuation, in all cases, of elementary education at evening schools. 5. Registration and inspection of all private educational establishments.

### RE-ORGANIZATION OF POOR LAW ADMINISTRATION

*Object*—To provide generously, and without stigma, for the aged, the sick, and those destitute through temporary want of employment, without relaxing the "tests" against the endowment of able-bodied idleness.

*Means*—1. The separation of the relief of the aged and the sick from the workhouse system, by a universal system of aged pensions, and public infirmaries. 2. The industrial organization and technical education of all able-bodied paupers. 3. The provision of temporary relief works for the unemployed. 4. The supersession of the Boards of Guardians by the local municipal authorities.

### EXTENSION OF MUNICIPAL ACTIVITY

*Object*—The gradual public organization of labor for all public purposes, and the elimination of the private capitalist and middleman.

*Means*—1. The provision of increased facilities for the acquisition of land, the destruction without compensation of all dwellings found unfit for habitation, and the provision of artisan dwellings by the municipality. 2. The facilitation of every extension of municipal administration, in London and all other towns, of gas, water, markets, tramways, hospitals, cemeteries, parks, museums, art galleries, libraries, reading-rooms, schools, docks, harbors, rivers, etc. 3. The provision of abundant facilities for the acquisition of land by local rural authorities, for allotments, common pastures, public halls, reading rooms, etc.

### AMENDMENT OF POLITICAL MACHINERY

*Object*—To obtain the most accurate representation and expression of the desires of the majority of the people at every moment.

*Means*—1. Reform of registration so as to give a vote, both Parliamentary and municipal, to every adult. 2. Abolition of any period of residence as a qualification for registration. 3. Biannual registration by special public officer. 4. Annual Parliaments. 5. Payment of election expenses, including postage of election addresses and polling cards. 6. Payment of all public representatives, parliamentary, county, or municipal. 7. Second ballot. 8. Abolition or painless extinction of the House of Lords.[29]

This is the programme to which a century of industrial revolution has brought the Radical working man. Like John Stuart Mill,[30] though less explicitly, he has turned from mere political Democracy to a complete, though unconscious, Socialism.[31]

### THE NEW SYNTHESIS

It need hardly be said that the social philosophy of the time did not remain unaffected by the political evolution and the industrial development. Slowly sinking into men's minds all this while was the conception of a new social nexus, and a new end of social life. It was discovered (or rediscovered) that a society is something more than an aggregate of so many individual units—that it possesses existence distinguishable from

[29] It need hardly be said that schemes of "free land," peasant proprietorship, or leasehold enfranchisement, find no place in the modern programme of the Socialist Radical, or Social Democrat. They are survivals of the Individualistic Radicalism which is passing away. Candidates seeking a popular "cry" more and more avoid these reactionary proposals.

[30] "Autobiography", p. 231–2. See also Book IV. of the "Principles of Political Economy" (Popular edition, 1865).

[31] For a forecast of the difficulties which this programme will have to encounter as its full scope and intention become more clearly realized, see the eighth essay in this volume, by Hubert Bland.

those of any of its components. A perfect city became recognized as something more than any number of good citizens—something to be tried by other tests, and weighed in other balances than the individual man. The community must necessarily aim, consciously or not, at its continuance as a community: its life transcends that of any of its members; and the interests of the individual unit must often clash with those of the whole. Though the social organism has itself evolved from the union of individual men, the individual is now created by the social organism of which he forms a part: his life is born of the larger life; his attributes are moulded by the social pressure; his activities, inextricably interwoven with others, belong to the activity of the whole. Without the continuance and sound health of the social organism, no man can now live or thrive; and its persistence is accordingly his paramount end. His conscious motive for action may be, nay always must be, individual to himself; but where such action proves inimical to the social welfare, it must sooner or later be checked by the whole, lest the whole perish through the error of its member. The conditions of social health are accordingly a matter for scientific investigation. There is, at any moment, one particular arrangement of social relations which involves the minimum of human misery then and there possible amid the "niggardliness of nature". Fifty years ago it would have been assumed that absolute freedom in the sense of individual or "manly" independence, plus a criminal code, would spontaneously result in such an arrangement for each particular nation; and the effect was the philosophic apotheosis of *Laisser Faire*. To-day every student is aware that no such optimistic assumption is warranted by the facts of life.[32] We know now that in natural

[32] See "Darwinism and Politics", by D. G. Ritchie, Fellow and Tutor of Jesus College, Oxford (London: Swan Sonnenschein and Co., 1889).

selection at the stage of development where the existence of civilized mankind is at stake, the units selected from are not individuals, but societies. Its action at earlier stages, though analogous, is quite dissimilar. Among the lower animals physical strength or agility is the favored quality: if some heaven-sent genius among the cuttle-fish developed a delicate poetic faculty, this high excellence would not delay his succumbing to his hulking neighbor. When, higher up in the scale, mental cunning became the favored attribute, an extra brain convolution, leading primitive man to the invention of fire or tools, enabled a comparatively puny savage to become the conqueror and survivor of his fellows.

Brain culture accordingly developed apace; but we do not yet thoroughly realize that this has itself been superseded as the "selected" attribute, by social organization. The cultivated Athenians, Saracens, and Provençals went down in the struggle for existence before their respective competitors, who, individually inferior, were in possession of a, at that time, more valuable social organization. The French nation was beaten in the last war, not because the average German was an inch and a half taller than the average Frenchman, or because he had read five more books, but because the German social organism was, for the purposes of the time, superior in efficiency to the French. If we desire to hand on to the afterworld our direct influence, and not merely the memory of our excellence, we must take even more care to improve the social organism of which we form part, than to perfect our own individual developments. Or rather, the perfect fitting development of each individual is not necessarily the utmost and highest cultivation of his own personality, but the filling, in the best possible way, of his humble function in the great social machine. We must abandon the self-conceit of imagining that we are independent units, and bend our jealous minds, absorbed in their own cultivation, to this subjection to the higher end, the Common Weal. Accordingly, conscious "direct adaptation" steadily supplants the unconscious and wasteful "indirect adaptation" of the earlier form of the struggle for existence; and with every advance in sociological knowledge Man is seen to assume more and more, not only the mastery of "things", but also a conscious control over social destiny itself.

This new scientific conception of the Social Organism has put completely out of countenance the cherished principles of the Political Economist and the Philosophic Radical. We left them sailing into Anarchy on the stream of *Laisser Faire*. Since then the tide has turned. The publication of John Stuart Mill's "Political Economy" in 1848 marks conveniently the boundary of the old individualist Economics. Every edition of Mill's book became more and more Socialistic. After his death the world learnt the personal history, penned by his own hand,[33] of his development from a mere political democrat to a convinced Socialist.

The change in tone since then has been such that one competent economist, professedly anti-Socialist,[34] publishes regretfully to the world that all the younger men are now Socialists, as well as many of the older Professors. It is, indeed, mainly from these that the world has learnt how faulty were the earlier economic generalizations, and above all, how incomplete as guides for social or political action. These generalizations are accordingly now to be met with only in leading articles, sermons, or the speeches of Ministers or

[33] "Autobiography", pp. 231–2.
[34] Rev. F. W. Aveling, Principal of Taunton Independent College, in leaflet "Down with the Socialists", August 1888. See also Professor H. Sidgwick on "Economic Socialism", *Contemporary Review*, November, 1886.

Bishops.[35] The Economist himself knows them no more.

The result of this development of Sociology is to compel a revision of the relative importance of liberty and equality as principles to be kept in view in social administration. In Bentham's celebrated "ends" to be aimed at in a civil code, liberty stands predominant over equality, on the ground that full equality can be maintained only by the loss of security for the fruits of labor. That exposition remains as true as ever; but the question for decision remains, how much liberty? Economic analysis has destroyed the value of the old criterion of respect for the equal liberty of others. Bentham, whose economics were weak, paid no attention to the perpetual tribute on the fruits of others' labor which full private property in land inevitably creates. In his view liberty and security to property meant that every worker should be free to obtain the full result of his own labor; and there appeared no inconsistency between them. The political economist now knows that with free competition and private property in land and capital, no individual can possibly obtain the full result of his own labor. The student of industrial development, moreover, finds it steadily more and more impossible to trace what is precisely the result of each separate man's toil. Complete rights of liberty and property necessarily involve, for example, the spoliation of the Irish cottier tenant for the benefit of Lord Clanricarde. What then becomes of the Benthamic principle of the greatest happiness of the greatest number? When the Benthamite comes to understand the Law of Rent, which of the two will he abandon? For he cannot escape the lesson of the century, taught alike by the economists, the statesmen, and the "practical men", that complete individual liberty, with unrestrained private

[35] That is to say, unfortunately, in nearly all the utterances which profess to guide our social and political action.

ownership of the instruments of wealth production, is irreconcileable with the common weal. The free struggle for existence among ourselves menaces our survival as a healthy and permanent social organism. Evolution, Professor Huxley [36] declares, is the substitution of consciously regulated co-ordination among the units of each organism, for blind anarchic competition. Thirty years ago Herbert Spencer demonstrated the incompatibility of full private property in land with the modern democratic State;[37] and almost every economist now preaches the same doctrine. The Radical is rapidly arriving, from practical experience, at similar conclusions; and the steady increase of the government regulation of private enterprise, the growth of municipal administration, and the rapid shifting of the burden of taxation directly to rent and interest, mark in treble lines the statesman's unconscious abandonment of the old Individualism, and our irresistible glide into collectivist Socialism.

It was inevitable that the Democracy should learn this lesson. With the masses painfully conscious of the failure of Individualism to create a decent social life for four-fifths of the people,[38] it might have been foreseen that Individualism could not survive their advent to political power. If private property in land and capital necessarily keeps the many workers permanently poor (through no fault of their own) in order to make the few idlers rich (from no merit of their own), private property in land and capital will inevitably go the way of the feudalism which it superseded. The economic analysis confirms the rough generalization of the suffering people. The history

[36] *Contemporary Review*, February 1888.
[37] "Social Statics", *passim*.
[38] See Professor Leone Levi's letter to the *Times*, 13th August, 1886, and Mr. Frederic Harrison's speech at the Industrial Remuneration Conference held in January 1885 (Report, p. 429).

of industrial evolution points to the same result; and
for two generations the world's chief ethical teachers
have been urging the same lesson. No wonder the
heavens of Individualism are rolling up before our
eyes like a scroll and even the Bishops believe and
tremble.[39]

It is, of course, possible, as Sir Henry Maine and
others have suggested, that the whole experience
of the century is a mistake, and that political power
will once more swing back into the hands of a monarch or an aristocratic oligarchy. It is, indeed, want
of faith in Democracy which holds back most educated sympathisers with Socialism from frankly
accepting its principles. What the economic side of
such political atavism would be it is not easy to forecast.
The machine industry and steam power could hardly
be dismissed with the caucus and the ballot-box. So
long, however, as Democracy in political administration continues to be the dominant principle, Socialism
may be quite safely predicted as its economic obverse,
in spite of those freaks or aberrations of Democracy
which have already here and there thrown up a short-
lived monarchy or a romantic dictatorship. Every increase in the political power of the proletariat will
most surely be used by them for their economic and
social protection. In England, at any rate, the history
of the century serves at once as their guide and their
justification.

[39] See Report of the Lambeth Episcopal Conference,
1888; subject, "Socialism": also the proceedings of the
Central Conference of Diocesan Councils, June 1889
(paper on Socialism by Canon Furse).

## 3. INDUSTRIAL

*By William Clarke, M.A.*

My object in the following paper is to present a brief narrative of the economic history of the last century or century and a half. From this I wish to draw a moral. That moral is that there has been and is proceeding an economic evolution, practically independent of our individual desires or prejudices; an evolution which has changed for us the whole social problem by changing the conditions of material production, and which *ipso facto* effects a revolution in our modern life. To learn clearly what that revolution is, and to prepare ourselves for taking advantage of it in due course—this I take to be briefly what is meant by Socialism. The ignorant public, represented by, let us say, the average bishop or member of Parliament, hears of the "Social Revolution" and instantly thinks of street riots, noyades, with a *coup d'état:* a 10th of August, followed perhaps by its nemesis in an 18th Brumaire. But these are not the Social Revolution. That great change is proceeding silently every day. Each new line of railway which opens up the trackless desert, every new machine which supplants hand labor, each fresh combination formed by capitalists, every new labor organization, every change in prices, each new invention—all these forces and many more are actually working out a social revolution before our eyes; for they are changing fundamentally the economic basis of life. There may possibly come some one supreme moment of time in which a great dramatic incident will reveal to men the significance of the changes which have led up to it, and of which it is merely the final expression. And future historians may write of that as The Revolution just as historians now write of the fall of the Bastille, or the execution of Louis XVI, as though these events constituted the French Revolution instead of being the final terms in a long series of events which had been loosening the fabric of French feudalism through several generations. The true prophet is not an ignorant soothsayer who foretells some Armageddon, but rather he who perceives the inevitable drift and tendency of things. Somewhat in this spirit we may consider the economic history of the modern industrial era in order to discern its meaning, to see what it has led up to, and what, consequently, are the problems with which we find ourselves confronted to-day.

Had we visited a village or small town in England where industrial operations were going on 150 years ago, what should we have found? No tall chimney, vomiting its clouds of smoke, would have been visible; no huge building with its hundred windows blazing with light would have loomed up before the traveller as he entered the town at dusk; no din of machinery would have been heard; no noise of steam hammers; no huge blast furnaces would have met his eye, nor would miles of odors wafted from chemical works have saluted his nostrils. If Lancashire had been the scene of his visit he would have found a number of narrow red-brick houses with high steps in front, and outside wooden shutters such as one may still see in the old parts of some Lancashire towns to-day. Inside each of these houses was a little family workshop, containing neither master nor servant, in which the family jointly contributed to produce by the labor of their hands a piece of cotton cloth. The father provided his own warp of linen yarn, and his cotton wool for weft. He had purchased the yarn in a prepared state, while the wool for the weft was carded and spun by his wife and daughters, and the cloth was woven by himself and his sons. There was a simple division of labor in the tiny cottage factory; but all the implements necessary to produce the cotton cloth were owned by the producers. There was neither capitalist nor wage-receiver: the weaver controlled his own labor, effected his own exchange, and received himself the equivalent of his own product. Such was the germ of the great English cotton manufacture. Ferdinand Lassalle said: "Society consists of ninety-six proletaires and four capitalists. That is your State." But in old Lancashire there was neither capitalist nor proletaire.

Or even much later had one visited—Stafford, let us say, one would not have found the large modern shoe-factory, with its bewildering variety of machines, each one with a human machine by its side. For shoemaking then was a pure handicraft, requiring skill, judgment, and some measure of artistic sense. Each shoemaker worked in his own little house, bought his own material from the leather merchant, and fashioned every part of the shoe with his own hand, aided by a few simple and inexpensive tools. He believed there was "nothing like leather", and had not yet learned the art of putting on cheap soles, *not* made of leather, to cheap boots, which, in a month's time, will be almost worn out. Very likely the shoemaker had no vote; but he was never liable to be locked out by his employer, or to be obliged to go on strike against a reduction of wages with his boy in prison for satisfying hunger at the expense of the neighboring baker, or his girl on the streets to pay for her new dress. Such was the simple industrialism of our great-great-grandfathers. But their mode of life was destined to change. All progress, says Mr. Herbert Spencer, is differentiation; and this formidable factor began to appear in the quiet sleepy English country. About 1760 a large share of calico-printing was transferred from London to Lancashire, where labor was then cheaper. There was a consequent fall in prices, and an increased demand for calicoes of linen warp and cotton weft. Then the Manchester dealers, instead of buying fustians and calicoes from the weaver, began to furnish him with the materials for his cloth, and to pay him a fixed price per piece for the work when executed. So the Manchester dealer became what the French call an *entrepreneur*; and the transformation of the independent weaver into a wage receiver began. The iron law of wages and the unemployed question also began to loom dimly up. For as the weaver came to hire himself to the dealer, so the weaver let out part of his work; and it frequently happened that the sum which the master weaver received from his employer was less than what he found himself compelled to pay to those whom he employed in spinning. "He durst not, however, complain," says Mr. Watts in his article on cotton ("Encyclopædia Britannica"), "much less abate the spinner's price, lest his looms should be unemployed." The quantity of yarn producible under this simple system by the aid of the one-thread wheel was very small. The whole did not exceed in quantity what 50,000 spindles of our present machinery can yield. As one man can now superintend 2,000 spindles, it will be seen that twenty-five men with machinery can produce as much as the whole population of old Lancashire. In 1750 the first important invention in the cotton industry was made in the shape of a fly-shuttle, invented by Kaye of Bury. In 1760 improvements were made in the carding process. In 1767 the spinning-jenny was invented by Hargreaves, and this was at length brought to work as many as eighty spindles. The ingenious Hargreaves had ample opportunity for practical study of the "unemployed" question; for the spinners, some of whom were forced into idleness by the new invention, broke into his house and destroyed his machine.

Shortly after, there was a general rising over industrial Lancashire; the poor hand-workers, whose prophetic souls were evidently dreaming on things to come, scouring the country and breaking in pieces every carding and spinning machine they could find.

Progress by differentiation, however, heeded not the second sight of Lancashire workers. In 1769, Arkwright contrived the spinning frame, and obtained his patent for spinning with rollers. In 1755, Crompton, of Bolton, invented the mule-jenny, enabling warps of the finest quality to be spun. In 1792, further improvements in this machine were made by Pollard, of Manchester, and Kelly, of Glasgow. In 1785, steam was first applied to the spinning of cotton in Nottinghamshire. In 1784 the Rev. E. Cartwright, of Kent, invented power-loom weaving, and completed and patented his invention in August, 1787. Here, then, within a period of about forty years, was a series of mechanical inventions which had the effect of absolutely changing the method of production, and enormously increasing the output; of dividing the labour of producing, which had formerly been effected by a single family within the walls of a single room, between scores and hundreds of people, each of whom only undertook a single process in a complex operation; of massing together hundreds of thousands of people under new conditions; of bringing a heretofore isolated district into intimate relations with distant foreign lands; and of separating the work of spinning or weaving from the ownership of the instruments by whose aid the work was done. The independent weaver was gone; or rather he was subjected, like an amœba, to a process of fission, but with this difference: that whereas the amœba produces by fission other similar amœbæ, the weaver was differentiated into a person called an employer and another called an employé or "hand". Multiply this "hand" by thousands, and we get the mill or factory,

divided into departments, each with its special detail
of work, each detail fitting into all the rest, each machine taking up the work where the last machine
left it, and each contributing its share to the joint
product. Multiply the employer; add enormously to
the aggregate of his capital; remove the barrier of
national frontiers from his operations; relieve him of
the duty of personal supervision; and we get the
joint-stock capitalist.

Pause a moment to consider the famous world-
events which made so much noise while these industrial processes were going on. The conquest of Canada,
the victories of Clive in India, the Seven Years' War,
the successful revolt of the American colonies, the
Declaration of Independence and formation of the
American Constitution, the deeds of Frederic the
Great, Pitt's accession to power, Washington's election
to the Presidency, the Fall of the Bastille, the death
of Mirabeau, the fall of the old French monarchy,
the National Convention—all these great events which
shook the world were contemporary with the industrial
revolution in England; and that revolution was in
promise and potency more important than them all.

I will glance at the development of another great
industry, that of iron. In former times iron was largely
worked in the south of England, notably in Sussex,
in a district now purely agricultural. By the middle
of the eighteenth century, important iron industries
had begun to cluster round Coalbrookdale; and here
many of the industrial changes in the working of
iron were first introduced. From 1766 to 1784 improvements were made in the mode of working
malleable iron and of transferring cast into wrought
iron. The puddling forge was invented in 1784; and
it gave an immense impetus to the manufacture. In
1828 the use of the hot blast was substituted for cold
air; in 1842 Nasmyth invented the steam-hammer;
and in 1856 the Bessemer process of making steel was

patented. Subsequently we have the Siemens regenerative furnace and gas producer, the use of machinery in lieu of hand labor for puddling, the casting of steel under great pressure, and the improvements in the Bessemer process. As a result of these inventions the increase in the production of steel during the last few years, especially in the United States and Great Britain, has been enormous. In all this we see the same series of phenomena, all tending to huge monopolies. Machinery supplants hand labor; production is greatly stimulated; the immense capital needed enables only the large producers to survive in the competitive conflict; and we get as the net result well defined aggregations of capital on the one hand, and dependent machine minders on the other.

I have alluded to the shoe industry as having been formerly a pure handicraft. Simple machine processes for fastening soles and heels to inner soles began to be adopted in 1809; and from that time onward successive inventions have converted the pure handicraft into one of the most mechanical industries in the world. In the United States in 1881 no less than 50,000,000 pairs of boots and shoes were sewn by the Blake-Mackay machines. A visitor to a shoe factory to-day will see the following machines: for cutting leather, for pressing rollers for sole leather, for stamping out sole and heel pieces, for blocking and crimping, for moulding uppers or vamps, for vamp-folding, for eyeletting, lasting, trimming and paring, scouring, sand papering and burnishing, for stamping, peg-cutting and nail-rasping. It is well to witness all these processes going on in one large factory in order to grasp fully the idea that the old individual industry of the last century is almost as extinct as the mastodon —that the worker in a shoe factory to-day is, so to speak, a machine in a vast complex system. The great industry has supplanted the small one; such great industry involves the aggregation of capital: conse-

quently competition on the part of the small producer
is hopeless and impossible. Thus in the proletarian class
the intensity of the struggle for existence is increased,
keeping down wages and ever widening the margin
of the unemployed class. The small producer must
become a wage earner either as manager, foreman, or
workman. As well attempt to meet Gatling guns with
bows and arrows, or steel cruisers armed with dynamite
bombs with the little cockle-shells in which Henry
V's army crossed over to win the field at Agincourt,
as to set up single shoe-makers or cotton-weavers
against the vast industrial armies of the world of
machinery. The revolution is confined to no one
industry, to no one land. While most fully developed
in England, it is extending to most industries and
to all lands. Prince Kropotkin, it is true, reminds
us in an interesting article in the *Nineteenth Century*
for October, 1888, that a number of small industries
can still be found in town and country. That is so,
no doubt; and it is not unlikely that for a long time
to come many small trades may exist, and some may
even flourish. But the countries in which small industries flourish most are precisely those in which there
is least machine industry, and where consequently
capitalism is least developed. In no country, says
Kropotkin, are there so many small producers as in
Russia. Exactly; and in no country is there so little
machinery or such an inefficient railway system in
proportion to population and resources. On the other
hand, in no country is machinery so extensively used
as in the United States; and it is precisely that country
which contains the fewest small industries in proportion to population and resources. Many of the small
industries, too, as Kropotkin admits, are carried on by
persons who have been displaced by machines, and
who have thus been thrown unemployed on the
labor market; or who have drifted into large towns,
especially into London, because in the country there

was no work for them. At best the great majority of these people earn but a scanty and precarious living; and, judging from the number of hawkers and vendors who wander about suburban streets and roads without selling anything, one would imagine that great numbers can scarcely make any living at all.

Furthermore, when Kropotkin refers to the sweaters' victims, and to the people in country places who make on a small scale clothes or furniture which they dispose of to the dealers in large towns, and so forth, let it be remembered that so long as human labor is cheaper than machinery it will be utilized by capitalists in this way. The capitalist uses or does not use machinery according as it pays or does not pay; and if he can draw to an unlimited extent on the margin of unemployed labor, paying a bare subsistence wage, he will do so, as the evidence given before the House of Lords Committee on Sweating shews. While admitting then that a good many small industries exist, and that some will continue to exist for an indefinite time, I do not think that such facts make against the general proposition that the tendency is to large production by machinery, involving the grouping of men and the massing of capital, with all the economic and social consequences thereby involved.

Even agriculture, that one occupation in which old-fashioned individualism might be supposed safe, is being subjected to capitalism. The huge farms of Dakota and California, containing single fields of wheat miles long, are largely owned by joint stock corporations and cultivated exclusively by machinery. It was the displacement of human labor by machinery on these farms as well as the crises in mining operations which helped to bring about the phenomenon of an unemployed class in the richest region of the world, and led Mr. Henry George to write his "Progress and Poverty". These huge farms, combined with the wheat "corners" in New York and Chicago and the great railway corporations of America, have played havoc with many of the small farmers of the Mississippi Valley, as the statistics respecting mortgaged farms will show. And when it is remembered that the American farmer will be more and more obliged to meet the growing competition of the wheat of India, produced by the cheapest labor in the world, his prospect does not appear to be very bright.

In order to perceive clearly the immense development of machine industry and the consequent displacement of labor, one must resort to figures, mere rhetoric being of no avail. The following figures are cited from the United States, because American public statistics are so much better than British, being both more complete and more accessible. The facts are taken from the first Annual Report of the United States Commissioner of Labor Statistics in Washington for 1886. The Commissioner, inquiring into the industrial crisis, finds that it is mainly due to the immense development of machine industry under the joint stock system; and he takes up various trades one after another to show how labor has been displaced by machinery. In the timber business, he says, twelve laborers with a Bucker machine will dress 12,000 staves. The same number of men by hand labour would have dressed in the same time only 2,500. In the manufacture of paper a machine now used for drying and cutting, run by four men and six girls, will do the work formerly done by 100 persons, and do it much better. In the manufacture of wall-paper the best evidence puts the displacement in the proportion of a hundred to one. In a phosphate mine in South Carolina ten men accomplish with machinery what 100 men handle without it in the same time. There has been a displacement of 50 per cent. in the manufacture of rubber boots and shoes. In South Carolina pottery the product is ten times greater by machine processes than by muscular labor. In the manufacture

of saws, experienced men consider that there has
been a displacement of three men out of five. In the
weaving of silk the displacement has been 95 per cent.,
and in the winding of silk 90 per cent. A large
soap manufacturing concern carefully estimates the
displacement of labor in its work at 50 per cent. In
making wine in California a crushing machine has
been introduced with which one man can crush and
stem 80 tons of grapes in a day, representing an amount
of work formerly requiring eight men. In woollen
goods modern machinery has reduced muscular labor
33 per cent. in the carding department, 50 per cent.
in the spinning, and 25 per cent. in the weaving.
In some kinds of spinning one hundred to one represents the displacement. In the whole United States
in 1886 the machinery was equal to 3,500,000 horse
power. If men only had been employed, it would have
required 21,000,000 to turn out the actual total product: the real number was four millions. To do the
work accomplished in 1886 in the United States by
power machinery and on the railways would have required men representing a population of 172,500,000.
The actual population of the United States in 1886
was something under 60,000,000, or a little more than
one-third.

Commenting on these very remarkable statistics, the
Labor Commissioner says: "The apparent evils resulting from the introduction of machinery and the
consequent subdivision of labor have to a large extent, of course, been offset by advantages gained; but
it must stand as a positive statement, which cannot be
successfully controverted, that this wonderful introduction and extension of power machinery is one of the
prime causes, if not the prime cause, of the novel
industrial condition in which the manufacturing
nations find themselves." One of the results of the
"novel industrial condition" in America in 1885 was an

unemployed class variously estimated at from one to
two millions of men, the condition of many of whom
as tramps furnished subjects for some very sorry jests
to the American press. Such facts as are here suggested
will show how a new country may soon be reduced to
a condition which aggregated capital on the one hand
and unemployed labor on the other render little better
than that of an old European State with its centuries
of misery and oppression. And incidentally they also
show that such a nostrum as emigration, if intended
not as a palliative but as a solution, is simply quackery.
The inference would seem to be irresistible. Just as
fast as capitalists find it profitable to introduce improved machinery, as fast also will the helplessness of
a growing number of the proletariat increase. The
"unemployed" question is the sphinx which will de-
vour us if we cannot answer her riddle.

The wonderful expansion of Lancashire perhaps
affords the best illustration of the change from individual to collective industry. A cotton mill in one of the
dismal "hell-holes" called towns in Lancashire is a
wonderful place, full of bewildering machines. Here
is a machine called an "opener," by which 15,000
lbs. of cotton can be opened in 56 hours. There is
a throstle, the spindles of which make from 6,000 to
7,000 revolutions per minute. Here is a man who,
with the aid of two piecers to take up and join the
broken ends, can work 2,000 spindles. Among the
distinct separate machines used are opener, scutcher
and lap machine, drawing frame, slubbing frame,
intermediate frame, roving frame, throstle, self-acting
mule and hand mule, doubling frame, and mule
doublers or twiners. By means of these appliances the
following results have been attained. Within eight
years, from 1792 to 1800, the quantity of cotton
exported from the United States to Lancashire had
increased from 138,000 lbs. to 18,000,000 lbs. In 1801

Lancashire took 84,000 bales of cotton from the United States: in 1876 she took 2,075,000 bales; and whereas in the former year only 14,000 bales came from India, in 1876 from that country came 775,000 bales, besides a great increase in Brazilian cotton, and a new import of 332,000 bales from Egypt. In 1805, one million pieces of calico were sold in the Blackburn market during the whole year; and that was considered a very large sale. In 1884, according to Ellison's Annual Review of the Cotton Trade, there were exported 4,417,000,000 yards of piece goods besides the vast quantity produced for home consumption. In 1875, in place of the little cottages with their hand-looms of a century before, Lancashire contained 2,655 cotton factories with 37,515,772 spinning spindles and 463,118 power looms; and she produced yarn and piece goods to the weight of 1,088,890,000 lbs., and of the value of £95,447,000. See too how through the use of machinery the cost of production has been lowered. In 1790 the price of spinning the yarn known technically as No. 100 was 4s. per lb.: in 1826 it had been reduced to 6½d. The sale price of yarn No. 100 in 1786 was 38s.: in 1793 it was reduced to 15s. 1d., in 1803 to 8s. 4d., in 1876 to 2s. 6d. The decreased cost in each case followed on economy in production, itself dependent on increased differentiation in machinery; that in turn involving larger and larger capital; and that again necessitating aggregation and the crushing out of small concerns which could not command machinery or sell at a profit in competition with it.

Speculating on the possibility of foreign competition destroying the industrial supremacy of Lancashire, Mr. Watts writes in the "Encyclopædia Britannica": "It may perhaps be sufficient to recall to our readers the small part of the cost of the commodity which now belongs to the labor of the land, and the daily diminution which is taking place even of that part, by the introduction of new mechanical substitutes".[1] Mr. Watts wrote as an expert; and the inference one is compelled to draw from his dictum is that concentration of capital and growth of monopoly must continue to develope; and that the "unemployed" problem must force itself on Lancashire. One who is not an expert will only venture to criticise with great diffidence Mr. Watts's optimistic tone; but it is well to point out that in India capitalists can command the cheapest labor in the world—labor, too, at present entirely unregulated by law. The cotton of India, and also of Asiatic Russia, is spun and woven near to where it is grown, and where it can easily command the great Asiatic market. One is not surprised to find therefore that the Bombay cotton mills are already giving cause for some anxiety in Lancashire; and there seems no rational ground for supposing that that anxiety will decrease; in which case the increasing competition would seem to involve in Lancashire either immense development of machinery or reduction in wages in order to cheapen the cost of production. Either alternative forces the social problem forward.

I now pass on to consider the social problem as it has actually been forced on the attention of the British Government through the new industrial conditions.

The unrestrained power of capitalism very speedily reduced a large part of England to a deplorable condition. The Mrs. Jellybys of the philanthropic world were busy ministering to the wants of Borioboola Gha by means of tracts and blankets, neither of which were of the slightest use to those for whom they were intended. But Borioboola Gha was an earthly paradise compared with civilized England. There was not a savage in the islands of the Pacific who was not better fed, happier, healthier, and more contented than the majority of the workers in the industrial parts of

[1] "Enc. Britt." art. "Cotton."

England. Children, it was discovered, were transferred
in large numbers to the north, where they were
housed in pent-up buildings adjoining the factories,
and kept to long hours of labor. The work was carried
on day and night without intermission; so that the
beds were said never to become cold, inasmuch as one
batch of children rested while another batch went
to the looms, only half the requisite number of beds
being provided for all. Epidemic fevers were rife in
consequence. Medical inspectors reported the rapid
spread of malformation of the bones, curvature of the
spine, heart diseases, rupture, stunted growth, asthma,
and premature old age among children and young
persons: the said children and young persons being
worked by manufacturers without any kind of restraint.
Manufacturing profits in Lancashire were being at
the same time reckoned at hundreds and even thousands per cent. The most terrible condition of things
existed in the mines, where children of both sexes
worked together, half naked, often for sixteen hours
a day. In the fetid passages, children of seven, six,
and even four years of age, were found at work.
Women were employed underground, many of them
even while pregnant, at the most exhausting labour.
After a child was born, its mother was at work again
in less than a week, in an atmosphere charged with
sulphuric acid. In some places women stood all day
knee-deep in water and subject to an intense heat.
One woman when examined avowed that she was
wet through all day long, and had drawn coal carts
till her skin came off. Women and young children of
six years old drew coal along the passages of the mines,
crawling on all fours with a girdle passing round their
waists, harnessed by a chain between their legs to
the cart. A sub-commissioner in Scotland reported that
he "found a little girl, six years of age, carrying half
a cwt., and making regularly fourteen long journeys
a day. The height ascended and the distance along

the road exceeded in each journey the height of St. Paul's Cathedral." "I have repeatedly worked," said one girl seventeen years of age, "for twenty-four hours." The ferocity of the men was worse than that of wild beasts; and children were often maimed and sometimes killed with impunity. Drunkenness was naturally general. Short lives and brutal ones were the rule. The men, it was said, "die off like rotten sheep; and each generation is commonly extinct soon after fifty." Such was a large part of industrial England under the unrestrained rule of the capitalist. There can be no doubt that far greater misery prevailed than in the Southern States during the era of slavery. The slave was property—often valuable property; and it did not pay his owner to ill-treat him to such a degree as to render him useless as a wealth-producer. But if the "free" Englishman were injured or killed, thousands could be had to fill his place for nothing.

Had this state of things continued we should have returned to a state of nature with a vengeance. Of man thus depicted we may say with Tennyson:

> "Dragons of the prime,
> That tare each other in their slime,
> Were mellow music match'd with him."

It was evident that capitalist monopoly must be restrained, reluctant as English statesmen brought up under the commercial system were to interfere. The zenith of *laisser faire* was at the close of the last century; but a great fabric often looks most imposing shortly before it begins to collapse. The first piece of labor legislation was the Morals and Health Act of 1802, which interfered with the accommodation provided to children by the employers, to which reference has been made. The Cotton Mills Act was passed in 1819, partly owing to the exertions of Robert Owen. It limited the age at which children might work in factories; and it limited the time of their labor to seventy-two hours per week. Seventy-two hours for a child of nine who ought to have been playing in the green fields! And even that was a vast improvement on the previous state of things. Saturday labor was next shortened by an Act passed by the Radical politician, Sir John Cam Hobhouse, in 1825. Workmen, Radicals, Tories, and philanthropists then joined in an agitation under Mr. Richard Oastler, a Conservative member of Parliament, to secure a Ten Hours' Bill. Hobhouse tried by a Bill introduced in 1831 to reduce the time in textile industries; but he was beaten by the northern manufacturers. However, Althorp the Whig leader, who had helped to defeat Hobhouse, was obliged himself to introduce a measure by which night work was prohibited to young persons, and the hours of work were reduced to sixty-nine a week. Cotton-mill owners were at the same time disqualified for acting as justices in cases of infringement of the law. This measure is regarded by Dr. E. Von Plener in his useful manual as the first real Factory Act. Mr. Thomas Sadler, who had succeeded Oastler as leader in the cause of the factory operatives, brought in a Bill in 1832 limiting the hours of labor for persons under eighteen; but it was met by a storm of opposition from manufacturing members and withdrawn.

To Sadler succeeded that excellent man, who has perhaps done more for the working-classes than any other public man of our time, Lord Ashley, better known as Lord Shaftesbury. And here let me pause to point out that it was the Radicals and a large section of the Tories who took the side of the operatives against the Whigs, official Conservatives and manufacturing class. The latter class is sometimes regarded as Liberal. I think the truth is, that it captured and held for some time the Liberal fort, and made Liberalism identical with its policy and interests. If the men of this class had the cynical candor of Mr. Jay Gould, they might have imitated his reply when examined by a legislative committee: "What are your politics, Mr. Gould?" "Well, in a Republican district I am Republican, in a Democratic district I am a Democrat; but I am always an Erie Railroad man". One of Lord Ashley's strong opponents was Sir Robert Peel, the son of a Lancashire capitalist; but the most bitter and persistent was Mr. John Bright. Lord Ashley introduced a Ten Hours' Bill which included adults. Lord Althorp refused to legislate for adults, but himself passed an Act in 1833 prohibiting night work to those under eighteen; fixing forty-eight hours per week as the maximum for children, and sixty-nine for young persons; also providing for daily attendance at school, and certain holidays in the year. As this Act repealed that of 1831, manufacturers were again eligible to sit as justices in factory cases; and although numerous infractions were reported by inspectors, the offenders in many cases got off scot free. In 1840 Lord Ashley brought to the notice of Parliament the condition of young people employed in mines; and through his activity was passed the first Mining Act, prohibiting underground work by women and by boys under ten. Peel then passed a consolidating Factory Act in 1844. Lord Ashley proposed to restrict to ten per day the working hours for young persons; but Peel defeated the proposal by threatening to resign if it were carried. By the Act of 1844 the labor of children was limited to six and a half hours per day; and they had to attend school three hours daily during the first five days of the week. The next year, 1845, Lord Ashley secured the passage of a Bill forbidding night work to women. In 1847 Mr. Fielden introduced a Bill limiting the time of labor for all women and young persons to eleven hours per day, and after May 1848 to ten hours. Peel and the factory owners opposed: but the Bill was carried. The Act of 1850 further reduced the legal working day for women and young persons; and an Act of 1853 prohibited the employment of children before 6 a.m., or after 6 p.m. In 1860 bleaching and dyeing works were subjected to the factory laws. Further legislation on this branch of industry took place in 1870. A Mines Act was passed in 1860, and made more stringent in 1862 with reference to safety and ventilation. Acts with reference to the lace industry were passed in the years 1861–64, to bakehouses in 1863, chimney-sweeping and pottery works in 1864. The Workshops Regulation Act, relating to small trades and handicrafts was passed in 1867, and a consolidating Factory and Workshops Act in 1871. The Act now in force is the Factory and Workshops Act 1878, modified in respect of certain industries by the Act of 1883. Further Acts relative to the regulations of mines were passed in 1872 and 1887.

This brief and imperfect survey of the legislation which has destroyed the regime of *laisser faire* is sufficient for my purpose to prove: (1) That with private property in the necessary instruments of production, individual liberty as understood by the eighteenth century reformers must be more and more restricted, *i.e.,* that in our existing economic condition individualism is impossible and absurd. (2) That even hostile or indifferent politicians have been compelled to recognise this. (3) That unrestrained capitalism tends as surely to cruelty and oppression as did feudalism or chattel slavery. (4) That the remedy has been, as a matter of fact, of a Socialistic character, involving collective checking of individual greed and the paring of slices off the profits of capital in the interests of the working community. These four propositions can scarcely be contested.

The immense development of English industry under the conditions previously set forth was due in great degree to the fact that England had secured an immense foreign market in which she had for a long time no formidable rival. Most of the wars in which England was engaged during the eighteenth century are quite unintelligible until it is understood that they were commercial wars intended to secure commercial supremacy for England. The overthrow of the Stuart monarchy was directly associated with the rise to supreme power of the rich market class, especially the London merchants. The revolution of 1688 marks the definite advent to political power of this class, which found the Whig party the great instrument for effecting its designs. The contrast between the old Tory squire who stood for Church and King, and the new commercial magnate who stood by the Whigs and the House of Hanover, is well drawn by Sir Walter Scott in "Rob Roy." The Banks of England and Scotland and the National Debt are among the blessings conferred on their descendants by the new mercantile rulers. They also began the era of corruption in politics which is always connected closely with predominance of capitalists in the State, as we see in France, the United States, and the British Colonies. "The desire of the moneyed classes", says Mr. Lecky,[2] "to acquire political power at the expense of the country gentlemen was the first and one of the chief causes of that political corruption which soon overspread the whole system of parliamentary government". What remained of the old aristocracy often found it convenient to form alliances with the new plutocracy; and it was this combination which governed England during the eighteenth century, and which specially determined her foreign policy. That policy was directed towards the securing of foreign markets and the extension of English trade. Napoleon's sneer at the "nation of shopkeepers" was not undeserved. The conquest of Canada, the conquest of India under Clive and Warren Hastings—the latter an agent of a great capitalist body, who illustrated well in his Indian career the methods of his class—the Colonial policy, the base destruction of Irish manufactures in the interest of English capi-

[2] "History of the Eighteenth Century," i, 202.

talists, were all part of the same scheme. The policy
was successfully consummated in the war waged by
Pitt against the French Revolution. That Revolution
was itself brought about mainly by poverty. Not only
was the French peasantry beggared; but some of the
new machinery which had been brought from England
had thrown many persons out of work. It was mainly
unemployed workmen who stormed and captured the
Bastille.[3] The chief counterblast to the Revolution was
prepared by Pitt. What were his motives? The Aus-
trian and Prussian monarchs, the emigrant nobles, the
imbecile English King and the Tory English bishops
may perhaps have seriously believed that England was
fighting for altar and throne. But Pitt was under no
such delusion. While he derived from his illustrious
father a real pride in England, his divinities were
rather the ledger and the cash-box. He was no bigot:
even while an undergraduate at Cambridge he was a
close student of Adam Smith; he started in public life
as a reformer, and his refusal to bow to the ignorant
prejudices of George III. cost him office in 1801. It
has been abundantly proved that at first he felt no
violent antipathy to the Revolution. A long period
elapsed before he was brought to join the monarchical
alliance. But he was essentially the great capitalist
statesman, the political successor of Walpole, the political predecessor of Peel. He saw that French conquest
might threaten seriously the English social fabric, and
that if England's chief rival were struck down, the
English commercial class might gain control of the
world's commerce. To secure that end he skilfully
welded together all the moneyed interests, the con-
tractors, landlords, financiers, and shopkeepers; and he
tried to persuade the simpler portion of the country
that he was fighting for the sacred cause of religion

[3] See the evidence contained in Vol. I. of Mr. Morse
Stephens' "History of the French Revolution."

and morality. Those who resisted him he flung into prison or transported beyond the seas. When the long war was brought to an end, the working-classes were in a wretched condition; although in those days also there were sophistical politicians who tried to prove that never had the people so much reason to be contented. When, in 1823, the Lancashire weavers petitioned Parliament to look into their grievances, an honorable member, who had presumably dined well if not wisely, had the audacity to declare that the weavers were better off than the capitalists—an observation not dissimilar to those we have heard in more recent times. As a matter of fact, the landlords, through protection and high rents—the capitalists, through enormous profits, were enriched "beyond the dreams of avarice." But the time had come for a conflict between these two classes: the conflict which is known as the Free Trade controversy. Protection was no longer needed by the manufacturers, who had supremacy in the world-market, unlimited access to raw materials, and a long start of the rest of the world in the development of machinery and in industrial organization. The landlord class on the other hand was absolutely dependent on Protection, because the economic isolation of England by means of import duties maintained the high prices of food which were the source of the high agricultural rents. Capitalist interests, on the contrary, were bound up with the interaction between England and the rest of the world; and the time had come when the barriers which had prevented that interaction must be pulled down. The triumph of Free Trade therefore signifies economically the decay of the old landlord class pure and simple, and the victory of capitalism. The capitalist class was originally no fonder of Free Trade than the landlords. It destroyed in its own interest the woollen manufacture in Ireland; and it would have throttled the trade of the Colonies had it not been for the successful resistance of Massachusetts and

Virginia. It was Protectionist so long as it suited its purpose to be so. But when cheap raw material was needed for its looms, and cheap bread for its workers: when it feared no foreign competitor, and had established itself securely in India, in North America, in the Pacific; then it demanded Free Trade. "Nothing in the history of political imposture", says Mr. Lecky, "is more curious than the success with which, during the Anti-Corn Law agitation, the notion was disseminated that on questions of Protection and Free Trade the manufacturing classes have been peculiarly liberal and enlightened, and the landed classes peculiarly selfish and ignorant. It is indeed true that when in the present century the pressure of population on subsistence had made a change in the Corn Laws inevitable, the manufacturing classes placed themselves at the head of a Free Trade movement from which they must necessarily have derived the chief benefit, while the entire risk and sacrifice were thrown upon others. But it is no less true that there is scarcely a manufacture in England which has not been defended in the spirit of the narrowest and most jealous monopoly; and the growing ascendancy of the commercial classes after the Revolution is nowhere more apparent than in the multiplied restrictions of the English Commercial Code".[4]

Cheap raw material having been secured by the English manufacturer through a series of enactments extending over a generation; and machinery having been so developed as to enormously increase production, England sent her textile and metal products all over the world; and her manufacturers supported exactly that policy which enabled them to secure markets for their goods or raw produce to work up in their mills. Cobdenism was in the ascendant; and the State was more and more regarded from the commercial point of view. The so-called "Manchester school"

[4] "History of the Eighteenth Century," iv. 450.

was in the main a peace party because war weakens
that confidence on which commerce is based. But this
attachment to peace principles did not prevent Cobden
himself from declaring for a powerful navy as an instrument of commercial insurance. Nor did it prevent
Manchester from supporting Palmerston's nefarious
Chinese policy in 1857, or the equally nefarious aggression in Egypt in 1882: both being regarded as
helpful to Manchester trade. In behalf of this extension
of English trade to new markets war has been made on
China, Egypt, the Soudan, Burmah, and Thibet. Germany follows England with cautious tread. Adventurers like Emin, Stanley, and Bartelott are employed
to "open up" Africa to the gentle influences of civilization by the agency of rum and revolver, under the
pretence of putting down the slave trade. France, not
to be behind, exploits Tonquin in the interests of Paris
speculators. An unscrupulous government in Italy attempts to divert the attention of the country from
domestic reforms to expeditions in Africa in the interests of moneyed people in Europe. Perhaps the greatest
move is yet to come: the move on the vast market of
China. For this England, America, France, and Germany will compete. Tentative steps are already being
taken. By her absorption of Burmah and her operations
in Thibet, England is approaching nearer to China.
By her acquisition of Tonquin, France has been
brought into actual contact with China. America will
probably, by a judicious reduction of her tariff, compete with England all over the Pacific, and will send
her goods from the Atlantic ports through the Panama
or Nicaragua Canal of the near future. In short, the
machinery for the wholesale exploitation of Asia and
Africa is in rapid progress. The whole globe will soon
be the private property of the capitalist class.

The appropriation of the planet has been powerfully
aided by the developments of transport and communi-
cations in our time: indeed, it would have been im-

possible without them. The mere application of machinery to production could not have produced the economic results of to-day but for the shrinkage of the globe caused by railways and telegraphs. For it is through these inventions that the capitalist class has become cosmopolitan, has broken up old habits, destroyed local associations, spared nothing either beautiful or venerable where profit was concerned. It has assimilated the conditions of life in various lands, and has brought about a general uniformity which accounts for much of the ennui felt in modern life.

As England was the first country to develope machine industry, so was she the first to develope railways and to form a powerful steam mercantile marine. Through the latter agency she has now in her hands about sixty-four per cent. of the carrying trade of the world. Within sixty years about 350,000 miles of railway have been built throughout the globe. Atlantic and Pacific are united by several lines of steel; while the locomotive has penetrated remote regions of Africa inhabited by barbarous tribes, and wastes of central Asia where it confronts the relics of dead and buried civilizations. This immense power, the greatest in the modern world, is mainly in the hands of monopolist corporations, among whom there is the same necessary tendency to aggregation, only far more marked, as is found in productive industries. The first small lines built to connect towns not far off have been added to others bit by bit; as from the original Stockton and Darlington Railway, less than twenty miles long, we get the great and wealthy North Eastern Railway of to-day. In America a single corporation controls as much as 7,000 miles of rail; and the end of the century will perhaps see the great Siberian-Pacific in actual existence. As in railways, so in steam vessels. Huge fleets like the Cunard, the Orient, the Messageries Maritimes, are owned by cosmopolitan capital, and sustain the traffic and commerce, not of a country, not even of a continent, but of the whole world. Such is the immense revolution in the methods of distribution effected in our time by the operation of capitalism.

We must now consider what the term "capitalist" is coming to signify. Had the term been used half a century ago it would have connoted a class, unscrupulous perhaps in the main, with low aims, little culture, and less fine sympathy or imagination. It was nevertheless a socially useful class, which at that time performed real services. It is a leading thought in modern philosophy that in its process of development each institution tends to cancel itself. Its special function is born out of social necessities: its progress is determined by attractions or repulsions which arise in society, producing a certain effect which tends to negate the original function. Thus early society among the Aryan peoples of Europe developes a leader in war or council who grows, by processes which in England, *e.g.*, can be clearly traced, into a king with genuine functions, a leader of the people in war like William I, or a powerful civil ruler and statesman like Henry I. The fact that such men were brutal or wicked is of little account: the important fact about them is, that in a barbarous chaotic society they performed some indispensable services. But the very putting forth of the kingly power arouses antagonism; then produces armed resistance by a combined group; and finally leads to overthrow either by the destruction of the king or by depriving him of all real power and reducing him to a mere ornamental puppet. The very power originally believed to be beneficent becomes tyrannical: it needs to be checked more and more, until finally it practically ceases to exist, and the curious paradox is seen of a monarch who does not rule. History proves abundantly that men do not rise and overthrow wicked and corrupt rulers merely because they are wicked and corrupt. It is part of the terrible irony of history that a Louis XV dies in his bed, while a

William the Silent or a Lincoln falls a victim to the assassin. What men do not long tolerate is either obstructiveness or uselessness.

Now, if we apply these ideas to the evolution of the capitalist, what is it we see? The capitalist was originally an *entrepreneur*, a manager who worked hard at his business, and who received what economists have called the "wages of superintendence". So long as the capitalist occupied that position, he might be restrained and controlled in various ways; but he could not be got rid of. His "wages of superintendence" were certainly often exorbitant; but he performed real functions; and society, as yet unprepared to take those functions upon itself, could not afford to discharge him. Yet, like the King, he had to be restrained by the legislation already referred to; for his power involved much suffering to his fellows. But now the capitalist is fast becoming absolutely useless. Finding it easier and more rational to combine with others of his class in a large undertaking, he has now abdicated his position of overseer, has put in a salaried manager to perform his work for him, and has become a mere rent or interest receiver. The rent or interest he receives is paid for the use of a monopoly which not he, but a whole multitude of people created by their joint efforts.

It was inevitable that this differentiation of manager and capitalist should arise. It is part of the process of capitalist evolution due to machine industry. As competition led to waste in production, so it led to the cutting of profits among capitalists. To prevent this the massing of capital was necessary, by which the large capitalist could undersell his small rivals by offering, at prices below anything they could afford to sell at, goods produced by machinery and distributed by a plexus of agencies initially too costly for any individual competitor to purchase or set on foot. Now for such massive capitals, the contributions of several capitalists are needed; and hence has arisen the Joint Stock

Company or *Compagnie Anonyme*. Through this new
capitalist agency a person in England can hold stock
in an enterprise at the Antipodes which he has never
visited and never intends to visit, and which, therefore, he cannot "superintend" in any way. He and the
other shareholders put in a manager with injunctions
to be economical. The manager's business is to earn
for his employers the largest dividends possible: if he
does not do so he is dismissed. The old personal relation between the workers and the employer is gone:
instead thereof remains merely the cash nexus. To
secure high dividends the manager will lower wages.
If that is resisted there will probably be either a strike
or lock-out. Cheap labor will be perhaps imported by
the manager; and if the workpeople resist by intimi-
dation or organised boycotting, the forces of the State
(which they help to maintain) will be used against
them. In the majority of cases they must submit. Such
is a not unfair picture of the relation of capitalist to
workman to-day: the former having become an idle
dividend-receiver. The dictum of orthodox political
economy, uttered by so competent an authority as the
late Professor Cairnes, runs:—

> "It is important, on moral no less than on economic
> grounds, to insist upon this, that no public benefit
> of any kind arises from the existence of an idle rich
> class. The wealth accumulated by their ancestors
> and others on their behalf, where it is employed as
> capital, no doubt helps to sustain industry; but
> what they consume in luxury and idleness is not
> capital, and helps to sustain nothing but their own
> unprofitable lives. By all means they must have their
> rents and interest, as it is written in the bond; but
> let them take their proper place as drones in the
> hive, gorging at a feast to which they have con-
> tributed nothing." [5]

[5] "Some Leading Principles of Political Economy", p. 32.

The fact that the modern capitalist may be not only useless but positively obstructive was well illustrated at a meeting of the shareholders of the London and South Western Railway on 7th February last. Three shareholders urged a reduction in third-class fares. The chairman pointed out the obvious fact that such a reduction would probably lower the dividend, and asked the meeting if that was what they wished. He was, of course, answered by a chorus of "No, no!"; and all talk of reduction of fares was at an end. Here is a plain sample (hundreds might be quoted) of the evident interests of the public being sacrificed to those of the capitalist.

That joint-stock capitalism is extending rapidly everyone knows. In the United States, according to Mr. Bryce, the wealth of joint-stock corporations is estimated at one-fourth of the total value of all property.[6] In England every kind of business, from breweries, banks, and cotton-mills down to automatic sweetmeat machines, is falling into the hands of the joint-stock capitalist, and must continue to do so. Twenty years ago who would have supposed that a brewery like that of Guinness or such a banking firm as Glyn, Mills, and Co. would become a joint-stock company? Yet we know it is so to-day. Capitalism is becoming impersonal and cosmopolitan. And the combinations controlling production become larger and fewer. Baring's are getting hold of the South African diamond fields: A few companies control the whole anthracite coal produce of Pennsylvania. Each one of us is quite "free" to "compete" with these gigantic combinations, as the Principality of Monaco is "free" to go to war with France should the latter threaten her interests. The mere forms of freedom remain; but monopoly renders them nugatory. The modern State, having parted with the raw material of the globe, cannot se-

[6] "The American Commonwealth", iii, note on p. 421.

cure freedom of competition to its citizens; and yet it was on the basis of free competition that capitalism rose. Thus we see that capitalism has cancelled its original principle—is itself negating its own existence. Before considering its latest forms, attention may here be conveniently directed to the Co-operative movement, which is, on one side at any rate, closely allied to the joint-stock development.

The Co-operative movement had in England a Socialistic origin; for its founder was Robert Owen. As Mr. Seligman says very truly in the *Political Science Quarterly*: "Owen was the founder of the Co-operative movement in England, a fact often ignored by those who glibly use the word to-day with an utter failure to discern its true significance." And Owen himself avowed that his grand ultimate object was "community in land", with which he hoped would be combined "unrestrained co-operation on the part of all, for every purpose of human life". It is thus important to associate Co-operation with Robert Owen—*clarum et venerabile nomen*—because there are many persons who suppose that Co-operation began with the Rochdale Pioneers in 1844. What the Rochdale movement really did was to commence the process of joint-stock shopkeeping, a very different thing from that which Owen had in view.

A powerful impetus was given to co-operation by the Christian Socialist movement under Maurice and Kingsley. "Of all narrow, conceited, hypocritical, anarchic and atheistic schemes of the Universe", said Kingsley, "the Cobden and Bright one is exactly the worst." The orthodox economic conclusions of the day fared badly at Kingsley's hands. "The man who tells us", said he, "that we ought to investigate Nature, simply to sit still patiently under her, and let her freeze, and ruin, and starve, and stink us to death, is a goose, whether he calls himself a chemist or a political economist". These Christian Socialist leaders felt deeply the anguish and poverty of the workers and the selfish apathy of the rich. "Mammon", says Kingsley, "shrieks benevolently whenever a drunken soldier is flogged; but he trims his paletot and adorns his legs with the flesh of men and the skins of women, with degradation, pestilence, heathendom, and despair; and then chuckles complacently over his tailor's bills. Hypocrite! straining at a gnat and swallowing a camel". All this is very admirable; but cheap clothes are not made solely or chiefly for Mammon, but for the masses, who are poor people. It is part of the sad irony of the situation that the great majority are obliged to accept the alternative of cheap clothes or none at all. And as the English climate and the British matron combine to exercise an absolute veto over the latter form of pre-historic simplicity, it follows that one portion of the working-classes must, in order to be clothed, connive at the sweating of another portion.

The *Christian Socialist,* which was the organ of Maurice and Kingsley, betrayed great simplicity as to the real nature of the economic problem. It neglected Owen's principle of "community in land", and supposed that by working together and selling articles of good quality at a fair price property could be eliminated, while yet every worker in the community was paying his tribute of economic rent to the owners of the instruments of production. Thus the movement had no economic basis; and when the moral idealism had departed from it, no wonder that it degenerated into mere "divvy" hunting and joint-stock shop-keeping. The economic advantages of joint-stock shop-keeping are thus summed up by Mr. Robert Somers in the "Encyclopædia Britannica" (Art., "Co-operation"): "Wholesome commodities, ready-money payments, a dividend of from five to ten per cent. on share capital, and a bonus to non-members on the amount of their purchases." As joint-stock shopkeeping, co-operation is a useful and cheap method of distribution, which has doubtless benefited a considerable number of persons; but the notion that it can solve the economic problem before society is "chimerical", as Dr. J. K. Ingram tells us is the opinion of modern economists.[7] This, indeed, might only be expected from the fact that 961 out of every 1,000 persons in England die without furniture, investments, or effects worth £300.[8] Economically considered, co-operation is, now that the initial enthusiasm has died out of it, a subsidiary branch of the great joint-stock enterprise. Ethically considered, its results are often doubtful. In its chief stronghold, Lancashire, one observes a narrow selfishness among its votaries which could not be surpassed in the most genteel quarters of Bayswater. Its ideal is not the raising of the working class as a whole, but the raising of certain persons out of the working into the middle class. If the advocates of co-operation will abate their pretensions, and claim merely (1) that their method is a useful and economic means of distribution among the lower-middle and upper-working classes; and (2) that by its agency working men can learn the important functions of organization and administration, their claim will be freely admitted. But if they go further their vaulting ambition will o'erleap itself. At the present rate of progress made by co-operative societies as compared with joint-stock capitalist companies, several generations will be in their graves before any deep or general impression is made. And meanwhile, unless economic rent is diverted from the class which at present absorbs it to the community which creates it, co-operators, like the rest of us, must pay tribute to the lords of the soil and of money. But the noteworthy fact about co-operation is that its very existence testifies to the process of industrial and capitalist aggregation here insisted on as the great social factor of our period.

[7] "Encyclopædia Britannica": Art., "Political Economy"
[8] Mulhall: "Dictionary of Statistics".

For co-operative societies supersede individual by social distribution, effecting it without the waste attendant on a number of little shops all competing against each other, the owners of none of which can make a decent living. Co-operation, therefore, well illustrates the economic evolution of the present age.

I now come to treat of the latest forms of capitalism, the "ring" and the "trust" whereby capitalism cancels its own principles, and, as a seller, replaces competition by combination. When capitalism buys labor as a commodity it effects the purchase on the competitive principle. Its indefinitely extended market enables it to do so; for it knows that the workman must sell his labor to secure the means to live. Other things being equal, therefore, it buys its labor in the cheapest market. But when it turns round to face the public as a seller, it casts the maxims of competition to the winds, and presents itself as a solid combination. Competition, necessary at the outset, is found ultimately, if unchecked, to be wasteful and ruinous. It entails great expense in advertising; it necessitates the employment of much unproductive labor; it tends to the indefinite lowering of prices; it produces gluts and crises, and renders business operations hazardous and precarious. To escape these consequences the competing persons or firms agree to form a close combination to keep up prices, to augment profits, to eliminate useless labor, to diminish risk, and to control the output. This is a "ring", which is thus a federation of companies. The best examples of "rings" and "pools" are to be found in America, where capitalism is more unrestrained and bolder in its operations than in Europe; and also where nearly all the active intellect is attracted to those commercial pursuits that dominate American life.

The individualist devotees of *laisser faire* used to teach us that when restrictions were removed, free competition would settle everything. Prices would go down, and fill the "consumer" with joy unspeakable; the fittest would survive; and as for the rest—it was not very clear what would become of them, and it really didn't matter. No doubt the "consumer" has greatly benefited by the increase in production and the fall in prices; but where is "free competition" now? Almost the only persons still competing freely are the small shopkeepers, trembling on the verge of insolvency, and the working-men, competing with one another for permission to live by work. Combination is absorbing commerce. Here are a few instances of the formation of rings.

A steel rail combination was some years ago formed among previously competing firms in America. This combination discovered that too many rails were being made and that prices were being cut. Accordingly, one of the mills in the combination—the Vulcan mill of St. Louis—was closed, and stood smokeless for years: its owners meanwhile receiving a subsidy of $400,000 a year from the other mills in the combination for *not* making rails. That is how the owners of the Vulcan mill earned their "wages of superintendence". It is needless to add that no payment was made to the men for *not* working: they were thrown on the streets to meditate on the right to "liberty and the pursuit of happiness", secured to them by the Declaration of Independence.

Or, again, take the case of the anthracite coal lands of Pennsylvania, occupying an area of some 270,000 acres, and held by the Reading Coal and Iron Company, the Lehigh Valley Railroad, the Delaware and Hudson Railroad, the Pennsylvania Railroad, the Pennsylvania Coal Company, and smaller firms and corporations tributary to these. The rich owners, popularly known as the "coal barons", agree to fix absolutely the wholesale price of coal, always securing an immense rise just before the winter sets in. There is no such thing known or possible as free trade or open competition in the anthracite coal produce of America.

Combinations in the United States have been made by the Western millers, the New York icemen, Boston fish dealers, manufacturers of sewer pipe, copper miners, makers of lamps, pottery, glass, hoop-iron, shot, rivets, candy, starch, sugar, preserved fruits, glucose, chairs, vapor stoves, lime, rubber, screws, chains, harvesting machinery, pins, salt, hardware, type, brass tubing, silk and wire. In these trades freedom of production and sale has been for a time partially or wholly destroyed. The American business man is very angry when boycotting is resorted to by workmen; but he is quite ready to boycott others when his interests lead that way. The stamped tinware makers in 1882 formed a ring and expelled members who sold at lower prices than the fixed rates, and refused to allow anyone in the pool to sell to the offenders. Some of the previous facts are taken from an article by Mr. Henry D. Lloyd,[9] who has investigated capitalist combinations with much knowledge and insight. From the same article I quote the following:

"On the 1st April, 1882, when the rest of us were lost in the reckless gaiety of All Fools' Day, forty-one tack manufacturers found out that there were too many tacks, and formed the Central Manufacturing Company of Boston with 3,000,000 dollars capital. The tack-mills in the combination ran about three days in the week. When this combination a few weeks ago silenced a Pittsburg rival by buying him out, they did not remove the machinery. The dead chimneys and idle machines will discourage new men from starting another factory, or can be run to ruin them if they are not to be discouraged in any other way. The first

[9] "Lords of Industry," *North American Review*, June 1884.

fruits of the tack-pool were an increase of prices to twice what they had been."

Again I quote Mr. Lloyd:

"The men who make our shrouds and coffins have formed a close corporation known as the 'National Burial Case Association', and held their annual convention in Chicago last year. Their action to keep up prices and keep down the number of coffins was secret, lest mortality should be discouraged."

From coffins to crackers is a short step in the study of capitalist methods:

"The Western Cracker Bakers' Association met in Chicago, in February, to consider among other things 'the reprehensible system of cutting prices' (*i.e.*, the reprehensible system of free competition which capitalists in buying labor tell us is our salvation). They first had a banquet. After their 'merriment and diversion' the revellers, true to Adam Smith's description, turned to consider 'some contrivance to raise prices.' 'The price lists were perfected,' said the newspaper report; 'and then they adjourned'."

In 1875 broke out a severe competition among the fire insurance companies, upon the collapse of a previous pool; and the competition cost them in New York City alone $17,500,000 in seven years. Consequently in 1882 they made a new combination which covered the whole country, and which Mr. Lloyd declares to be wealthy, cohesive, and powerful. Though there is no pool or ring, I am credibly informed that there is a common understanding among the fire insurance companies of London. One of the most noted of combinations has been the great Copper Syndicate which attracted world-wide attention early in 1888. It was formed by some French speculators in October, 1887, and during the eighteen months of its existence, maintained copper at a purely arbitrary price in all the markets of the world. At its head was M. Eugéne Secretan, managing director of the So- ciété des Métaux, the world's largest buyer of, and dealer in, manufactured copper. The syndicate's agents bought all the copper that was visible and for sale, the result of their speculation being that the price of copper in the London market rose from less than £40 to over £80 a ton, and the price of Lake Superior copper in America rose from 10½ cents to 17¾ cents per pound. M. Secretan informed a London journal that his designs were purely philanthropic. "Our only purpose", he said, "is that every miner, dealer and manufacturer should have fair remuneration for his work." Thanks to M. Secretan's philanthropy, copper, tin, lead and spelter rose enormously in price; several trades were more or less paralysed; and in France large numbers of workmen were thrown out of em- ployment. And let it not be supposed that the suicide of M. Denfert-Rochereau, which heralded the collapse of this first attempt to corner the world's copper—a collapse due to a miscalculation of the extent to which the supply of copper could increase under the stimulus of high prices—offers us any security against a repe- tition of the attempt. On the contrary, it has shewn how the thing may be safely done. The metal hoarded by the unlucky speculators is still so far cornered that it has been kept off the market up to the present, prices being not yet normal. "To a regular trust it must and will come at last", says Mr. E. Benjamin Andrews, of Cornell University. "Nor has aught taken place to indicate that a Copper Trust, organized like the Standard Oil Trust, with its energy and re- lentless methods, would fail".[10]

[10] *Quarterly Journal of Economics,* July, 1889.

The individualist who supposes that Free Trade plus private property will solve all economic problems is naturally surprised at these "rings", which upset all his crude economic notions; and he very illogically asks for legislation to prevent the natural and inevitable result of the premises with which he starts. It is amusing to note that those who advocate what they call self-reliance and self-help are the first to call on the State to interfere with the natural results of that self-help, of that private enterprise, when it has overstepped a purely arbitrary limit. Why, on ordinary commercial principles, should not a copper syndicate grasp all the copper in the world? It is merely the fittest surviving. The whole case against Socialism is assumed by its most intelligent opponents to lie in that Darwinian theory. And yet when the copper syndicate or the "coal barons" survive, they arouse against themselves the fiercest and, from the commercial point of view, the most unreasonable antagonism. As sin when it is finished is said to bring forth death, so capitalism when it is finished brings forth monopoly. And one might as well quarrel with that plain fact as blame thorns because they do not produce grapes, or thistles because they are barren of figs.

The story of the growth of capitalism is not yet complete. The "ring" is being succeeded by a more elaborate organization known as the "trust". Although in England great combinations like the Salt Union are rapidly rising, yet we must again travel to America to learn what the so-called "trust" is. The fullest information on the subject of trusts is contained in a report of a Committee of the New York State Legislature, which was appointed to investigate the new combination. The following trusts were inquired into: Sugar, milk, rubber, cotton-seed oil, envelope, elevator, oil cloth, Standard oil, butchers, glass, and furniture. A trust is defined by the Committee as a combination "to destroy competition and to restrain trade through the stockholders therein combining with other corporations or stockholders to form a joint-stock company of corporations, in effect renouncing the powers of such several corporations, and placing all powers in the hands of trustees". The general purposes and effects are stated to be "to control the supply of commodities and necessities; to destroy competition; to regulate the quality; and to keep the cost to the consumer at prices far beyond their fair and equitable value". It is unnecessary to deal with all these trusts, which possess certain features in common. I will select one or two, particularly the great Standard Oil Trust and the Cotton-seed Oil Trust.

The Standard Oil Trust is probably the largest single business monopoly in the world, the value of all its included interests being estimated, according to the evidence submitted, at £29,600,000. In the report it is described as "one of the most active and possibly the most formidable monied power on this continent. Its influence reaches into every State, and is felt in remote villages; and the products of its refineries seek a market in almost every seaport on the globe." The germ of this huge monopoly was a small petroleum refinery near Cleveland, bought by one Rockefeller, a book-keeper in a store, and a friend of his, a porter, with borrowed money. Rockefeller formed an acquaintance with a rich whiskey distiller, who advanced money and put his son-in-law Flagler into the business. This person's doctrines are thus described: "He says that there is no damned sentiment about business; that he knows no friendship in trade; and that if he gets his business rival in a hole he means to keep him there". Such a man is eminently fitted to be the founder of a monopoly: he is a hero of self-help; for he helps himself to anything he can lay his hands on. A second refinery was established in Ohio, and a warehouse opened in New York. The concern grew, and was incorporated as the Standard Oil Company. It is charged with having secured special legislation by judicious expenditure in the lobbies of the Ohio and Pennsylvania Legislatures. By entering into arrangements with the trunk railway lines, it secured special rates for transit. New refineries were established and new oil lands in Pennsylvania acquired; the capital was increased; and an enormous yearly business was done. After a time the company controlled every avenue of transportation; managed all the largest refineries in the land; and was able to shut off every competitor from either receiving supplies or shipping its products. New companies, nominally distinct, but all under the control of the same men, were incorporated in New Jersey, Ohio, West Virginia, and other States. The monopoly elected one of its chief stockholders into the United States Senate, it is said, through bribery in the Ohio Legislature, over which body it certainly acquired strong hold. These tactics were known as "coal oil politics". All the dirty work was, of course, done through agents, the directors pretending perfect innocence. In 1882 the Standard Oil Companies were consolidated into the Standard Oil Trust.[11] The stockholders surrendered their stock to the trustees, nine in number, created under the agreement, and received certificates in the place thereof, the representatives of the Trust and the stockholders in the refineries making a joint valuation of the refineries, and the certificates being issued to that amount. Thus the separate concerns were merged in one gigantic business, controlled by nine men (owning a majority of the stock), having a monopoly of nearly all the oil lands in America, controlling legislative votes, forming a solid alliance with the railway and shipping interests, and determining to a gallon how much oil

[11] Report of Senate Committee, p. 419.

shall be produced and refined, and to a fraction of a cent what shall be its price. In 1887 there was a cash dividend of 10 per cent. declared, besides a stock dividend of 20 per cent. on the certificates of four years' aggregation. In addition to the enormous stock they hold, the trustees receive an annual salary of £5,000. What are the economic results of this combination? It has not raised prices, as the trusts were charged by the committee with doing. On the contrary there has been a steady decrease in price during the decade 1877-1887. The consumption of oil has also enormously increased. The working and producing expenses have been greatly lowered by the dismissal of needless labor and vast improvements in machinery; the pipe lines controlled by the trust having displaced 5,700 teams of horses and 11,400 men in handling the oil. Thus of this trust we may say that though the means used to establish it were morally doubtful or even bad, the political results disastrous, the economic results have been beneficial, except in the matter of helping to form an unemployed class through the dismissal of needless labor consequent on the development of machinery.

The Cotton-seed Oil Trust was organized two or three years ago in the State of Arkansas.[12] Upwards of seventy different companies had been competing with each other, and consequently suffering heavy losses. Their mills being comparatively small and equipped with imperfect machinery, they were glad to combine; and those that did not were forced to close. The seventy corporations, the vast majority of the members of which had agreed to the combination, surrendered their stock to a body of trustees and received in return $100 certificates. The various mills send a monthly report to the trust; and if the officers in a given mill do not sell at the terms im-

[12] Report of Senate Committee, p. 233, *et seq.*

posed, they are dismissed by the trust.[13] The object
of the trust was declared by a witness to be to prevent
bankruptcy, to improve methods, to find markets,
to develop the enterprise and to make money. The
economic result has been displacement of labor by
machinery and great economy in production. Incidentally it came out that much cotton-seed oil was
sold to French and Italian buyers, who mix it with
a little olive oil and export it back to America and
to England, where a confiding public purchases it
as pure Tuscan olive oil—an interesting illustration
of international trade morality.

An examination of the milk and butchers' trusts
ought to be a revelation to those who imagine that
trade is "free", and that competition rules. On April
29th, 1885, the directors of the Milk Exchange met
in New York and unanimously resolved:

> "That on the first day of May next, and until
> otherwise ordered, the market price of milk pro-
> duced from meadow hay and sound cereals be 2½
> cents per quart, and that produced from brewers'
> grains and glucose and corn starch refuse be 2 cents
> per quart." [14]

A representative of the Sheep and Lamb Butchers'
Mutual Benefit Association testified that the members of that body agreed that they would only buy
sheep and calves from the Sheep Brokers' Association,
a penalty for violation of this rule being imposed at
the rate of 15 cents a head per sheep or calf. The
absolute despotism, and the system of espionage involved in such regulation is obvious. Here is a copy
of a document issued by this body:

> "New York, January 9th, 1888. Permission has
> been granted by the board of trustees of this Asso-

[13] Report, p. 244.
[14] Report of Senate Committee, p. 305.

ciation to Simon Strauss to buy sheep and lambs in New York markets, providing he buys no sheep and lambs from outsiders, under penalty of 15 cents per head fine. Richard S. Tobin, secretary." [15]

Occasionally the Association relaxed. On November 5th, 1887, according to its minutes,

"The application of John Healey, No. 2, to be granted the privilege of buying a few sheep and lambs without the 15 cents being charged to the brokers, was favorably acted upon."

This is not a record of Bagdad under the caliphs, but of the Republican State of New York! The threatened despotism of Socialism has been often eloquently dwelt on: but what of the actual despotism of to-day?

Now what does this examination of trusts show? That, granted private property in the raw material out of which wealth is created on a huge scale by the new inventions which science has placed in our hands, the ultimate effect must be the destruction of that very freedom which the modern democratic State posits as its first principle. Liberty to trade, liberty to exchange products, liberty to buy where one pleases, liberty to transport one's goods at the same rate and on the same terms enjoyed by others, subjection to no *imperium in imperio*: these surely are all fundamental democratic principles. Yet by monopolies every one of them is either limited or denied. Thus capitalism is apparently inconsistent with democracy as hitherto understood. The development of capitalism and that of democracy cannot proceed without check on parallel lines. Rather are they comparable to two trains approaching each other from different directions on the same line. Collision between the opposing forces seems inevitable.

[15] Report of Senate Committee, p. 497.

But both democracy and the new capitalist combinations which threaten it are inevitable growths of an evolutionary process. We are therefore brought to consider the question whether the ring, syndicate, or trust either can or ought to be destroyed. These combinations can be shown to be the most economical and efficient methods of organizing production and exchange. They check waste, encourage machinery, dismiss useless labor, facilitate transport, steady prices, and raise profits—i.e., they best effect the objects of trade from the capitalist's point of view. Now, the opponents of Socialism say that without this enterprising capitalist we cannot live. He "provides employment", they say. Well, if we need him, we must obviously pay his price. If he has a natural monopoly of a function indispensable to social progress, society must concede the terms he imposes. These terms are briefly large combinations of capitalist ownership. In this way he can best organize business: if we do not choose to let him do it in this way, he will not do it for us at all. From his point of view that is a fair position to take up; and it places the Individualist opponent of trusts in an awkward dilemma. For he must either submit to trusts or give up capitalists, in which latter case he becomes a Socialist. The answer of Socialism to the capitalist is that society can do without him, just as society now does without the slave-owner or feudal lord, both of whom were formerly regarded as necessary to the well-being and even the very existence of society. In organizing its own business for itself, society can employ, at whatever rate of remuneration may be needed to call forth their powers, those capitalists who are skilled organizers and administrators. But those who are mere dividend-receivers will no longer be permitted to levy a contribution on labor, but must earn their living by useful industry as other and better people have to do.

It may be said that society is not yet ripe for this transformation, nor is it. The forms of the democratic State are not yet perfected, nor has the economic evolution yet proceeded generally far enough, even in England, not to speak of the less advanced European countries. Much yet remains to be done through both the education of the intellect and the development of a nobler public spirit. But on the other hand we seem to be rapidly approaching such an *impasse* that some very large and definite extension of collective authority must be made. This would seem to involve on one side general reduction of the hours of labor, and on the other an attempt to absorb by the community a portion of those social values which it creates. In reference to ground values it may be anticipated that local democratic authorities will secure them for the benefit of the people by any means which may be found expedient.

As regards the great combinations of capital, State action may take one of three courses. It may prohibit and dissolve them; it may tax and control them; or it may absorb and administer them. In either case the Socialist theory is *ipso facto* admitted: for each is a confession that it is well to exercise a collective control over industrial capital. If the first of these courses is taken a distinctly retrogressive policy is definitely adopted, a policy of alarm at what Mr. Cleveland called the "communism of capital", a policy of reversion to the chaos of "free competition", and of cession of the undoubted benefits which combination has secured. Such a policy would signify the forcible prevention of acquisition of property, the very thing dearest to the individualist. If the powers of acquisition, now evidently dependent on combination, are to be restricted, what becomes of the "incentive to industry", the "reward of abstinence", and all the rest of the worn out phrases which have so often done duty in the place of argument? If the syndicate or the trust represents the legitimate outcome of capitalism—if it is necessary to give order to trade and to prevent the ruinous waste of unrestricted competition, how absurd it is for the State to say to the capitalist: "You shall carry your privileges of acquisition just up to the point where competition is likely to ruin you; but there you shall stop. Immediately you and your friends combine to prevent waste, to regulate production and distribution, to apply new methods of manufacture, we shall absolutely prevent you or restrain you by vexatious regulations". To which the capitalist may be supposed to reply: "I cannot fulfil my function in society at this serious risk. I shall never know security— never be even moderately sure of reaping that reward to which I am admittedly entitled. If you intend to fetter my action in this way after having proclaimed me free to own the raw material out of which wealth is made—if you compel me to stop at a purely arbitrary line, I must inform you that I am not going to undertake business on such terms". Would not the capitalist say something like this: and from his point of view would he not be right?

If it were instantly possible to do so, we should take the capitalist at his word; appropriate the necessary instruments of production; and make them common property, the values they create accruing to the community. But the human race generally contrives to exhaust every device which stupidity can suggest before the right line of action is ultimately taken. I think therefore that some probably inefficient method of taxation and public control over combinations will, as a matter of fact, be adopted. Such legislation will immensely restrict individual liberty in certain directions, will produce much friction, and may possibly hamper production; until by a long series of experiments men shall discover what is the most reasonable way of acquiring for the community as a whole the wealth which it produces. But in any case individualism

or anything whatever in the nature of *laisser faire* goes
by the board.

And now, finally, what is the immediate policy for
rational students of economics and genuine social
reformers to adopt? Their motto must be, *Nulla vestigia
retrorsum*. To all quack proposals they must offer
a steady resistance. These proposals will take the form
of attempts to bring back some economic condition
out of which society has emerged. One quack will
desire to revive the old British yeomanry; another will
talk nonsense about "Fair Trade"; a third will offer
to the rustic "three acres and a cow"; while a fourth
will see salvation in getting rid of primogeniture and
entail and "planting" properous laborers on the soil—
as though the laborers grew there like trees. Those
who understand the economic crisis may be ready and
eager to support any reform, however small, which is
a genuine step forward; but they cannot support any
effort to call back the past. They may help to build a
new bridge across the gulf that separates us from the
Co-operative Commonwealth; but they can never
repair the old broken-down structure which leads
back to Individualism. Instead, therefore, of attempting to undo the work which capitalists are unconsciously doing for the people, the real reformer will
rather prepare the people, educated and organized as
a true industrial democracy, to take up the threads
when they fall from the weak hands of a useless
possessing class. By this means will the class struggle,
with its greed, hate, and waste, be ended, and the life
hinted at by Whitman in his "Song of the Exposition" be attained:

"Practical, peaceful life, the people's life, the People
     themselves,
   Lifted, illumined, bathed in peace—elate, secure in
     peace."

# 4. MORAL

## By Sydney Olivier

The argument of this fourth instalment of Socialist criticism may be provisionally described as an attempt to justify Socialist ideals by the appeal to canons of moral judgment accepted generally and supported by the results of positive ethical science. The previous essays have made it clear that we are dealing with Socialism in that restricted sense in which it is defined by Schaeffle,[1] as having for its aim "the re-placement of private capital by collective capital: that is, by a method of production which, upon the basis of the collective property of the sum of all the members of the society in the instruments of production, seeks to carry on a co-operative organization of national work". We are not dealing with Socialism as a religion, nor as concerned with questions of sex or family: we treat it throughout as primarily a property-form, as the scheme of an industrial system for the supply of the material requisites of human social existence.

If it were admitted that the establishment of such a system would guarantee just this much—that abject poverty should be done away, and that every man and woman should be ensured the opportunity of obtaining sufficient food and covering in return for a moderate day's work, we might still be far from

[1] "The Quintessence of Socialism." Swan Sonnenschein and Co.

convincing some people that the realization of that ideal would be a good thing for the world. There are still a great many who, though they may not join in the common prophecy that the chief result of such a system would be an increase in beer-drinking and other stupid self-indulgence,[2] yet regard starvation and misery as part of the inevitable order of nature, and as necessary conditions of progress, conducive to the survival of what they are pleased to call the "fittest" types of life. Such critics see danger to progress in any attempt to enrol intelligence and adaptiveness into conscious combination against starvation and misery, to extinguish by concerted effort survivals of the accidents of primitive barbarism against which as individuals we are always struggling. This aim of Socialism, accordingly, does not wholly commend itself to their moral judgment, to their opinion of what is *good* in the widest sense, although they may willingly admit that the aim possesses a certain element of shortsighted good intention. Other persons, influenced by religious conceptions older than that of progress, and regarding morality less as determined by reference to that end than as a concern of the individual, a certain state of the soul of each man, are inclined to view the material evils which Socialists desire to get rid of, as a necessary schooling and discipline without which individual morality would decay.

Against these doctrines Socialists would maintain that the ordering of our national life, and of the relations between individuals and social groups throughout the world in accordance with the principles of Socialism, is the effectual and indispensable process for ensuring to the mass of mankind the advantages of progress already effected and its continued and orderly development, and for the realisation, in individuals

[2] *E.g.*, see "Communism and Socialism", by Theodore D. Woolsey. Sampson Low and Co., London.

and the State, of the highest morality as yet imagined by us.

It may be well at this point to anticipate a challenge to define what is meant by the word "Morality", and to briefly explain the position which will be assumed, and the method which will be followed, throughout the succeeding observations. It must be remembered that the subject of this essay is "The Moral Aspect of the Basis of Socialism", and not "The Socialist View of the Basis of Morals". We may therefore conscientiously steer clear of the whirlpool of agelong controversy as to what that basis is, merely noting as we pass that any metaphysic of Ethics being necessarily universal, there is in this sense no special ethic or morality of Socialism. By such cautious procedure we sacrifice indeed the fascinating ambition to exhibit, by impressive dialectic pageant of deduction from first principles, the foundation of formal Socialism in the Idea that informs the universe. But we also avoid the certainty of losing, at the very outset of our attempted demonstration, the company of all but that minority who might assent to our fundamental propositions. A further sacrifice we shall make, in descending to the unpretentious methods of empiricism; for we thereby renounce the right of appeal to that theologic habit of mind common to Socialists with other pious persons. Mr. Henry George, educated under the American Constitution, may share the familiarity of its framers with the intentions of the Creator and the natural rights of Man. He may prove, as did Mr. Herbert Spencer in his generous youth, that private property in land is incompatible with the fundamental right of each individual to live and to own the product of his labor. But positive ethical science knows nothing of natural and fundamental rights: it knows nothing of individual liberty, nothing of equality, nothing of underlying unity. Yet here again our loss has some redress; for a brief survey will assure us that various

schools of moral philosophy, differing in their characteristic first principles, are converging in the justification of Socialism; and that the practical judgments of
contemporary mankind as to what sort of conduct is
"moral", and what conditions make for the increase
of "common morality", are in practice largely coinci-
dent. They offer, at least, a body of provisional opinion,
or prejudice, to which we can appeal in presenting
Socialism for criticism of its morality. The tribunal is
by no means infallible: still, the common contemporary
sense of humanity may count for something. But in
approaching the criticism of Socialism from the point
of view of ethics, we are bound to go a little deeper
than this. While accepting the phenomena of current
opinion on morality as part of our material, we must
follow the explorations of ethical speculation into
the causes and history of the development of those
opinions. By examining the genesis of convictions that
this or that kind of action is good or bad, moral or
immoral, we shall be helped to form a judgment as
to which appears likely to persist and be strengthened,
and which to be modified, weakened, or forgotten. If
the claim of Socialism rests on judgments of the latter
class, we may know that it is a moribund bantling;
if they preponderate among the obstacles to its credit,
we may prophesy encouragingly of it; if it is supported
by those judgments whose persistence seems essential to the survival of the individual and of society,
we may be assured of its realisation in the future.

Socialism appears as the offspring of Individualism,
as the outcome of individualist struggle, and as the
necessary condition for the approach to the Individualist ideal. The opposition commonly assumed in
contrasting the two is an accident of the now habitual confusion between personality and personalty,
between a man's life and the abundance of things
that he has. Socialism is merely Individualism ra-
tionalised, organised, clothed, and in its right mind.

Socialism is taking form in advanced societies and the social revolution must be brought to its formal accomplishment through the conscious action of innumerable individuals seeking an avenue to rational and pleasant existence for themselves and for those whose happiness and freedom they desire as they do their own. All conscious action, all conscious modification of conditions, is inspired by the desire of such personal relief, satisfaction, or expression, by the attempt to escape from some physical or intellectual distress. "Subjective volition, passion it is", says Hegel, "that sets men in activity: men will not interest themselves for anything unless they find their individuality gratified by its attainment". This common end, this desire of personal relief or satisfaction, we see throughout recorded or indicated history impelling every living creature on the earth; merging itself, as we trace it backwards, in the mere apparent will to live of organisms not recognised as conscious, and in the indestructible energy of the inorganic. The field of activity thus conceived presents a panorama of somewhat large extent; but a very small division of it is all that we shall have to do with. For morality, whatever be its nature and basis, certainly does not become recognisable to us, we cannot attribute the quality of rightness or wrongness, until the formation of society has begun, until individuals are in conscious relation with individuals other than themselves.

If we could imagine an individual absolutely isolated, and having no relation at all with other sentient beings, *we* could not say that it was moral or immoral for him to eat, drink, sleep, breathe, wash himself, take exercise, cough, sneeze, and the like, just as much or as little, when or where he felt inclined. His conduct in these activities must appear to us absolutely indifferent. We may have some vague reflected suppositions as to what is necessary for the dignity and development of the man's "self", as we might call it; but this is a matter about which the man may pretend to know as much as we do; and we have really no valid ground for prejudice against the habits of the recluse Indian fakir, who has, on the other hand, considerable claims to be regarded as a peculiarly holy individual. But of every man living in society we can say, that if he starves himself into inefficiency; if he gorges or fuddles himself; if he sleeps unseasonably; if he abstains from the fresh air, the cleanliness, and the exercise, necessary to keep his body healthy and his presence pleasant; if he destroys his powers by over-work; then he is acting wrongly, immorally, unreasonably, in extreme cases insanely. (Insanity is only the name we give to abnormal deviation from what are accepted as reasonable and intelligible desires and behavior.) And if this is the case with actions of the kind loosely described as self-regarding, with those which most nearly concern the agent's own person, much more is it so with the kind of actions which necessarily and invariably affect other persons. Those relations of the individual with his fellows in which subjective morality is chiefly recognised, have no existence at all apart from society. Subjective morality, then, being only distinguishable in the State, the extent of our panorama is already much diminished; for in every gentile or national society, and to some degree in the World-State of to-day, we find the individualist activity, the desire and passion of the human unit, very largely exercising itself in accordance with what we call a moral habit. Innumerable types of society have been formed in the process of life-development. In the oldest of these we recognise the elements of a conventional morality, similar to that by which our own human society is held together. We consider the ways of the ant; and we see that they are wise.

We find that in all societies those actions and habits are approved as moral which tend to preserve the existence of society and the cohesion and convenience of its members; and that those which are or seem to be fraught with contrary tendencies are considered immoral. It is plain that no society in which these judgments were habitually reversed could continue in existence; and this fact will account for much of that general inherited disposition to actions socially beneficial, and inherited repugnance to those presumably the reverse, which form so large a part of what we speak of as conscience. So deep in grain have many of these common judgments come to be that their influence has passed out of consciousness; and they are obeyed automatically or instinctively without any reflexion as to their moral aspect arising in the agent's mind. It is, for example, so necessary for the existence of society that the citizen should abstain from slaughtering at large, such self-restraint is so evidently reasonable, its non-observance so contrary to common sense, that when we find a murder done for mere desire of bloodshed and under the impulse of no other passion whatsoever, we do not think of the murderer as immoral, but rather as insane, judging the man who would destroy the life of society as coroners' juries by their habitual verdict upon suicides pronounce of the man who destroys his own.

Most of the habits of activity and avoidance, necessary for the mere physical existence of the individual as moral actions and abstentions are necessary for the existence of society, have long ago become automatic, and are sunk, so far as common opinion is concerned, permanently out of the purview of moral criticism. All the involuntary functions of the human body which conduce to its nutrition and maintenance in health have been gradually acquired in the course of ages, as the conditions necessary for the expression of the mere animal will to live the largest and freest life permitted by the physical environment. And as the bodily form and functions of the typical individual of each species have accrued and become established as the indispensable mechanic of the mere determination to exist, so the form and institutions of society, and the relations and mutual behavior of its individuals, have been adjusted and established as the equally indispensable conditions for the expression of the determination to exist more fully, for the enlargement of freedom and opportunity for the gratification of those passions and aspirations, the display of those energies and activities which characterise the more complex forms of life as it passes from the inorganic and vegetative to the conscious and self-conscious stages of its evolution.

The primitive forms of human society we must infer to have grown up and survived simply because they increased the efficiency of man as a feeding and a fighting animal, just as did those of the wolf, the beaver, and the ant. Society has now grown to be for man the indispensable guarantee not only of nutrition and protection, but of the opportunity to imagine and attain a thousand varieties of more refined satisfaction. So far as man has attained freedom to do and be as he desires, he has attained it only through the evolution of society. When a society perishes, as societies organically weak among stronger competitors have done and will do, the individual perishes with it, or is forced backwards with impaired freedom until a fresh social integration renews and extends his powers of self-development. Societies as has been pointed out by Sidney Webb on page 79 must safeguard their existence to-day for the very same reasons for which society has formed itself. It has grown up for the convenience of individuals, for their defence and relief under the pressure of all that was not themselves —of Nature, as we call it—beasts, and competing men, to give a little breathing space, a little elbow room, amid the storm and stress of primæval existence; and from that beginning it has been unfolded and elaborated, each step of progress effected for the convenience of active individuals, until the individual of to-day is born as a leaf upon a mighty tree, or a coral insect in a sponge, himself to live his individual life, and in living it to modify the social organism in which he has his being.

Reviewing the development in society of the conditions for the satisfaction of the individual will to live, and to live in the best way conceivable, we see in the progress of moral ideas the progress of discovery of the most reasonable manner of ordering the life of the individual and the form of social institutions under the contemporary environment. It has already been pointed out that some kinds of anti-social action are so unreasonable, so obviously prejudicial to the attainment of the common end of conscious individuals, that we brand them unhesitatingly as insane. Instances suggested were extreme personal uncleanliness or dissipation, and extreme cruelty or blood-thirstiness. The reason why other anti-social or indirectly suicidal kinds of action are not yet classed as madness, though there is a steady tendency towards so treating them, is plainly that some activities of the individual, though hurtful to other citizens just as the activity of a pack of wolves or a predatory tribe is hurtful to adjacent societies, are commonly aimed at gratifying impulses and passions which are not yet grown so rare as blood-thirst, are not yet recognized as irrational or valueless, or even are acknowledged to be in their proper scope harmless, desirable, or necessary.

It is an established social convention (in England) that it is immoral to steal or to defraud. Only in very extreme cases do we account these pursuits as evidence of mania; for though injustice and dishonesty are incompatible with the health of society, and thus actually unreasonable and indirectly suicidal, the desires which prompt men to them are only at worst exaggerations of the desire for wealth or subsistence, which everyone recognizes as a necessary

condition of the mere continuance of life. Nay,
where the alternative is death for lack of subsistence,
many consider that neither are immoral. At the other
extreme, when the instinct prompts aggression in
defiance of the conscious reason and without assigna-
ble purpose of gain, when Jean Valjean robs the little
Savoyard, or a noble earl pockets the sugar-tongs, we
speak of mental aberration or of kleptomania.

The case of self-defence is similar. Quarrelsome-
ness and violence are destructive of social existence,
or at best impede its higher elaboration. But readiness
of resentment and quickness of fist were for ages and
ages necessities for individual survival; and for ages
and ages more their kindred social qualities of spirit
and valor were necessary for social survival, and accordingly ranked as virtues. The instruction to turn
the other cheek to the smiter is even now, perhaps, an
exaggeration of the precept commendable to Socialists
when charged by the London police: to suffer one-
self to be killed without reason is clearly and unmis-
takably immoral. As the western world advances out
of warfare into industry, more and more of what was
once military virtue becomes immorality in the individual; until an habitual ferocity which might
once have qualified its subject for chieftainship
may nowadays consign him to penal servitude or
Bedlam.

The foregoing illustrations have been treated, for
the present purpose, with reference only to the effect
of the behavior of the individual upon society. It is
indeed certain that anti-social action does not, as a
rule, effect permanent satisfaction for the individual
(isolated instances, of the type of Shelley's Count
Cenci, notwithstanding); but, independently of this,
the actions and propensities of the individual have
always, it appears, been judged by his fellows moral or
immoral chiefly according to their supposed effects upon
society. The object of every living creature being to

do as he pleases, if what he pleases to do incommodes other people they will take measures to restrain him from doing it. This they strive to effect by means of laws and conventional codes of morality, the main difference between the two being that the code of law is enforced by the infliction of direct personal punishment by officers of the State. This acceptance of codes of laws and conventions of morality leads to a secondary series of judgments as to right and wrong: for it comes to be accounted immoral to break the law whether the law itself be good or not, and reprehensible to depart from convention whether convention be any longer reasonable or not. This secondary morality is as it were the bud-sheath of the individual, which support he cannot dispense with until he has come to his full powers, but which he must dispense with if he is to fully realise his own freedom. Customary morality prevents him during the process of his education from pursuing his own satisfaction across the corns of his fellow creatures. In the process of education he learns that for the unit in society the word *self* includes more than the individual: the infant very soon finds out that what disagrees with his mother disagrees with him; the child, that the failure of his father's income means misery and hunger to the family. To say nothing of the facts of sympathy, every man born into an advanced society is early made aware that the satisfaction of his mere material needs depends upon the activities of that society around him quite as much as upon his own. All through the growth of nations and societies the complexity of this interdependence of individuals has increased, the areas of social consciousness have been extended and unified, from the solitary cave-dweller to the family or horde, from the tribe to the nation, and from the nation, by commerce, to the world, till the fortunes of each people have power over the hopes and fears of workers in every other, and the arts, the learning, and the literature of a hundred painful civilizations are available for us to-day, all the kingdoms of the earth and their glory displayed in a moment of time.

But not by bread alone does mankind live. Very early in the course of human evolution must the type of individual to whom all society was repugnant have been eliminated and suppressed by natural selection. The social instinct, the disposition to find comfort in comradeship independently of its material advantages, is of such evident antiquity in Man that we are justified in speaking of it as one of his fundamental and elementary characteristics. It is easy enough to suggest theories of the origin of this adhesiveness, this affection, this sympathy, in the conditions of racial survival: the important fact for us is its remarkable susceptibility of cultivation and extension. The individual in society does that which is pleasant to his friends, and abstains from doing that which is unpleasant, not because he likes to be thought a good fellow, or expects benefits in return, but simply because it gives him immediate pleasure so to act. He is sensitive to that which hurts them, not because he fears that his own defences are weakened by their injury, but because they have actually become part of himself by the extension of his consciousness over them. This social instinct, this disposition to benevolent sympathy, appears almost as inextinguishable as the personal desire of life: in innumerable instances it has proved far stronger.

The recognition by each individual of his dependence on society or sensitiveness to his own interest, and his affection towards society or sensitiveness to its interest: these two faces of the same fact represent an intricate tissue of social consciousness extremely sensitive to all kinds of anti-social, or immoral, action. The moral education of the individual appears formally as the process of learning, by sheer extension of knowledge and experience, and nothing else, how

he may harmonise and follow out his own desires
in these two aspects and their combinations. He has
to learn how to provide for the needs of his bodily
life in a manner that will not interfere with the freedom
of others to do the same. Laws and conventions of
morality guide him at first in this respect; but the
man cannot be said to be free until he acts morally
because, foreseeing that on the satisfaction of these
primary needs new desires will emerge whose satisfaction will give him a more exquisite contentment,
he perceives that it is reasonable so to act. The
existence and stability of society are the indispensable guarantee for the general satisfaction of the primary
desires of individuals, therefore it is unreasonable to
weaken society by immoral action; but much more are
the existence and health of society indispensable conditions for the common birth and satisfaction of the
secondary desires, the desires which have created all
that is most valuable in civilization and which find
their satisfaction in art, in culture, in human intercourse, in love. The moral education of the individual
is the lesson, not that desire is evil, and that he can only
attain his freedom by ceasing to desire, for this is
death, or desertion, and the army of the living presses
on to fuller life; but that the wider, fuller satisfaction
is built upon the simpler, and common morality a condition of its possibility; that there are certain manners
and methods in which, if he goes about to save his
life, he most infallibly will lose it; and that love, the
social instinct, and science, which is ordered knowledge, are his only reliable tutors in practical morality.

But man in society not only lives his individual life:
he also modifies the form of social institutions in the
direction indicated by reason—in such a manner, that
is, as it seems to his understanding will render them
more efficient for securing freedom for that life of his.
And just as certain forms of individual activity, in their
passage into and through the field of positive criticism,

appear first as indifferent, because they seem to concern the individual only, then as moral or immoral, because recognized as affecting society, later as simply rational or insane, morality having here formally attained its identification with reason and immorality with folly, and at last become habitual, instinctive, and unconscious; so institutions, originating in modes apparently accidental, come to be recognized as useful and valuable additions to the machinery of existence, are buttressed with all the authority and sanction of religion, and finally pass into unquestioned acceptance by the common-sense of men. In time some fundamental change in the conditions of the life of individuals is introduced by causes similarly unforeseen: the form of the old institution ceases to subserve the common end: it begins to cramp the freedom of the majority, who no longer require its support. Meanwhile it has established a minority, ostensibly controlling it for the common weal, in a position to administer it in the sole interest of their class. These, as their existence appears dependent on their so administering it, cannot be untaught the habit except by such modification of the institution as will render it again impossible for any class to have a special interest in its contemporary form.

This process is so familiar in history that it would be a waste of time here to illustrate it by tracing it in the growth of monarchies, aristocracies, priesthoods, chattel slavery, feudal bondage, representative government, or others of its innumerable manifestations. The institution of private property in certain things is in many respects so reasonable and convenient for the majority of mankind, and was so conspicuously advantageous for those stronger individuals under whose leadership the beginnings of tribal civilisations were developed, that very early in their history it received the sanction of moral convention, religion, and law. It was obviously necessary for the establish-

ment of industrial society that each man should own
the product of his labor and the tools necessary for
him to labor effectually. But the Industrial Revolution
described in the third paper of this series has entirely
changed the conditions under which men produce
wealth, and the character of the tools with which they
work, while the sanctions of law and conventional
morality still cling to all that has been imported under
the old definition of property. If the idea so constantly
appealed to in justification of property law is to be
realised; if the fruits of each man's labor [3] are to be
guaranteed to him and he is to own the instruments
with which he works; if the laws of property are not
to establish a parasitic class taking tribute from the
labor of others in the forms of Rent and Interest,
then we must modify our administration of property.
We must admit that as the agricultural laborer cannot
individually own the farm he works on and its stock,
as the factory hand cannot individually own the mill,
land and industrial capital are things in which private
property is impossible except on condition of a small
minority owning all such property and the great
majority none at all.

Socialists contend that this system of private property
in land and capital is actively destructive of the conditions in which alone the common morality necessary
for happy social life is possible. Without any demand
upon the faith of those persons who deny the capacity
of average human nature for the temperance and
kindliness indispensable for the success of a true co-
operative commonwealth, they assert that this modern
development of the property system (a development
of the last few generations only, and unprecedented in
the history of the world) is more and more forcing the

[3] To the intelligent Socialist this phrase has, of course, no
meaning. But against the non-Socialist who employs it it
may be legitimately used, *ad captandum*.

individual into anti-social disposition and action, and thereby destroying the promise of free and full existence which only the health and progressive development of the social organism can give him. It has become plainly reasonable that when this is the effect of our property system we should modify our institutions in the direction which will give us freedom, just as we modified the institutions which subjected us to a feudal aristocracy, and abolished for ever the laws which enabled one man to hold another as his chattel slave.

There is on record a Greek proverb, that so soon as a man has ensured a livelihood, then he should begin to practise virtue. We all protest that he will do well to practise virtue under any circumstances; but we admit on reflexion that our judgment as to what virtuous action depends upon the circumstances under which action is to be taken. Whether we approve the killing of one man by another depends entirely on the circumstances of the case; and there is scarcely one of the acts which our laws regard as criminal, which could not, under imaginable circumstances, be justified. Our laws, and our conventional opinions as to what conduct is moral or immoral, are adapted to the ordinary circumstances of the average man in society, society being in them presumed to be homogeneous, not to contain in itself essential distinctions between classes, or great contrasts between the conditions of individuals.

But that element in our private property system which is at present the main object of the Socialist attack, the individual ownership of the instruments of production, land and capital, in an age when the use of those instruments has become co-operative, results, and must inevitably result, as the foregoing dissertations have sought to prove, in the division of society into two classes, whose very livelihood is ensured to them by methods essentially different. The livelihood of the typical proletarian is earned by the exercise of his faculties for useful activity: the livelihood of the typical capitalist, or owner of property, is obtained, without any contribution of his or her activity, in the form of a pension called rent, interest, or dividend, guaranteed by law out of the wealth produced from day to day by the activities of the proletariat.

Observe the effect of this distinction in moral phenomena. Most of our common opinions as to social morality are adapted to a society in which every citizen is contributing active service. The most ancient and universal judgments of mankind as to the virtues of industry, of honesty, of loyalty and forbearance between man and man, of temperance, fortitude and just dealing, point to the elementary conditions necessary for the survival and strengthening of societies of equal and free individuals dependent for their subsistence upon the exercise of each one's abilities, and upon his fitness for co-operation with his fellows. But where a class or society exists, not dependent upon its own industry, but feeding like a parasite upon another society or class; when the individuals of such a parasitic society in no way depend for their livelihood or their freedom upon their fitness for co-operation one with another among themselves, or upon any personal relation with the class that feeds them; then the observation of the moral conventions of industrial and co-operative societies is in many respects quite unnecessary for the continuance of the life of the parasitic society, or for the pleasant existence of the individuals composing it. All that is necessary is that the established laws and conventions should continue to be observed by the industrial class ("it is required *in stewards* that a man be found faithful"); and as the existence of the propertied class in modern societies does depend ultimately upon the observance by the bulk of the people of this conventional morality, the propertied class professes publicly to venerate and observe conventions which in its private practice it has long admitted to be obsolete. This complication is a perennial source of cant. To this we owe the spectacle of Sir William Harcourt advocating total abstinence, of Mr. Arthur Balfour commending Christianity; to this the continual inculcation of industry and thrift by idle and extravagant people, with many another edifying variation on the theme of Satan's reproval of sin. Temperance, Christian morality, industry, and economy are of considerable social utility; but for the members of a propertied class they are not necessitated by the conditions of its existence, and consequently in such classes are neither observed nor commonly made the subject of moral criticism.

Consider the case of industry alone—of the moral habit of earning one's subsistence by useful activity. Assuming sustenance to be guaranteed, there is no obvious and pressing social necessity for such exertion. No doubt the paradise of the maid-of-all-work—where she means to do *nothing* for ever and ever—is the paradise of an undeveloped intelligence. A society relieved of the function of providing its own material sustenance need not relapse into general torpor, though the result is very commonly that an individual so circumstanced relapses into uselessness. It will be vain to preach to such an individual that he will find his fullest satisfaction in honest toil: he will simply laugh in your face, and go out partridge shooting, hunting, or yachting, or to Monte Carlo or the Rocky Mountains, finding in such an exercise of his capacities the keenest imaginable enjoyment for months in succession. He may feel no inclination at all to work for the benefit of the people whose work is supporting him: all that he, like the rest of us, requires is to find some means of passing his time in an agreeable or exciting manner. Accordingly, in that section of our nation which speaks of itself as "society," being indeed a society separated by economic parasitism from the common mass, we find that the characteristic activity is the provision of agreeable and exciting methods of passing time. This being the end of fashionable society, its code of morality is naturally quite different from the code suitable for industrial societies. Truthfulness is preached in these as a cardinal virtue. Lying is of course common enough in all classes, and is generally immoral; but in the fashionable world it is not only a perfectly legitimate means of avoiding an undesired visitor, or almost any other unpleasant experience: it is a positive necessity of conventional politeness and good manners. It is really harmless here, almost a virtue. To return to the virtue of industry: though the conventional morality of the people, necessary for the life of the nation, permeates with its vibrations this parasitic society which it enfolds; and though the unfailing contentment which a really intelligent man finds in social activity keeps a good many of the propertied class usefully occupied, the actual public opinion of that class is absolutely in accordance with the conditions of their life. The clerk in a Government office is congratulated by middle-class acquaintances on his luck in obtaining a berth where he need do no more work than he chooses; and it is habitually assumed that he will choose, like the Trafalgar Square fountains, to play from ten to four, with an interval for lunch. That may or may not be an adequate account of his activities: the significant thing is that such an assumption should not be considered insulting. But how indignantly will the very same acquaintances denounce the idleness and untrustworthiness of a British working man suspected, in the service of a private master, of interpreting his time work as most servants of the public are good humoredly assumed, without hint of disapproval, to interpret theirs!

This obsolescence of elementary social morality is most noticeable in women dependent upon incomes from property. They are doubly removed from the primary conditions of life; they are less likely than their men folk to be engaged in any work of perceptible social utility outside of their own homes; and their intellectual education being generally far more imperfect, it is only natural that their ideas of morality should be still more intimately adapted to the conditions of their class, and less to the general conditions of human society. The angels of heaven, we have always understood, are exempt from the apparatus of digestion, and are clothed as freely as the lilies of the field. In any society where all common needs are so supplied it would be immoral, surely, because a waste of time, to work as for a living. Now the universal ideal of capitalism is that man, being created a little lower than the angels, should raise himself to their level in this respect by the acquisition of property, a process pleasantly described as attaining a competence or independence, that is to say the right to be dependent and incompetent. The result of this has been a prejudice, which only within quite recent years has begun to be seriously shaken, that it is humiliating, even disgraceful, for a lady to have to earn her own living at all, for a gentleman to practise a handicraft for money, for a nobleman to go into trade: a prejudice for which, in a class society, there was much justification, but which is obviously a fragment of class morality directly antagonistic to the common social morality which recognises all useful industry as praiseworthy. It is now yielding to economic pressure and to the stimulus of the desire to get rich. Ladies are being driven, and in spite of Mr. Walter Besant's protestations will continue to be driven, into most of the female handicrafts, though some are still outside the pale of respectability. Ranching in America, though not yet drovering and butchering in England, is suitable occupation for the aristocracy. The "directing" of companies and the patronizing of nitrogenous Volunteer Colonels are legitimate modes of exploiting of a title.

The prejudice against useful employments is balanced for decency's sake by a hypocritical laudation of useless ones. The fiction so dear to the Primrose Dame, that the rich are the employers of the poor, the idlers the supporters of the industrious, takes nowadays forms more insidious than the rugged proposition that private vices are public benefits. The amusements, the purely recreational activities, of country gentlemen are glorified in the *National Review* [4] as "hard work". It is pretended that the leisured class is the indispensable patron and promoter of culture and the fine arts. The claim that such functions are virtues is a direct concession to the feeling that some effort must be made to exhibit the practices of parasitic society as compatible with its preaching of the common social morality.

The same necessity causes an exaggerated tribute of praise to be paid to such really useful work as is done under no compulsion but that of the social instinct. This kind of activity is habitually pointed to, by the friends of those who are engaged in it, as evidence of extraordinary virtue. A few hours of attention every week to the condition of the poor, a few gratuitously devoted to local administration, a habit of industry in any branch of literature or science: these are imputed as an excess of righteousness by persons who denounce the wage laborer as an idler and a shirk. Such activity is work of supererogation, approved but not required or expected. The motto of "noblesse oblige" has not been adopted by the plutocracy. Similar approbation and admiration are extended to those who, while already earning their living by a reasonable day's work, employ their spare time, or a part of it, in gratuitous activities of the kinds referred to. It may be safely said that by far the greater portion of this kind of

[4] See *National Review* for February, 1888, "Are Rich Landowners Idle?" by Lady Janetta Manners (now Duchess of Rutland).

work is done by people who are simultaneously earning an income in middle class professions or by the
less exhausting forms of wage labor. Most of them
have probably had experience of the ridiculous in-
appropriateness of the commendation usually paid to
their gratuitous energy by well-to-do friends. The activity is moral, no doubt; but its exercise gives no sensa-
tion of virtue or praiseworthiness: it is followed because
it is seen to be reasonable, because it is the path indicated by common sense towards the satisfaction of the
individual passion for the extension of freedom and
love.

The phenomena of class morality are ancient and
familiar enough. They have varied throughout history
with the changing character of the basis of class distinctions. The great permanent distinction of sex, and
the social relations between man and woman which
have arisen thereout in the period of civilisation from
which the world is now emerging, have resulted not
only in the establishment of distinct codes of chastity
for the sexes, but also in innumerable prejudices
against the participation of one sex or the other in
activities having nothing whatever to do with physio-
logical distinction. They have even succeeded in producing, through inequality of freedom and education,
well marked differences in mental habit, which show
themselves continually when men and women are
confronted with the same questions of truthfulness,
honor, or logic. It is hardly necessary to observe that
most of these differences are distinctly traceable to the
institution of private property, and to its concentration
in the hands of the male as the stronger individual in
a competitive society. The class moralities of societies
whose orders have been based immediately on status
or caste have formed the subject of an extensive
literature. The tracing of all such distinctions to their
root in economic circumstances is scarcely less interesting than the investigation of the same foundation

for sex morality. But even the interpreters of the Church Catechism have abandoned the appeal to status as the basis of duty; the idea of hereditary aristocracy is dead; and class distinctions and their appurtenant ethics are now founded directly and obviously on property.

We have glanced at some effects of our present property system which work continually for the destruction of the traditions of social morality in the capitalist class. The fundamental idea of that system, that man can live without working, as the angels of heaven, is (fortunately) self-contradictory in this respect, that in human society no class can so live except by the double labor of another class or classes. The would-be angelic society on earth must either own chattel slaves, or be a military caste taking tribute, or a parasitical and exploiting class extracting rent and interest by the operation of the industrial system analysed in the preceding papers. Such a class and such a system are, as we are all becoming aware, more virulently revolutionary in their operation, and more certain to bring about their own destruction than either chattel slavery or feudalism. Of these three phases of human injustice that of wage slavery will surely be the shortest. But meanwhile the propertied class assumes to represent civilisation; its approved morality is preached and taught in church and schools; it debases our public opinion; and it directly poisons all that host of workers who are at present hangers-on of the rich, whether as menial servants or as ministering to their especial amusements and extravagance. There is no such snob as a fashionable dressmaker; and there is no class of the proletariat so dehumanised as the class of domestic servants.

Now if these results are effected in the class whose livelihood is assured, and whose education and culture have given it a hold on the higher inducements to morality—if we here find morality strangled at the

root and starving, what shall we find when we turn
to the masses whose livelihood is not assured them?
Our Greek, perhaps, would say that it was impossible
for them to practise virtue, just as Plato in his "Republic" suggested that only the philosophic class could
be really moral, since slaves and the proletariat could
not receive the intellectual education necessary to
train the reason. The great bulk of the wage earning
class in modern civilised countries is so far assured
of its livelihood that it remains thoroughly permeated
with common social morality. It is, from habit and
preference, generally industrious and kindly, thus exhibiting the two most important qualifications for the
social life. It remains to a great extent honest, though
competition and capitalism are directly antagonistic
to honesty. The decalogue of commercial morality
has its own peculiar interpretation of stealing, murder,
false witness and coveting; and yet the most unscrupulous wrecker in the City will be outraged in his
finest feelings by the class morality of the plumber,
who, called in to bring the gas to reason, takes the
opportunity to disorganise the water-supply and introduce a duster into the drain. The employer is aghast
at the increase of idleness and bad workmanship under
a system in which the good workman knows that
to work his best will not only not be worth his while
but will lead to the exaction of heavier tasks from his
fellows.

But it is not in the mass of the proletariat that the
action of our property system in destroying elementary
morality is most conspicuous. It is in those whom it
excludes even from the proletariat proper that this
extreme result is clearest. The characteristic operation
of the modern industrial economy is continually and
repeatedly to thrust out individuals or bodies of the
workers from their settlement in the social organism—
to eject, as it were, the coral insect from the cell in
which he is developing. The capitalist farming system

expels the agricultural laborer from the village: the machine expels the craftsman from the ranks of skilled labor: the perpetual competition and consolidation of capital in every trade alternately destroys employment in that trade and disorganises others. Overproduction in one year leaves thousands of workers wageless in the next. The ranks of unskilled labor, the army of the unemployed, are day by day recruited in these fashions. An inveterate social habit, an almost indestructible patience, a tenacious identification of his own desire with the desire of those whom he loves, in most cases preserve the worker from accepting the sentence of exclusion from society. If he is able-bodied, intelligent and fortunate, he will struggle with hard times till he finds fresh occupation among strange surroundings; but woe to him if he be weakly, or old, or unpractical. In such a case he will almost infallibly become a pauper or an outcast, one of that residuum of unskilled, unemployed, unprofitable and hopeless human beings which in all great cities festers about the base of the social pyramid. And his children will become the street Arabs and the corner-boys and the child-whores and the sneak-thieves who, when they come of age, accept their position as outside of social life and resume the existence of the wild beasts that fathered man—the purely predatory and unsocial activity of harrying their neighbors for their own support. Before society was, morality was not: those who have no part nor lot in the ends for which society exists will adapt their morality to suit their outcast state: there will indeed be honor among thieves, just as there will be cant and insincerity among the parasitic rich; but the youth who has been nurtured between the reformatory and the slum has little chance of finding a foothold, if he would, in the restless whirl of modern industry, and still less of retaining permanently such foothold as he may manage to find.

When the conditions of social life are such that the individual may be excluded through no unfitness of his own for co-operation, or may be born without a chance of acquiring fitness for it, we are brought face to face with the conditions of primitive ages. And if you force him back upon the elemental instincts, one of two things will happen. Either, if the individual is weak through physical deterioration or incapacity to combine with his fellow outcasts, he will be crushed and killed by society and putrefy about its holy places; or, if he has indomitable life and vigor, he will revert to the argument of elemental forces: he will turn and explode society. Here, then, we should fear explosion, for we are not as submissive in extremities as the proletariats of arrested Indian civilisations. But with us the class whose freedom is incessantly threatened by the operation of private capitalism is the class which by its political position holds in its hands the key to the control of industrial form: that is to say, its members can modify, as soon as they elect to, the laws of property and inheritance in this State of Britain. They can, as soon as they see clearly what is needed, supersede institutions now immoral because useless and mischievous by institutions which shall re-establish the elementary conditions of social existence and the possibility of the corresponding morality—namely, the opportunity for each individual to earn his living and the compulsion upon him to do so.

Returning from the consideration of the "residuum" and the "criminal classses", we find that even the workers of the employed proletariat are by no means wholly moral. In spite of the massive healthiness of their behavior in ordinary relations, they are generally coarse in their habits; they lack intelligence in their amusements and refinement in their tastes. The worst result of this is the popularity of boozing and gambling and allied forms of excitement, with their outcomes in violence and meanness. But when once society has ensured for man the opportunity for satisfying his primary needs—once it has ensured him a healthy body and a wholesome life, his advance in the refinements of social morality, in the conception and satisfaction of his secondary and more distinctly human desires, is solely and entirely a matter of education. This will be attested by every man and woman who has at all passed through the primary to the secondary passions. But education in the sense alluded to is impossible for the lad who leaves school at fourteen and works himself weary six days in the week ever afterwards.

The oldest socialistic institution of considerable importance and extent is the now decrepit Catholic Church. The Catholic Church has always insisted on the duty of helping the poor, not on the ground of the social danger of a "residuum", but by the nobler appeal to the instinct of human benevolence. The Catholic Church developed, relatively to the enlightenment of its age, the widest and freest system of education the world has ever seen before this century. Catholic Christianity, by its revolutionary conception that God was incarnated in Man, exploding the hideous superstition that the imagination of the thoughts of man's heart was only to do evil continually, and substituting the faith in the perfectibility of each individual soul; by its brilliant and powerful generalisations that God must be Love, because there is nothing better, and that man is freed from the law by the inward guidance of grace, has done more for social morality than any other religion of the world.

Protestant Individualism in England shattered the Catholic Church; founded the modern land system upon its confiscated estates; destroyed the mediæval machinery of charity and education; and in religion rehabilitated the devil, and the doctrines of original sin and the damnable danger of reason and good works.

Out of the wreckage of the Catholic Church, and amid the dissolution of the Protestant religion, there successively emerged, at an interval of some three hundred years, the two great socialistic institutions of the Poor Law and the People's Schools. As the pretence of a foundation of Christian obligation withered from out of the Poor Law, till it has come to be outspokenly recognised as nothing but a social safety-valve, the individualist and commercial administration of this rudimentary socialistic machinery deprived it of its efficiency even in this elementary function. He to whom the workhouse means the break up of his home, and his own condemnation to a drudgery insulting because useless and wasteful, would as lief take his exclusion from Society in another and a less degrading way, either by death, or by reluctant enrolment in the "residuum"; and so it has come to pass that outside of their use as hospitals for the aged and infirm, the poor houses are principally employed as the club-houses and hotels of the great fraternity of habitual tramps and cadgers; and not till he has sunk to this level does the struggling proletarian seek "work" there.

Socialists would realize the idea of the Poor Law, regarding that society as deadly sick in which the individual cannot find subsistence by industry, in the only way in which it can be realized: namely, by the organization of production and the resumption of its necessary instruments. It is not so great a matter in their eyes that the perpetual toll of rent and interest deprives the workers of the wealth which their activities produce; nor is it the actual pressure of this heavy tribute that would force on the Social Revolution, if the system only left men the assurance of the comforts of tame beasts. It is the constant disquiet and uncertainty, the increasing frequency of industrial crises, that are the revolutionary preachers of our age; and it is the disappearance at the base and at

the summit of society of the conditions of social morality
that rouses those whose mere material interests remain
unaffected.

But though it is not envy or resentment at this
tribute that mostly moves us to our warfare, this tribute
we must certainly resume if the ideal of the school
is to effect its social purpose. For the ideal of the school
implies, in the first place, leisure to learn: that is to
say, the release of children from all non-educational
labor until mind and physique have had a fair start
and training, and the abolition of compulsion on the
adult to work any more than the socially necessary
stint. The actual expenditure on public education must
also be considerably increased, at any rate until parents
are more generally in a position to instruct their own
children. But as soon as the mind has been trained
to appreciate the inexhaustible interest and beauty
of the world, and to distinguish good literature from
bad, the remainder of education, granted leisure, is a
comparatively inexpensive matter. Literature is become dirt-cheap; and all the other educational arts
can be communally enjoyed. The schools of the adult
are the journal and the library, social intercourse, fresh
air, clean and beautiful cities, the joy of the fields, the
museum, the art-gallery, the lecture-hall, the drama,
and the opera; and only when these schools are free
and accessible to all will the reproach of proletarian
coarseness be done away.

Yet the most important influence in the repairing of
social morality may perhaps be looked for not so much
from the direct action of these elements of the higher
education as from those very socialist forms of property and industry which we believe to be the primary
condition for allowing such higher education to affect
the majority at all. Nothing so well trains the individual to identify his life with the life of society as the
identification of the conditions of his material sustenance with those of his fellows, in short, as industrial

co-operation. Not for many centuries has there been such compulsion as now for the individual to acknowledge a social ethic. For now, for the first time since the dissolution of the early tribal communisms, and over areas a hundred times wider than theirs, the individual worker earns his living, fulfils his most elementary desire, not by direct personal production, but by an intricate co-operation in which the effect and value of his personal effort are almost indistinguishable. The apology for individualist appropriation is exploded by the logic of the facts of communist production: no man can pretend to claim the fruits of his own labor; for his whole ability and opportunity for working are plainly a vast inheritance and contribution of which he is but a transient and accidental beneficiary and steward; and his power of turning them to his own account depends entirely upon the desires and needs of other people for his services. The factory system, the machine industry, the world commerce, have abolished individualist production; and the completion of the co-operative form towards which the transition stage of individualist capitalism is hurrying us will render a conformity with social ethics a universal condition of tolerable existence for the individual.

This expectation is already justified by the phenomena of contemporary opinion. The moral ideas appropriate to Socialism are permeating the whole of modern society. They are clearly recognisable not only in the proletariat, but also in the increasing philanthropic activity of members of the propertied class, who, while denouncing Socialism as a dangerous exaggeration of what is necessary for social health, work honestly enough for alleviatory reforms which converge irresistibly towards it. The form, perhaps, does not outrun the spirit, any more than the spirit anticipates the form; and it may have been sufficient in this paper to have shown some grounds for the conviction that

Socialist morality, like that of all preceding systems, is only that morality which the conditions of human existence have made necessary; that it is only the expression of the eternal passion of life seeking its satisfaction through the striving of each individual for the freest and fullest activity; that Socialism is but a stage in the unending progression out of the weakness and the ignorance in which society and the individual alike are born, towards the strength and the enlightenment in which they can see and choose their own way forward—from the chaos where morality is not to the consciousness which sees that morality is reason; and to have made some attempt to justify the claim that the cardinal virtue of Socialism is nothing else than Common Sense.

*THE ORGANIZATION OF SOCIETY*

## 5. PROPERTY UNDER SOCIALISM

### By Graham Wallas

In the early days of Socialism no one who was
not ready with a complete description of Society as
it ought to be, dared come forward to explain any point
in the theory. Each leader had his own method of organizing property, education, domestic life, and the
production of wealth. Each was quite sure that mankind had only to fashion themselves after his model in
order, like the prince and princess in the fairy story,
to live happily ever after. Every year would then be
like the year before; and no more history need be
written. Even now a thinker here and there like Gronlund or Bebel sketches in the old spirit an ideal commonwealth; though he does so with an apology for
attempting to forecast the unknowable. But Socialists
generally have become, if not wiser than their spiritual
fathers, at least less willing to use their imagination.
The growing recognition, due in part to Darwin, of
causation in the development of individuals and societies; the struggles and disappointments of half a
century of agitation; the steady introduction of Socialistic institutions by men who reject Socialist ideas,
all incline us to give up any expectation of a final
and perfect reform. We are more apt to regard the
slow and often unconscious progress of the Time spirit
as the only adequate cause of social progress, and to
attempt rather to discover and proclaim what the

future *must* be, than to form an organization of men determined to make the future what it should be.

But the new conception of Socialism has its dangers as well as the old. Fifty years ago Socialists were tempted to exaggerate the influence of the ideal, to expect everything from a sudden impossible change of all men's hearts. Now-a-days we are tempted to under-value the ideal—to forget that even the Time Spirit itself is only the sum of individual strivings and aspirations, and that again and again in history changes which might have been delayed for centuries or might never have come at all, have been brought about by the persistent preaching of some new and higher life, the offspring not of circumstance but of hope. And of all the subjects upon which men require to be brought to a right mind and a clear understanding, there is, Socialists think, none more vital to-day than Property.

The word Property has been used in nearly as many senses as the word Law. The best definition I have met with is John Austin's "any right which gives to the entitled party such a power or liberty of using or disposing of the subject . . . as is merely limited generally by the rights of all other persons".[1] This applies only to private property. It will be convenient in discussing the various claims of the State, the municipality, and the individual, to use the word in a wider sense to denote not only the "power or liberty" of the individual, but also the "rights of all other persons". In this sense I shall speak of the property of the State, or municipality. I shall also draw a distinction, economic perhaps rather than legal, between property in things, or the exclusive right of access to defined material objects, property in debts and future services, and property in ideas (copyright and patent right).

[1] Lectures on Jurisprudence. Lecture XLVIII.

The material things in which valuable property rights can exist, may be roughly divided into means of production and means of consumption. Among those lowest tribes of savages who feed on fruit and insects, and build themselves at night a rough shelter with boughs of trees, there is little distinction between the acts of production and consumption. But in a populous and civilised country very few even of the simplest wants of men are satisfied directly by nature. Nearly every commodity which man consumes is produced and renewed by the deliberate application of human industry to material objects. The general stock of materials on which such industry works is "Land". Any materials which have been separated from the general stock or have been already considerably modified by industry, are called capital if they are either to be used to aid production or are still to be worked on before they are consumed. When they are ready to be consumed they are "wealth for consumption". Such an analysis, though generally employed by political economists, is of necessity very rough. No one can tell whether an object is ready for immediate consumption or not, unless he knows the way in which it is to be consumed. A pine forest in its natural condition is ready for the consumption of a duke with a taste for the picturesque; for he will let the trees rot before his eyes. Cotton wool, a finished product in the hands of a doctor, is raw material in the hands of a spinner. But still the statement that Socialists work for the owning of the means of production by the community and the means of consumption by individuals, represents fairly enough their practical aim. Not that they desire to prevent the community from using its property whenever it will for direct consumption, as, for instance, when a piece of common land is used for a public park, or the profits of municipal waterworks are applied to keep up a municipal library. Nor do they contemplate any need for preventing individuals from working at will on their possessions in such a way as to make them more valuable. Even Gronlund, with all his hatred of private industry, could not, if he would, prevent any citizen from driving a profitable trade by manufacturing bread into buttered toast at the common fire. But men are as yet more fit for association in production, with a just distribution of its rewards, than for association in the consumption of the wealth produced. It is true indeed that the economies of associated consumption promise to be quite as great as those of associated production; and it was of these that the earlier Socialists mainly thought. They believed always that if a few hundred persons could be induced to throw their possessions and earnings into a common stock to be employed according to a common scheme, a heaven on earth would be created. Since then, an exhaustive series of experiments has proved that in spite of its obvious economy any system of associated consumption as complete as Fourier's "Phalanstère" or Owen's "New Harmony" is, except under very unusual conditions, distasteful to most men as they now are. Our picture galleries, parks, workmen's clubs, or the fact that rich people are beginning to live in flats looked after by a common staff of servants, do indeed shew that associated consumption is every year better understood and enjoyed; but it remains true that pleasures chosen by the will of the majority are often not recognised as pleasures at all.

As long as this is so, private property and even private industry must exist along with public property and public production. For instance, each family now insists on having a separate home, and on cooking every day a separate series of meals in a separate kitchen. Waste and discomfort are the inevitable result; but families at present prefer waste and discomfort to that abundance which can only be bought by organisation and publicity. Again English families

constitute at present isolated communistic groups, more
or less despotically governed. Our growing sense of
the individual responsibility and individual rights of
wives and children seems already to be lessening both
the isolation of these groups and their internal coher-
ency; but this tendency must go very much further
before society can absorb the family life, or the industries of the home be managed socially. Thus, associated
production of all the means of family life may be developed to a very high degree before we cease to feel that
an Englishman's home should be his castle, with free
entrance and free egress alike forbidden. It is true
that the ground on which houses are built could
immediately become the property of the community;
and when one remembers how most people in England
are now lodged, it is obvious that they would gladly
inhabit comfortable houses built and owned by the
State. But they certainly would at present insist on
having their own crockery and chairs, books and pictures, and on receiving a certain proportion of the
value they produce in the form of a yearly or weekly
income to be spent or saved as they pleased. Now
whatever things of this kind we allow a man to
possess, we must allow him to exchange, since exchange never takes place unless both parties believe
themselves to benefit by it. Further, bequest must be
allowed, since any but a moderate probate duty or
personalty would, unless supported by a strong and
searching public opinion, certainly be evaded. Moreover, if we desire the personal independence of women
and children, then their property, as far as we allow
property at all, must for a long time to come be most
carefully guarded.

There would remain therefore to be owned by the
community the land in the widest sense of the word,
and the materials of those forms of production, distribution, and consumption, which can conveniently
be carried on by associations larger than the family

group. Here the main problem is to fix in each case the area of ownership. In the case of the principal means of communication and of some forms of industry, it has been proved that the larger the area controlled the greater is the efficiency of management; so that the postal and railway systems, and probably the materials of some of the larger industries, would be owned by the English nation until that distant date when they might pass to the United States of the British Empire or the Federal Republic of Europe. Land is perhaps generally better held by smaller social units. The rent of a town or an agricultural district depends only partly on those natural advantages which can be easily estimated once for all by an imperial commissioner. The difference in the rateable value of Warwick and of Birmingham is due, not so much to the sites of the two towns, as to the difference in the industry and character of their inhabitants. If the Birmingham men prefer, on the average, intense exertion resulting in great material wealth, to the simpler and quieter life lived at Warwick, it is obviously as unjust to allow the Warwick men to share equally in the Birmingham ground rents, as it would be to insist on one standard of comfort being maintained in Paris and in Brittany.

At the same time, those forms of natural wealth which are the necessities of the whole nation and the monopolies of certain districts, mines for instance, or harbors, or sources of water-supply, must be "nationalised". The salt and coal rings of to-day would be equally possible and equally inconvenient under a system which made the mining populations absolute joint owners of the mines. Even when the land was absolutely owned by local bodies, those bodies would still have to contribute to the national exchequer some proportion of their income. The actual size of the units would in each case be fixed by convenience; and it is very likely that the development of the County

Government Act and of the parochial and municipal systems will soon provide us with units of government which could easily be turned into units of ownership.

The savings of communities—if I may use the word community to express any Social Democratic unit from the parish to the nation—would probably take much the same form that the accumulation of capital takes nowadays: that is to say, they would consist partly of mills, machinery, railways, schools, and the other specialised materials of future industry, and partly of a stock of commodities such as food, clothing, and money by which workers might be supported while performing work not immediately remunerative. The savings of individuals would consist partly of consumable commodities or of the means of such industry as had not been socialised, and partly of deferred pay for services rendered to the community, such pay taking the form of a pension due at a certain age, or of a sum of commodities or money payable on demand.

Voluntary associations of all kinds, whether joint stock companies, religious corporations, or communistic groups would, in the eyes of the Social Democratic State, consist simply of so many individuals possessing those rights of property which are allowed to individuals. They might perform many very useful functions in the future as in the past; but the history of the city companies, of the New River company, the Rochdale Pioneers, or the Church of England shews the danger of granting perpetual property rights to any association not co-extensive with the community, although such association may exist for professedly philanthropic objects. Even in the case of universities, where the system of independent property-owning corporations has been found to work best, the rights of the State should be delegated and not surrendered.

On this point the economic position of modern Social Democrats differs widely from the transfigured joint stockism of the present co-operative movement or from the object of the earlier Socialists, for whose purposes complete community was always more important than complete inclusiveness. Even Socialist writers of to-day do not always see that the grouping of the citizens for the purpose of property holding must be either on the joint stock basis or on the territorial basis. Gronlund, in spite of contradictory matter in other parts of his "Co-operative Commonwealth", still declares that "each group of workers will have the power of distributing among themselves the whole exchange value of their work", which either means that they will, as long as they are working, be the absolute joint owners of the materials which they use, or means nothing at all. Now the proposal that any voluntary association of citizens should hold absolute and perpetual property rights in the means of production, seems to be not a step towards Social Democracy, but a negation of the whole Social Democratic idea. This of course brings us to the following difficulty. If our communities even when originally inclusive of the whole population are closed: that is, are confined to original members and their descendants, new comers will form a class like the plebeians in Rome, or the "metoeci" in Athens, without a share in the common property though possessed of full personal freedom; and such a class must be a continual social danger. On the other hand, if all newcomers receive at once full economic rights, then any country in which Socialism or anything approaching it is established will be at once overrun by proletarian immigrants from those countries in which the means of production are still strictly monopolised. If this were allowed, then, through the operation of the law of diminishing return and the law of population based on it, the whole body of the inhabitants even of a Socialist State, might conceivably be finally brought down to the bare means of subsistence. It does not seem necessary to conclude that Socialism must be established

over the whole globe if it is to be established anywhere. What is necessary is that we face the fact, every
day becoming plainer, that any determined attempt
to raise the condition of the proletariat in any single
European country must be accompanied by a law of
aliens considerate enough to avoid cruelty to refugees,
or obstruction to those whose presence would raise
our intellectual or industrial average, but stringent
enough to exclude the unhappy "diluvies gentium",
the human rubbish which the military empires of
the continent are so ready to shoot upon any open
space. Such a law would be in itself an evil. It might
be unfairly administered; it might increase national
selfishness and would probably endanger international
good will; it would require the drawing of a great
many very difficult lines of distinction; but no sufficient
argument has been yet advanced to disprove the
necessity of it.

On the question of private property in debts, the attitude of the law in Europe has changed fundamentally
in historical times. Under the old Roman law, the
creditor became the absolute owner of his debtor. Now-
a-days, not only may a man by becoming bankrupt
and surrendering all his visible property repudiate his
debts and yet retain his personal liberty; but in Factory Acts, Employers' Liability Acts, Irish Land Acts,
etc., certain contracts are illegal under all circumstances. With the growth of Socialism, this tendency
would be quickened. The law would look with extreme jealousy upon any agreement by which one party
would be reduced even for a time to a condition of
slavery, or the other enabled to live even for a time
without performing any useful social function. And
since it has been clearly recognized that a certain access
to the means of industry is a first condition of personal
freedom, the law would refuse to recognize any agreement to debar a man from such access, or deprive him
of the results of it. No one would need to get into

debt in order to provide himself with the opportunity of work, nor would anyone be allowed to give up the opportunity of work in order to obtain a loan. This, by making it more difficult for creditors to recover debts, would also make it more difficult for would-be debtors to obtain credit. The present homestead law would, in fact, be extended to include everything which the State thought necessary for a complete life. But as long as private industry and exchange go on to such an extent as to make a private commercial system convenient, so long will promises to pay circulate, and, if necessary, be legally enforced under the conditions above marked out.

To whatever extent private property is permitted, to that same extent the private taking of Rent and Interest must be also permitted. If you allow a selfish man to own a picture by Raphael, he will lock it up in his own room unless you let him charge something for the privilege of looking at it. Such a charge is at once Interest. If we wish all Raphael's pictures to be freely accessible to everyone, we must prevent men not merely from exhibiting them for payment, but from owning them.

This argument applies to other things besides Raphael's pictures. If we allow a man to own a printing press, or a plough, or a set of bookbinders' tools, or a lease of a house or farm, we must allow him so to employ his possession that he may, without injuring his neighbor, get from it the greatest possible advantage. Otherwise, seeing that the community is not responsible for its intelligent use, any interference on the part of the community may well result in no intelligent use being made of it at all; in which event all privately owned materials of industry not actually being used by their owners would be as entirely wasted as if they were the subjects of a chancery suit. It is easy to see that the Duke of Bedford is robbing the community of the rent of Covent Garden.

It is not so easy to see that the owners of the vacant
land adjoining Shaftesbury Avenue have been robbing
the community for some years past of the rent which
ought to have been made out of the sites which they
have left desolate. I know that it has been sometimes
said by Socialists: "Let us allow the manufacturer to
keep his mill and the Duke of Argyle to keep his
land, as long as they do not use them for exploitation
by letting them out to others on condition of receiving
a part of the wealth created by those others". Then,
we are told, the manufacturer or Duke will soon discover that he must work hard for a living. Such senti-
ments are seldom ill received by men in the humor
to see dukes and capitalists earning, as painfully as
may be, their daily bread. Unluckily, there are no
unappropriated acres and factory sites in England
sufficiently advantageous to be used as efficient substitutes for those upon which private property has
fastened; and the community would be wise if it paid
the Duke of Argyle and Mr. Chamberlain anything
short of the full economic rent of their properties rather
than go further and fare worse. Therefore, if we refused either to allow these gentlemen to let their
property to those who would use it, or hesitated to
take it and use it for ourselves, we should be actually
wasting labor. The progressive socialization of land
and capital must proceed by direct transference of them
to the community through taxation of rent and interest
and public organization of labor with the capital so
obtained: not solely by a series of restrictions upon their
use in private exploitation. Such concurrent private
exploitation, however unrestricted, could not in any
case bring back the old evils of capitalism; for any
change in the habits of the people or in the methods
of industry which made associated production of any
commodity on a large scale convenient and profitable,
would result at once in the taking over of that industry

by the State exactly as the same conditions now in America result at once in the formation of a ring.

It is because full ownership is necessary to the most intelligent and effective use of any materials, that no mere system of taxation of Rent and Interest, even when so drastic as Mr. Henry George's scheme of universal State absentee landlordism, is likely to exist except as a transition stage towards Social Democracy. Indeed the anarchist idea which allows the State to receive Rent and Interest, but forbids it to employ labor, is obviously impracticable. Unless we are willing to pay every citizen in hard cash a share of the State Rent of the future, it, like the taxes of to-day, must be wholly invested in payments for work done. It would always be a very serious difficulty for a Socialist legislature to decide how far communities should be allowed to incur debts or pay interest. Socialism once established, the chief danger to its stability would be just at this point. We all know the inept attack on Socialism which comes from a debating-society orator who considers the subject for the first time, or from the cultured person who has been brought up on the *Saturday Review*. He tells us that if property were equally divided to-morrow, there would be for the next ten years forty men out of every hundred working extremely hard, and the other sixty lazy. After that time, the sixty would have to work hard and keep the forty, who would then be as lazy as the sixty were before. It is very easy to explain that we do not want to divide all property equally; but it is not so easy to guard against any result of that tendency in human nature on which the argument is grounded. Men differ so widely in their comparative appreciation of present and future pleasures, that wherever life can be supported by four hours' work a day, there will always be some men anxious to work eight hours in order to secure future benefits for themselves or their children, and others anxious to avoid their four hours' work for

the present by pledging themselves or their children
to any degree of future privation. As long as this is
so, communities as well as individuals will be tempted
to avail themselves of the freely offered services of the
exceptionally energetic and farsighted, and to incur
a common debt under the excuse that they are spreading the payment of such services over all those benefited by them. The Municipalities, Boards of Works,
School Boards, etc., of England have already created
enormous local debts; and unless men grow wiser
in the next few months the new County Councils will
probably add to the burden. As we sit and think, it
may seem easy to prevent any such trouble in the
future by a law forbidding communities to incur
debts under any circumstances. But in the case of a
central and supreme government such a law would,
of course, be an absurdity. No nation can escape a
national debt or any other calamity if the majority
in that nation desire to submit to it. It is reassuring
to see how the feeling that national governments
should pay their way from year to year grows stronger
and stronger. National debts no longer even in France
go up with the old light-hearted leaps and bounds.
But local debts still increase. In Preston the local debt
is said to amount to seven times the annual rating
valuation. And although at present (November, 1888),
since the "surf at the edge of civilisation" is only
thundering to the extent of three small colonial wars,
our own national debt is slowly going down; still
if war were declared to-morrow with any European
State no ministry would dare to raise all the war expenses by immediate taxation either on incomes or on
property. It may be objected that no such danger
would arise under Socialism; for there would be no
fund from which a loan could be offered that would
not be equally easily reached by a direct levy. But
if we are speaking of society in the near future there
would certainly be plenty of members of non-Socialist

States, or English holders of property in them, ready to lend money on good security to a timid or desperate or dishonest Socialist government. Again, in times of extreme stress a government might believe itself to require even personal possessions; and it might be difficult under such circumstances not to offer to restore them with or without interest. In any case there would be no more economic difference between the new fund-holders and the old landlords than between Lord Salisbury as owner of the Strand district and Lord Salisbury now that he has sold his slums and bought consols. Perhaps the most serious danger of the creation of a common debt would arise from the earnings of exceptional ability. Modern Socialists have learnt, after a long series of co-operative experiments and failures, that the profits of private adventure will withdraw men of exceptional business talent from communal service unless work of varying scarcity and intensity is paid for at varying rates. How great this variation need be in order to ensure full efficiency can only be decided by experience; and as the education and moralization of society improves, and industry becomes so thoroughly socialized that the alternative of private enterprise will be less practicable, something like equality may at last be found possible. But, meanwhile, comparatively large incomes will be earned by men leading busy lives, but often keenly anxious to secure leisure and comfort for their old age and aggrandizement for their family.[2] I have already suggested that some of the earnings of a man employed by the community might be left for a time in the common treasury to accumulate without interest. Now, it would suit both these men and the lazier of their contemporaries that the reward of their services should

[2] Happily, the ordinary anxieties as to the fate of children left without property, especially weaklings or women unlikely to attract husbands, may be left out of account in speculations concerning socialized communities.

be fixed at a very high rate, and be left to the next
generation for payment; while the next generation
might prefer a small permanent charge to any attempt
to pay off the capital sum. It is often hinted that one
way to obviate this would be for each generation to
cultivate a healthy indifference to the debts incurred
on its behalf by its forefathers. But the citizens of
each new generation attain citizenship not in large
bodies at long intervals, but in small numbers every
week. One has only to warn sanguine lenders that
veiled repudiations may always be effected in such
emergencies by a judicious application of the Income
Tax, and to hope that the progress of education under
Socialism would tend to produce and preserve on such
matters a certain general minimum of common sense.
If this minimum is sufficient to control the central
government the debts of local bodies can be easily and
sternly restricted.

Property in services means of course property in
future services. The wealth which past services may
have produced can be exchanged or owned; but the
services themselves cannot. Now all systems of law
which we know have allowed private persons to contract with each other for the future performance
of certain services, and have punished, or allowed to
be punished, the breach of such contracts. Here as in
the case of debts, our growing respect for personal
liberty has made the law look jealously on all onerous
agreements made either by the citizen himself or for
him by others. In fact, as Professor Sidgwick points out:
"In England hardly any engagement to render personal service gives the promisee a legal claim to more
than pecuniary damages—to put it otherwise, almost
all such contracts, if unfulfilled, turn into mere debts
of money so far as their legal force goes".[3] The marriage contract forms the principal exception to this

[3] "Principles of Political Economy," p. 435.

rule; but even in this case there seems to be a tendency in most European countries to relax the rigidity of the law.

On the other hand the direct claims of the State to the services of its citizens shew at present no signs of diminishing. Compulsory military service and compulsory attendance at school already take up a not inconsiderable share of the life of every male inhabitant of France and Germany. So far in England the compulsion of grown men to serve in any capacity has been condemned for a century past, because it is considered wasteful and oppressive as compared with the free contract system of the open market. Most English Socialists seem inclined to believe that all work for the State should be voluntarily engaged and paid for out of the produce of common industry.

In considering how far the State has a claim upon the services of its members, we come upon the much larger question—How far are we working for Socialism; and how far for Communism? Under pure Socialism, to use the word in its narrowest sense, the State would offer no advantage at all to any citizen except at a price sufficient to pay all the expenses of producing it. In this sense the Post Office, for example, is now a purely Socialistic institution. Under such conditions the State would have no claim at all on the services of its members; and compulsion to work would be produced by the fact that if a man chose not to work he would be in danger of starvation. Under pure Communism, on the other hand, as defined by Louis Blanc's dictum: "From every man according to his powers: to every man according to his wants", the State would satisfy without stint and without price all the reasonable wants of any citizen. Our present drinking fountains are examples of the numerous cases of pure communism which surround us. But since nothing can be made without labor, the commodities provided by the State must be produced by the services, voluntary or forced, of the citizens. Under pure communism, if any compulsion to work were needed, it would have to be direct. Some communistic institutions we must have; and as a matter of fact there is an increasing number of them already in England. Indeed, if the whole or any part of that Rent Fund which is due to the difference between the best and worst materials of industry in use be taken for the State, by taxation or otherwise, it, or rather the advantages produced by its expenditure, can hardly be distributed otherwise than communistically. For, as men are now, saturated with immoral principles by our commercial system, the State would have to be exceedingly careful in deciding what wants could be freely satisfied without making direct compulsion to labor necessary. It would cost by no means an impossible sum to supply a tolerable shelter with a bed, and a sufficient daily portion of porridge, or bread and cheese, or even of gin and water, to each citizen; but no sane man would propose to do so in the existing state of public morals. For more than a century the proletarians of Europe have been challenged by their masters to do as little work as they can. They have been taught by the practical economists of the Trades Unions, and have learnt for themselves by bitter experience, that every time any of them in a moment of ambition or goodwill does one stroke of work not in his bond, he is increasing the future unpaid labor not only of himself but of his fellows. At the same time every circumstance of monotony, ugliness, and anxiety has made the work as wearisome and disgusting as possible. All, almost without exception, now look upon the working day as a period of slavery, and find such happiness as they can get only in the few hours or minutes that intervene between work and sleep. For a few, that happiness consists in added toil of thought and speech in the cause of themselves and their comrades. The rest care only for such rough pleasures as are possible to men both poor and overworked. There would be plenty of excuse if under these circumstances they dreamt, as they are accused of dreaming, of some universal division of the good things of the earth— of some means of being utterly at leisure, if only for a week or two.

But there are products of labor which the workmen in their time of triumph might freely offer each other without causing the weakest brother to forego any form of useful social work. Among such products are those ideas which we have brought under the dominion of private property by means of copyright and patent right. Luckily for us the dominion is neither complete nor permanent. If the Whig landlords who are responsible for most of the details of our glorious constitution had been also authors and inventors for profit, we should probably have had the strictest rights of perpetual property or even of entail in ideas; and there would now have been a Duke of Shakespere to whom we should all have had to pay two or three pounds for the privilege of reading his ancestor's works, provided that we returned the copy uninjured at the end of a fortnight. But even for the years during which copyright and patents now last, the system which allows an author or inventor a monopoly in his ideas is a stupid and ineffective way either of paying for his work or of satisfying the public wants. In each case the author or inventor obtains a maximum nett return by leaving unsatisfied the wants, certainly of many, probably of most of those who desire to read his book or use his invention. We all know that the public got a very good bargain when it paid the owners of Waterloo Bridge more than they could possibly have made by any scheme of tolls. In the same way it is certain that any government which aimed at the greatest happiness of the greatest number could afford to pay a capable artist or author possibly even more than he gets from the rich men who are his present patrons, and certainly more than he could get by himself selling or exhibiting his productions in a society where few possessed wealth for which they had not worked. Although the State could thus afford to pay an extravagantly large reward for certain forms of intellectual labor, it does not therefore follow that it would be obliged to do so in the absence of any other important bidder.

There would always remain the sick, the infirm, and the school children, whose wants could be satisfied from the general stock without asking them to bear any part of the general burden. In particular, it would be well to teach the children by actual experience the economy and happiness which arise in the case of those who are fitly trained from association applied to the direct satisfaction of wants, as well as from association in the manufacture of material wealth. If we wish to wean the children from the selfish isolation of the English family, from the worse than savage habits produced by four generations of capitalism, from that longing for excitement, and incapacity for reasonable enjoyment, which are the natural results of workdays spent in English factories, and English Sundays spent in English streets, then we must give freely and generously to our schools. If this generation were wise it would spend on education not only more than any other generation has ever spent before, but more than any generation would ever need to spend again. It would fill the school buildings with the means not only of comfort, but even of the higher luxury; it would serve the associated meals on tables spread with flowers, in halls surrounded with beautiful pictures, or even, as John Milton proposed, filled with the sound of music; it would seriously propose to itself the ideal of Ibsen, that every child should be brought up as a nobleman. Unfortunately, this generation is not wise.

In considering the degree in which common owning of property would be possible among a people just at that stage of industrial and moral development at which we now find ourselves, it is expedient to dwell, as I have dwelt, rather upon the necessary difficulties and limitations of Socialism, than upon its hopes of future development. But we must always remember that the problems which Socialism attempts to solve, deal with conditions which themselves are constantly changing. Just as anything like what we call Socialism would be impossible in a nation of individualist savages like the Australian blacks, and could not, perhaps, be introduced except by external authority among a people like the peasants of Brittany, for whom the prospect of absolute property in any portion of land, however small, is at once their strongest pleasure and their only sufficient incentive to industry; so among a people further advanced, socially and industrially, than ourselves, a social condition would be possible which we do not now dare to work for or even try to realise. The tentative and limited Social-Democracy which I have sketched is the necessary and certain step to that better life which we hope for. The interests which each man has in common with his fellows tend more and more to outweigh those which are peculiar to himself. We see the process even now beginning. Already, as soon as a public library is started, the workman finds how poor a means for the production of happiness are the few books on his own shelf, compared with the share he has in the public collection, though that share may have cost even less to produce. In the same way the score or two of pounds which a workman may possess are becoming daily of less and less advantage in production; so that the man who a few years ago would have worked by himself as a small capitalist, goes now to work for wages in some great business, and treats his little savings as a fund to provide for a few months of sickness or years of old age. He will soon see how poor a means for the production of food is his own fire when compared with the public kitchen; and he will perhaps at last not only get his clothes from the public store, but the delight of his eyes from the public galleries and theatres, the delight of his ears from the public opera, and it may be, when our present anarchy of opinion be overpast, the refreshment of his mind from the publicly chosen teacher. Then at last such a life will be possible for all as not even the richest and most powerful can live to-day. The system of property holding which we call Socialism is not in itself such a life any more than a good system of draining is health, or the invention of printing is knowledge. Nor indeed is Socialism the only condition necessary to produce complete human happiness. Under the justest possible social system we might still have to face all those vices and diseases which are not the direct result of poverty and over-work; we might still suffer all the mental anguish and bewilderment which are caused, some say by religious belief, others by religious doubt; we might still witness outbursts of national hatred and the degradation and extinction of weaker peoples; we might still make earth a hell for every species except our own. But in the households of the five men out of six in England who live by weekly wage, Socialism would indeed be a new birth of happiness. The long hours of work done as in a convict prison, without interest and without hope; the dreary squalor of their homes; above all that grievous uncertainty, that constant apprehension of undeserved misfortune which is the peculiar result of capitalist production: all this would be gone; and education, refinement, leisure, the very thought of which now maddens them, would be part of their daily life. Socialism hangs above them as the crown hung in Bunyan's story above the man raking the muck heap—ready for them if they will but lift their eyes. And even to the few who seem to escape and even profit by the misery of our century, Socialism offers a new and nobler life, when full sympathy with those about them, springing from full knowledge of their condition, shall be a source of happiness, and not, as now, of constant sorrow—when it shall no longer seem either folly or hypocrisy for a man to work openly for his highest ideal. To them belongs the privilege that for each one of them the revolution may begin as soon as he is ready to pay the price. They can live as simply as the equal rights of their fellows require: they can justify their lives by work in the noblest of all causes. For their reward, if they desire any, they, like the rest, must wait.

## 6. INDUSTRY UNDER SOCIALISM

### By Annie Besant

There are two ways in which a scheme for a future organisation of industry may be constructed. Of these, by far the easier and less useful is the sketching of Utopia, an intellectual gymnastic in which a power of coherent and vivid imagination is the one desideratum. The Utopist needs no knowledge of facts: indeed such a knowledge is a hindrance: for him the laws of social evolution do not exist. He is a law unto himself; and his men and women are not the wayward, spasmodic, irregular organisms of daily life, but automata, obeying the strings he pulls. In a word, he creates, he does not construct: he makes alike his materials and the laws within which they work, adapting them all to an ideal end. In describing a new Jerusalem, the only limits to its perfection are the limits of the writer's imagination.

The second way is less attractive, less easy, but more useful. Starting from the present state of society, it seeks to discover the tendencies underlying it; to trace those tendencies to their natural outworking in institutions; and so to forecast, not the far-off future, but the next social stage. It fixes its gaze on the vast changes wrought by evolution, not the petty variations made by catastrophes; on the Revolutions which transform society, not the transient riots which merely upset thrones and behead kings. This second way I elect to follow; and this paper on industry under Socialism therefore starts from William Clarke's exposition of the industrial evolution which has been in progress during the last hundred and fifty years. In thus building forward—in thus forecasting the transitions through which society will probably pass, I shall scarcely touch on the ideal Social State that will one day exist; and my sketch must lay itself open to all the criticisms which may be levelled against a society not ideally perfect. It is therefore necessary to bear in mind that I am only trying to work out changes practicable among men and women as we know them; always seeking to lay down, not what is ideally best, but what is possible; always choosing among the possible changes that which is on the line towards the ideal, and will render further approach easier. In fact this paper is an attempt to answer the "How?" so often heard when Socialism is discussed. Large numbers of people accept, wholly or in part, the Socialist theory: they are intellectually convinced of its soundness or emotionally attracted by its beauty; but they hesitate to join in its propaganda, because they "don't see where you are going to begin", or "don't see where you are going to stop". Both difficulties are disposed of by the fact that we are not "going to begin". There will never be a point at which a society crosses from Individualism to Socialism. The change is ever going forward; and our society is well on the way to Socialism. All we can do is to consciously co-operate with the forces at work, and thus render the transition more rapid than it would otherwise be.

The third Fabian essay shews us the success of capitalism bringing about a position which is at once intolerable to the majority, and easy of capture by them. At this point the destruction of the small industries has broken down most of the gradations which used to exist between the large employer and the hired laborer, and has left in their place a gulf across which a few capitalists and a huge and hungry proletariat face each other. The denial of human sympathy by the employer in his business relations with his "hands" has taught the "hands" to regard the employer as outside the pale of their sympathy. The "respect of the public conscience for the rights of property", which was at bottom the private interest of each in his own little property, has diminished since the many lost their individual possessions, and saw property accumulate in the hands of the few: it is now little more than a tradition inherited from a former social state. The "public conscience" will soon condone, nay, it will first approve, and then demand, the expropriation of capital which is used anti-socially instead of socially, and which belongs to that impersonal abstraction, a company, instead of to our next door neighbor. To the average person it is one thing for the State to seize the little shop of James Smith who married our sister, or the thriving business of our Sam who works early and late for his living; and quite another when James and Sam, ruined by a big Company made up of shareholders of whom nobody knows anything but that they pay low wages and take high dividends, have been obliged to become hired servants of the Company, instead of owning their own shops and machinery. Whose interest will it be to protest against the State taking over the capital, and transforming James and Sam from wage-slaves at the mercy of a foreman, into shareholders and public functionaries, with a voice in the management of the business in which they are employed?

Let us suppose, then, that the evolution of the capitalist system has proceeded but a little further along the present lines, concentrating the control of industry, and increasingly substituting labor-saving machinery for human beings. It is being accompanied, and must continue to be accompanied, by a growth of the numbers of the unemployed. These numbers may ebb and flow, as some of the waves of a rising tide run forward some feet and then a few touch a lower level; but as the tide rises despite the fluctuations of the ripples, so the numbers of the unemployed will increase despite transient mountings and fallings. With these, probably, will begin the tentative organisation of industry by the State; but this organisation will soon be followed by the taking over by the community of some of the great Trusts.

The division of the country into clearly defined areas, each with its elected authority, is essential to any effective scheme of organisation. It is one of the symptoms of the coming change, that, in perfect unconsciousness of the nature of his act, Mr. Ritchie has established the Commune. He has divided England into districts ruled by County Councils, and has thus created the machinery without which Socialism was impracticable. True, he has only made an outline which needs to be filled in; but Socialists can fill in, whereas they had no power to outline. It remains to give every adult a vote in the election of Councillors; to shorten their term of office to a year; to pay the Councillors, so that the public may have a right to the whole of their working time; to give the Councils power to take and hold land—a reform already asked for by the Liberal and Radical Union, a body not consciously Socialist; and to remove all legal restrictions, so as to leave them as free to act corporately as an individual is to act individually. These measures accomplished, the rapidity with which our institutions are socialised depends on the growth of Socialism among the people. It is essential to the stability of the changed forms of industry that they shall be made by the people, not imposed upon them: hence the value of Mr. Ritchie's gift of Local Government, enabling each locality to move swiftly or slowly, to experiment on a comparatively small scale, even to blunder without widespread disaster. The *mot d'ordre* for Socialists now is, "Convert the electors; and capture the County Councils". These Councils, administering local affairs, with the national Executive, administering national affairs, are all destined to be turned into effective industrial organisers; and the unit of administration must depend on the nature of the industry. The post, the telegraph, the railways, the canals, and the great industries capable of being organised into Trusts, will, so far as we can see now, be best administered each from a single centre for the whole kingdom. Tramways, gas-works, water-works, and many of the smaller productive industries, will be best managed locally. In marking the lines of division, convenience and experience must be our guides. The demarcations are of expediency, not of principle.

The first great problem that will press on the County Council for solution will be that of the unemployed. Wisely or unwisely, it will have to deal with them: wisely, if it organises them for productive industry; unwisely, if it opens "relief works", and tries, like an enlarged Bumble, to shirk the difficulty by enforcing barren and oppressive toil upon outlawed wretches at the expense of the rest of the community. Many of the unemployed are unskilled laborers: a minority are skilled. They must first be registered as skilled and unskilled, and the former enrolled under their several trades. Then can begin the rural organisation of labor on county farms, held by the County Councils. The Council will have its agricultural committee, charged with the administrative details; and this committee will choose well-trained, practical agriculturists, as directors of the farm business. To the County Farm will be drafted from the unemployed in the towns the agricultural laborers who have wandered townwards in search of work, and many of the unskilled laborers. On these farms every advantage of machinery, and every discovery in agricultural science, should be utilised to the utmost. The crops should be carefully chosen with reference to the soil and aspect—cereals, fruit, vegetables—and the culture adapted to the crop, the one aim being to obtain the largest amount of produce with the least expenditure of human labor. Whether land is most profitably cultivated in large or small parcels depends on the crop; and in the great area of the County Farm, *la grande et la petite culture* might each have its place. Economy would also gain by the large number of laborers under the direction of the head farmer, since they could be concentrated when required at any given spot, as in harvest time, and dispersed to work at the more continuous kinds of tillage when the seasonal task was over.

To these farms must also be sent some skilled laborers from among the unemployed, shoemakers, tailors, smiths, carpenters, &c.; so that the County Farm may be self-supporting as far as it can be without waste of productive power. All the small industries necessary in daily life should be carried on in it, and an industrial commune thus built up. The democracy might be trusted to ordain that an eight hours' day, and a comfortable home, should be part of the life-conditions on the County Farm. Probably each large farm would soon have its central store, with its adjacent railway station, in addition to the ordinary farm buildings; its public hall in the centre of the farm village to be used for lectures, concerts, and entertainments of all sorts; its public schools, elementary and technical; and soon, possibly from the outset, its public meal-room, saving time and trouble to housewives, and, while economising fuel and food, giving a far greater choice and variety of dishes. Large dwellings, with suites of rooms, might perhaps replace old-fashioned cottages; for it is worth noting, as showing the tendency already existing among ourselves to turn from isolated self-dependence to the advantages of associated living, that many modern flats are being built without servants' rooms, the house-cleaning, &c. being done by persons engaged for the whole block, and the important meals being taken at restaurants, so as to avoid the trouble and expense of private cooking. It will surely be well

in initiating new organisations of industry to start
on the most advanced lines, and take advantage of every
modern tendency towards less isolated modes of living.
Socialists must work hard to make municipal dealings
with the unemployed avenues to the higher life, not
grudging utilisation of pauper labor. And as they
know their aim, and the other political parties live
but from hand to mouth, they ought to be able to
exercise a steady and uniform pressure, which, just
because it is steady and uniform, will impress its
direction on the general movement.

The note of urban industrial organisation, as of all
other, must be that each person shall be employed to
do what he can do best, not what he does worst. It may
be desirable for a man to have two trades; but watch-
making and stone-breaking are not convenient alternative occupations. Where the skilled unemployed belong
to trades carried on everywhere, such as baking, shoemaking, tailoring, etc., they should be employed at
their own trades in municipal workshops, and their
products garnered in municipal stores. These workshops
will be under the direction of foremen, thoroughly
skilled workmen, able to superintend and direct as
though in private employment. The working-day must
be of eight hours, and the wages, for the present,
the Trades Union minimum. Then, instead of tailors
and shoemakers tramping the streets ragged and bare-
foot, the tailors will be making clothes and the shoe-
makers boots and shoes; and the shoemaker with the
wages he earns will buy the tailor's products, and the
tailor the shoemaker's. Then, instead of supporting the
unemployed by rates levied on the employed, they
will be set to work to supply their own necessities,
and be producers of the wealth they consume instead
of consuming, in enforced idleness or barren penal
exercises in the stoneyard, the wealth produced by
others. Masons, bricklayers, plumbers, carpenters, etc.,
might be set to work in building decent and pleasant

dwellings—in the style of the blocks of flats, not of the barracks called model dwellings—for the housing of the municipal industrial army. I lay stress on the pleasantness of the dwellings. These places are to be dwellings for citizens, not prisons for paupers; and there is no possible reason why they should not be made attractive. Under Socialism the workers are to be the nation, and all that is best is for their service; for, be it remembered, our faces are set towards Socialism, and our organisation of labor is to be on Socialist lines.

It is very likely that among the unemployed some will be found whose trade can only be carried on by large numbers, and is not one of the industries of the town into which their unlucky fate has drifted them. These should be sent into municipal service in the towns where their trade is the staple industry, there to be employed in the municipal factory.

Concurrently with this rural and urban organisation of non-centralised industries will proceed the taking over of the great centralised industries, centralised for us by capitalists, who thus unconsciously pave the way for their own supersession. Everything which has been organised into a Trust, and has been worked for a time in the Trust fashion, is ripe for appropriation by the community. All minerals would be most properly worked in this centralised way; and it will probably be found most convenient to work all the big productive industries—such as the textile—in similar fashion. It is idle to say that it cannot be done by the State when it is being done by a ring of capitalists: a Local Board, an Iron Board, a Tin Board, can as easily be responsible to the nation as to a casual crowd of shareholders. There need be no dislocation of production in making the transference: the active organisers and directors of a Trust do not necessarily, or even usually, own the capital invested in it. If the State finds it convenient to hire these organisers and directors, there is nothing to prevent its doing so for as long

or as short a period as it chooses. The temporary
arrangements made with them during the transition
period must be governed by expediency.

Let us pause for a moment to estimate the position
so far. The unemployed have been transformed into
communal workers—in the country on great farms,
improvements of the Bonanza farms in America—in
the towns in various trades. Public stores for agricultural and industrial products are open in all convenient
places, and filled with the goods thus communally
produced. The great industries, worked as Trusts, are
controlled by the State instead of by capitalist rings.
The private capitalist, however, will still be in business,
producing and distributing on his own account in
competition with the communal organisations, which
at present will have occupied only part of the industrial
field. But apart from a pressure which will be recognised
when we come to deal with the remuneration of
labor, these private enterprises will be carried on under
circumstances of ever-increasing difficulty. In face of
the orderly communal arrays, playing into each other's
hands, with the credit of the country behind them,
the ventures of the private capitalist will be at as great
a disadvantage as the cottage industries of the last
century in face of the factory industries of our own
period. The Trusts have taught us how to drive competing capitals out of the market by associated capitals.
The Central Boards or County Councils will be able
to utilise this power of association further than any
private capitalists. Thus the economic forces which
replaced the workshop by the factory will replace
the private shop by the municipal store and the private factory by the municipal one. And the advantages
of greater concentration of capital and of association
of labour will not be the only ones enjoyed by the
communal workers. All waste will be checked, every
labor-saving appliance utilised to the utmost, where the
object is the production of general wealth and not

the production of profit to be appropriated by a class; for in the one case it is the interest of the producers to produce—inasmuch as their enjoyment depends on the productivity of their labor—whereas in the other it is their interest to sterilise their labor as far as they dare in order to render more of it necessary and so keep up its price. As the organisation of the public industry extends, and supplants more and more the individualist producer, the probable demand will be more easily estimated, and the supply regulated to meet it. The Municipalities and Central Boards will take the place of the competing small capitalists and the rings of large ones; and production will become ordered and rational instead of anarchical and reckless as it is to-day. After awhile the private producers will disappear, not because there will be any law against individualist production, but because it will not pay. No one will care to face the worries, the harassments, the anxieties, of individual struggling for livelihood, when ease, freedom, and security can be enjoyed in the communal service.

The best form of management during the transition period, and possibly for a long time to come, will be through the Communal Councils, which will appoint committees to superintend the various branches of industry. These committees will engage the necessary manager and foreman for each shop, factory, etc., and will hold the power of dismissal as of appointment. I do not believe that the direct election of the manager and foreman by the employees would be found to work well in practice, or to be consistent with the discipline necessary in carrying on any large business undertaking. It seems to me better that the Commune should elect its Council—thus keeping under its own control the general authority—but should empower the Council to select the officials, so that the power of selection and dismissal within the various sub-divisions should lie with the nominees of the whole Commune instead of with the particular group immediately concerned.

There is no practical difficulty in the way of the management of the ordinary productive industries, large or small. The Trusts and Co-operation have, between them, solved, or put us in the way of solving, all problems connected with these. But there are difficulties in connexion with the industries concerned in the production of such commodities as books and newspapers. During the transitional stage these difficulties will not arise; but when all industries are carried on by the Commune, or the Nation, how will books and newspapers be produced? I only throw out the following suggestions. Printing, like baking, tailoring, shoemaking, is a communal rather than a national industry. Suppose we had printing offices controlled by the Communal Council. The printing committee might be left free to accept any publication it thought valuable, as a private firm to-day may take the risk of publication, the arrangement with the author being purchase outright, or royalty on copies sold, in each case so much to be put to his credit at the Communal Bank. But there are many authors whose goods are desired by no one: it would be absurd to force the community to publish all minor poetry. Why not accept the principle that in every case where the printing committee declines to print at the communal risk, the author may have his work printed by transferring from his credit at the Communal Bank to the account of the printing committee sufficient to cover the cost of printing? The committee should have no power to refuse to print, where the cost was covered. Thus liberty of expression would be guarded as a constitutional right, while the community would not be charged with the cost of printing every stupid effusion that its fond composer might deem worthy of publicity.

Newspapers might be issued on similar terms; and it

would always be open to individuals, or to groups of individuals, to publish anything they pleased on covering the cost of publication. With the comparative affluence which would be enjoyed by each member of the community, anyone who really cared to reach the public ear would be able to do so by diminishing his expenditure in other directions.

Another difficulty which will meet us, although not immediately, is the competition for employment in certain pleasanter branches of industry. At present an unemployed person would catch eagerly at the chance of any well-paid work he was able to perform. If he were able both to set type and to stitch coats, he would not dream of grumbling if he were by chance offered the job he liked the less of the two: he would be only too glad to get either. But it is quite possible that as the vast amelioration of life-conditions proceeds, Jeshurun will wax fat and kick if, when he prefers to make microscope lenses, he is desired to make mirrors. Under these circumstances, Jeshurun will, I fear, have to accommodate himself to the demand. If the number of people engaged in making lenses suffices to meet the demand for lenses, Jeshurun must consent to turn his talents for the time to mirror-making. After all, his state will not be very pitiable, though Socialism will have failed, it is true, to make $2 + 2 = 5$.

This, however, hardly solves the general question as to the apportioning of laborers to the various forms of labor. But a solution has been found by the ingenious author of "Looking Backward, from A.D. 2000". Leaving young men and women free to choose their employments, he would equalise the rates of volunteering by equalising the attractions of the trades. In many cases natural bent, left free to develop itself during a lengthened educational term, will determine the choice of avocation. Human beings are fortunately very varied in their capacities and tastes: that which attracts one repels another. But there are unpleasant and indispensable forms of labor which, one would imagine, can attract none—mining, sewer-cleaning, &c. These might be rendered attractive by making the hours of labor in them much shorter than the normal working day of pleasanter occupations. Many a strong, vigorous man would greatly prefer a short spell of disagreeable work to a long one at a desk. As it is well to leave the greatest possible freedom to the individual, this equalising of advantages in all trades would be far better than any attempt to perform the impossible task of choosing an employment for each. A person would be sure to hate any work into which he was directly forced, even though it were the very one he would have chosen had he been left to himself.

Further, much of the most disagreeable and laborious work might be done by machinery, as it would be now if it were not cheaper to exploit a helot class. When it became illegal to send small boys up chimneys, chimneys did not cease to be swept: a machine was invented for sweeping them. Coal-cutting might now be done by machinery, instead of by a man lying on his back, picking away over his head at the imminent risk of his own life; but the machine is much dearer than men, so the miners continue to have their chests crushed in by the falling coal. Under Socialism, men's lives and limbs will be more valuable than machinery; and science will be tasked to substitute the one for the other.

In truth the extension of machinery is very likely to solve many of the problems connected with differential advantages in employment; and it seems certain that, in the very near future, the skilled worker will not be the man who is able to perform a particular set of operations, but the man who has been trained in the use of machinery. The difference of trade will be in the machine rather than in the man: whether the produce is nails or screws, boots or coats, cloth or silk, paper-folding or type-setting, will depend on the internal arrangements of the mechanism and not on the method of applying the force. What we shall probably do will be to instruct all our youth in the principles of mechanics and in the handling of machines; the machines will be constructed so as to turn the force into the various channels required to produce the various articles; and the skilled workman will be the skilled *mechanic,* not the skilled printer or bootmaker. At the present time a few hours', or a few days', study will make the trained mechanician master of any machine you can place before him. The line of progress is to substitute machines for men in every department of production: let the brain plan, guide, control; but let iron and steel, steam and electricity, that do not tire and cannot be brutalised, do the whole of the heavy toil that exhausts human frames to-day. There is not the slightest reason to suppose that we are at the end of an inventive era. Rather are we only just beginning to grope after the uses of electricity; and machinery has before it possibilities almost undreamed of now, the men produced by our system being too rough-handed for the manipulation of delicate and complicated contrivances. I suggest this only as a probable simplification of balancing the supply and demand in various forms of labor in the future: our immediate method of regulation must be the equalising of advantages in them.

One may guess that in each nation all the Boards and communal authorities will ultimately be represented in in some central Executive, or Industrial Ministry; that the Minister of Agriculture, of Mineral Industries, of Textile Industries, and so on, will have relations with similar officers in other lands; and that thus, internationally as well as nationally, co-operation will replace competition. But that end is not yet.

We now approach a yet more thorny subject than the organisation of the workers. What should be the remuneration of labor—what the share of the product taken respectively by the individual, the municipality, and the State?

The answer depends on the answer to a previous question. Is the organisation of the unemployed to be undertaken in order to transform them into self-supporting, self-respecting citizens; or is it to be carried on as a form of exploitation, utilising pauper labor for the production of profit for non-paupers? The whole matter turns on this point; and unless we know our own minds, and fight for the right method and against the wrong from the very beginning, the organisation of the unemployed will be a buttress for the present system instead of a step towards a better. Already there is talk of establishing labor colonies in connexion with workhouses; and there is no time to be lost if we are to take advantage of the good in the proposal and exclude the bad. The County Councils also will lead to an increase of municipal employment; and the method of that employment is vital.

The ordinary vestryman, driven by the force of circumstances into organising the unemployed, will try to extract a profit to the ratepayers from pauper farms by paying the lowest rates of wages. He would find this way of proceeding very congenial, and would soon, if permitted, simply municipalise slave-driving. In this way the municipal and rural organisation of labour, even when its necessity and its advantages are realised, can do nothing but change the form of exploitation of labour if the workers in public employ are to be paid a wage fixed by the competition of the market, and the profits of their labor used only for the relief of the rates. Under such circumstances we should have the whole of the rates paid by the communal workers, while the private employers would go free. This would not be a transition to Socialism, but only a new way of creating a class of municipal serfs, which would make our towns burlesques of the ancient Greek

slaveholding "democracies". We shall find surer ground
by recalling and applying the principle of Socialism
that the laborers shall enjoy the full product of their
toil. It seems to me that this might be worked out
somewhat in the following way:

Out of the value of the communal produce must
come rent of land payable to the local authority, rent
of plant needed for working the industries, wages
advanced and fixed in the usual way, taxes, reserve
fund, accumulation fund, and the other charges necessary for the carrying on of the communal business.
All these deducted, the remaining value should be
divided among the communal workers as a "bonus".
It would be obviously inconvenient, if not impossible,
for the district authority to sub-divide this value and
allot so much to each of its separate undertakings—
so much left over from gas works for the men employed
there, so much from the tramways for the men employed on them, and so on. It would be far simpler
and easier for the municipal employees to be regarded
as a single body, in the service of a single employer,
the local authority; and that the surplus from the
whole of the businesses carried on by the communal
council should be divided without distinction among
the whole of the communal employees. Controversy
will probably arise as to the division: shall all the
shares be equal; or shall the workers receive in proportion to the supposed dignity or indignity of their
work? Inequality, however, would be odious; and I
have already suggested (p. 198) a means of adjusting
different kinds of labor to a system of equal division
of net product. This meets the difficulty of the varying
degrees of irksomeness without invidiously setting up
any kind of socially useful labor as more honorable
than any other—a distinction essentially unsocial and
pernicious. But since in public affairs ethics are apt
to go to the wall, and appeals to social justice too often
fall on deaf ears, it is lucky that in this case ethics

and convenience coincide. The impossibility of esti-
mating the separate value of each man's labor with any
really valid result, the friction which would arise,
the jealousies which would be provoked, the inevitable discontent, favoritism and jobbery that would pre-
vail: all these things will drive the Communal Council
into the right path, equal remuneration of all workers.
That path once entered on, the principle of simplification will spread; and presently it will probably be
found convenient that all the Communal Councils
shall send in their reports to a Central Board, stating
the number of their employees, the amount of the
values produced, the deductions from rent and other
charges, and their available surplus. All these surpluses
added together would then be divided by the total
number of communal employees, and the sum thus
reached would be the share of each worker. The national trusts would at first be worked separately on lines
analogous to those sketched for the Communes; but
later these would be lumped in with the rest, and
still further equalise the reward of labor. As private
enterprises dwindle, more and more of the workers
will pass into communal employ, until at last the
Socialist ideal is touched of a nation in which all
adults are workers, and all share the national product.
But be it noted that all this grows out of the first
organisation of industry by Municipalities and County
Councils, and will evolve just as fast or just as slowly
as the community and its sections choose. The values
dealt with, and the numbers employed at first, would
not imply as much complexity of details as is involved
in many of the great businesses now carried on by
individuals and by companies. The same brains will
be available for the work as are now hired by individuals; and it is rather the novelty of the idea than
the difficulty of its realisation which will stand in the
way of its acceptance.

It is probable, however, that for some time to come,

the captains of industry will be more highly paid than the rank and file of the industrial army, not because it is just that they should receive higher remuneration, but because they, having still the alternative of private enterprise, will be able to demand their ordinary terms, at which it will pay the community better to engage them than to do without them —which would be indeed impossible. But their remuneration will fall as education spreads: their present value is a scarcity value, largely dependent on their monopoly of the higher education; and as the wider training is thrown open to all, an ever-increasing number will become qualified to act as organisers and directors.

The form in which the worker's share is paid to him is not a matter of primary importance. It would probably be convenient to have Communal Banks, issuing cheques like those of the Cheque Bank; and these banks could open credits to the workers to the amount of their remuneration. The way in which each worker expended his wealth would of course be his own business.

The above method of dealing with the surplus remaining from communal labor after rent and other charges had been paid to the Municipality, would prove the most potent factor in the supersession of private enterprise. The amounts produced by the communal organisations would exceed those produced under individualist control; but even if this were not so, yet the shares of the communal workers, as they would include the produce now consumed by idlers, would be higher than any wage which could be paid by the private employer. Hence competition to enter the communal service, and a constant pressure on the Communal Councils to enlarge their undertakings.

It should be added that children and workers incapacitated by age or sickness should receive an equal

share with the communal employees. As all have
been children, are at times sick, and hope to live
to old age, all in turn would share the advantage;
and it is only just that those who have labored honestly in health and through maturity should enjoy the
reward of labor in sickness and through old age.

The share of individuals and of Municipalities
being thus apportioned, there remains only a word to
say as to the Central National Council—the "State"
*par excellence*. This would derive the revenues necessary for the discharge of its functions, from contributions levied on the Communal Councils. It is evident
that in the adjustment of these contributions could
be effected the "nationalisation" of any special natural
resources, such as mines, harbors, &c., enjoyed by
exceptionally well situated Communes. The levy would
be, in fact, of the nature of an income tax.

Such a plan of Distribution—especially that part
of it which equalizes the shares in the product—is
likely to provoke the question: "What will be the
stimulus to labor under the proposed system? Will
not the idle evade their fair share of labor, and live
in clover on the industry of their neighbors?"

The general stimulus to labor will be, in the first
place, then as now, the starvation which would follow
the cessation of labor. Until we discover the country
in which jam-rolls grow on bushes, and roasted
sucking-pigs run about crying "Come eat me!" we
are under an imperious necessity to produce. We shall
work because, on the whole, we prefer work to starvation. In the transition to Socialism, when the organisation of labor by the Communal Councils begins, the
performance of work will be the condition of employment; and as non-employment will mean starvation—
for when work is offered, no relief of any kind need
be given to the healthy adult who refuses to perform
it—the strongest possible stimulus will force men to
work. In fact, "work or starve" will be the alternative

set before each communal employee; and as men now prefer long-continued and ill-paid work to starvation, they will certainly, unless human nature be entirely changed, prefer short and well-paid work to starvation. The individual shirker will be dealt with much as he is to-day: he will be warned, and, if he prove incorrigibly idle, discharged from the communal employ. The vast majority of men now seek to retain their employment by a reasonable discharge of their duty: why should they not do the same when the employment is on easier conditions? At first, discharge would mean being flung back into the whirpool of competition, a fate not lightly to be challenged. Later, as the private enterprises succumbed to the competition of the Commune, it would mean almost hopelessness of obtaining a livelihood. When social reorganisation is complete, it would mean absolute starvation. And as the starvation would be deliberately incurred and voluntarily undergone, it woud meet with no sympathy and no relief.

The next stimulus would be the appetite of the worker for the result of the communal toil, and the determination of his fellow-workers to make him take his fair share of the work of producing it. It is found at the present time that a very small share of the profits arising from associated labor acts as a tremendous stimulus to each individual producer. Firms which allot a part of their profits for division among their employees find the plan profitable to themselves. The men work eagerly to increase the common product, knowing that each will have a larger bonus as the common product is larger: they become vigilant as to waste in production; they take care of the machinery; they save gas, etc. In a word, they lessen the cost as much as they can, because each saving means gain to them. We see from the experiments of Leclaire and Godin that inventiveness also is stimulated by a share in the common produce. The workers in these businesses are ever trying to discover better methods, to improve their machinery, in a word to progress, since each step forward brings improvement of their lot. Inventions come from a desire to save trouble, as well as from the impulse of inventive genius, the joy in accomplishing an intellectual triumph, and the delight of serving the race. Small inventions are continually being made by clever workmen to facilitate their operations, even when they are not themselves personally gainers by them; and there is no reason to fear that this spontaneous exercise of inventiveness will cease when the added productivity of labor lightens the task or increases the harvest of the laborer. Is it to be argued that men will be industrious, careful, and inventive when they get only a fraction of the result of their associated labor, but will plunge into sloth, recklessness and stagnation when they get the whole? that a little gain stimulates, but any gain short of complete satisfaction would paralyse? If there is one vice more certain than another to be unpopular in a Socialist community, it is laziness. The man who shirked would find his mates making his position intolerable, even before he suffered the doom of expulsion.

But while these compelling motives will be potent in their action on man as he now is, there are others, already acting on some men, which will one day act on all men. Human beings are not the simple and onesided organisms they appear to the superficial glance of the Individualist—moved only by a single motive, the desire for pecuniary gain—by one longing, the longing for wealth. Under our present social system, the struggle for riches assumes an abnormal and artificial development; riches mean nearly all that makes life worth having—security against starvation, gratification of taste, enjoyment of pleasant and cultured society, superiority to many temptations, self-respect, consideration, comfort, knowledge, freedom, as far as these things are attainable under existing conditions. In a society where poverty means social discredit, where misfortune is treated as a crime, where the prison or the workhouse is the guerdon of failure, and the bitter carking harassment of daily wants unmet by daily supply is ever hanging over the head of each worker, what wonder that money seems the one thing needful, and that every other thought is lost in the frenzied rush to escape all that is summed up in the one word Poverty?

But this abnormal development of the gold-hunger would disappear upon the certainty for each of the means of subsistence. Let each individual feel absolutely secure of subsistence—let every anxiety as to the material wants of his future be swept away; and the longing for wealth will lose its leverage. The daily bread being certain, the tyranny of pecuniary gain will be broken; and life will begin to be used in living and not in struggling for the chance to live. Then will come to the front all these multifarious motives which are at work in the complex human organism even now, and which will assume their proper importance when the basis of physical life is assured. The desire to excel, the joy in creative work, the longing to improve, the eagerness to win social approval, the instinct of benevolence: all these will start into full life, and will serve at once as the stimulus to labor and the reward of excellence. It is instructive to notice that these very forces may already be seen at work in every case in which subsistence is secured, and they alone supply the stimulus to action. The soldier's subsistence is certain, and does not depend on his exertions. At once he becomes susceptible to appeals to his patriotism, to his *esprit de corps,* to the honor of his flag: he will dare anything for glory, and value a bit of bronze, which is the "reward of valor", far more than a hundred times its weight in gold. Yet many of the private soldiers come from the worst of the population; and military glory and success in murder are but poor objects to aim at. If so much can be done under circumstances so unpromising, what may we not hope from nobler aspirations? Or take the eagerness, self-denial, and strenuous effort, thrown by young men into their mere games! The desire to be captain of the Oxford eleven, stroke of the Cambridge boat, victor in the foot-race or the leaping—in a word, the desire to excel—is strong enough to impel to exertions which often ruin physical health. Everywhere we see the multiform desires of humanity assert themselves when once livelihood is secure. It is on the devotion of these to the service of Society, as the development of the social instincts teaches men to identify their interests with those of the community, that Socialism must ultimately rely for progress; but in saying this we are only saying that Socialism relies for progress on human nature as a whole, instead of on that mere fragment of it known as the desire for gain. If human nature should break down, then Socialism will break down; but at least we have a hundred strings to our Socialist bow, while the Individualist has only one.

But Humanity will not break down. The faith which is built on it is faith founded on a rock. Under healthier and happier conditions, Humanity will rise to heights undreamed of now; and the most exquisite Utopias, as sung by the poet and idealist, shall, to our children, seem but dim and broken lights compared with their perfect day. All that we need are courage, prudence, and faith. Faith, above all, which dares to believe that justice and love are not impossible; and that more than the best that man can dream of shall one day be realised by men.

*THE TRANSITION TO SOCIAL DEMOCRACY*

## 7.  TRANSITION [1]

*By G. Bernard Shaw*

When the British Association honored me by an invitation to take part in its proceedings, I proposed to do so by reading a paper entitled *"Finishing* the Transition to Social Democracy". The word "finishing" has been, on consideration, dropped. In modern use it has gathered a certain sudden and sinister sense which I desire carefully to dissociate from the process to be described. I suggested it in the first instance only to convey in the shortest way that we are in the middle of the transition instead of shrinking from the beginning of it; and that I propose to deal with · the part of it that lies before us rather than that which we have already accomplished. Therefore, though I shall begin at the beginning, I shall make no apology for traversing centuries by leaps and bounds at the risk of sacrificing the dignity of history to the necessity for coming to the point as soon as possible.

Briefly, then, let us commence by glancing at the Middle Ages. There you find, theoretically, a much more orderly England than the England of to-day. Agriculture is organised on an intelligible and consistent system in the feudal manor or commune: handicraft is ordered by the gilds of the towns. Every man has his class, and every class its duties. Payments and privileges are fixed by law and custom, sanctioned

[1] An address delivered on the 7th September, 1888, to the Economic Section of the British Association at Bath.

by the moral sense of the community, and revised by the light of that moral sense whenever the operation of supply and demand disturbs their adjustment. Liberty and Equality are unheard of; but so is Free Competition. The law does not suffer a laborer's wife to wear a silver girdle: neither does it force her to work sixteen hours a day for the value of a modern shilling. Nobody entertains the idea that the individual has any right to trade as he pleases without reference to the rest. When the townsfolk, for instance, form a market, they quite understand that they have not taken that trouble in order to enable speculators to make money. If they catch a man buying goods solely in order to sell them a few hours later at a higher price, they treat that man as a rascal; and he never, as far as I have been able to ascertain, ventures to plead that it is socially beneficent, and indeed a pious duty, to buy in the cheapest market and sell in the dearest. If he did, they would probably burn him alive, not altogether inexcusably. As to Protection, it comes naturally to them.

This Social Order, relics of which are still to be found in all directions, did not collapse because it was unjust or absurd. It was burst by the growth of the social organism. Its machinery was too primitive, and its administration too naïve, too personal, too meddlesome to cope with anything more complex than a group of industrially independent communes, centralized very loosely, if at all, for purely political purposes. Industrial relations with other countries were beyond its comprehension. Its grasp of the obligations of interparochial morality was none of the surest: of international morality it had no notion. A Frenchman or a Scotchman was a natural enemy: a Muscovite was a foreign devil: the relationship of a negro to the human race was far more distant than that of a gorilla is now admitted to be. Thus, when the discovery of the New World began that economic

revolution which changed every manufacturing town
into a mere booth in the world's fair, and quite altered
the immediate objects and views of producers, English
adventurers took to the sea in a frame of mind
peculiarly favorable to commercial success. They were
unaffectedly pious, and had the force of character
which is only possible to men who are founded on
convictions. At the same time, they regarded piracy
as a brave and patriotic pursuit, and the slave trade
as a perfectly honest branch of commerce, adventurous
enough to be consistent with the honor of a gentleman, and lucrative enough to make it well worth the
risk. When they stole the cargo of a foreign ship, or
made a heavy profit on a batch of slaves, they regarded
their success as a direct proof of divine protection.
The owners of accumulated wealth hastened to "venture" their capital with these men. Persons of all the
richer degrees, from Queen Elizabeth downward,
took shares in the voyages of the merchant adventurers.
The returns justified their boldness; and the foundation of the industrial greatness and the industrial
shame of the eighteenth and nineteenth centuries was
laid: modern Capitalism thus arising in enterprises
for which men are now, by civilized nations, hung
or shot as human vermin. And it is curious to see still,
in the commercial adventures of our own time, the
same incongruous combination of piety and rectitude
with the most unscrupulous and revolting villainy.
We all know the merchant princes whose enterprise,
whose steady perseverance, whose high personal honor,
blameless family relations, large charities, and liberal
endowment of public institutions mark them out
as very pillars of society; and who are nevertheless
grinding their wealth out of the labor of women and
children with such murderous rapacity that they have
to hand over the poorest of their victims to sweaters
whose sole special function is the evasion of the Factory
Acts. They have, in fact, no more sense of social

solidarity with the wage-workers than Drake had with the Spaniards or negroes.

With the rise of foreign trade and Capitalism, industry so far outgrew the control, not merely of the individual, but of the village, the gild, the municipality, and even the central government, that it seemed as if all attempt at regulation must be abandoned. Every law made for the better ordering of business either did not work at all, or worked only as a monopoly enforced by exasperating official meddling, directly injuring the general interest, and reacting disastrously on the particular interest it was intended to protect. The laws, too, had ceased to be even honestly intended, owing to the seizure of political power by the capitalist classes, which had been prodigiously enriched by the operation of economic laws which were not then understood.[2] Matters reached a position in which legislation and regulation were so mischievous and corrupt, that anarchy became the ideal of all progressive thinkers and practical men. The intellectual revolt formerly inaugurated by the Reformation was reinforced in the eighteenth century by the great industrial revolution which began with the utilization of steam and the invention of the spinning jenny.[3] Then came chaos. The feudal system became an absurdity when its basis of communism with inequality of condition had changed into private property with free contract and competition rents. The gild system had no machinery for dealing with division of labor, the factory system, or international trade; it recognized in competitive individualism only something to be repressed as diabolical. But competitive individualism simply took possession of the gilds, and turned them into refectories for aldermen, and notable additions to the grievances and laughing stocks of posterity.

The desperate effort of the human intellect to un-

[2] Explained in the first essay in this volume.

[3] See the third essay in this volume.

ravel this tangle of industrial anarchy brought modern
political economy into existence. It took shape in
France, where the confusion was thrice confounded;
and proved itself a more practical department of
philosophy than the metaphysics of the schoolmen,
the Utopian socialism of More, or the sociology of
Hobbes. It could trace its ancestry to Aristotle; but
just then the human intellect was rather tired of
Aristotle, whose economics, besides, were those of
slave holding republics. Political economy soon declared
for industrial anarchy; for private property; for individual recklessness of everything except individual
accumulation of riches; and for the abolition of all
the functions of the State except those of putting
down violent conduct and invasions of private property. It might have echoed Jack Cade's exclamation,
"But then are we in order, when we are most out of
order".

Although this was what political economy decreed,
it must not be inferred that the greater economists
were any more advocates of mere licence than Prince
Kropotkin, or Mr. Herbert Spencer, or Mr. Benjamin
Tucker of Boston, or any other modern Anarchist.
They did not admit that the alternative to State
regulations was anarchy: they held that Nature had
provided an all-powerful automatic regulator in Competition; and that by its operation self-interest would
evolve order out of chaos if only it were allowed
its own way. They loved to believe that a right and
just social order was not an artificial and painfully
maintained legal edifice, but a spontaneous outcome
of the free play of the forces of Nature. They were
reactionaries against feudal domineering and mediæval
meddling and ecclesiastical intolerance; and they were
able to shew how all three had ended in disgraceful
failure, corruption and self-stultification. Indignant
at the spectacle of the peasant struggling against the
denial of those rights of private property which his

feudal lord had successfully usurped, they strenuously affirmed the right of private property for all. And whilst they were dazzled by the prodigious impulse given to production by the industrial revolution under competitive private enterprise, they were at the same time, for want of statistics, so optimistically ignorant of the condition of the masses, that we find David Hume, in 1766, writing to Turgot that "no man is so industrious but he may add some hours more in the week to his labor; and scarce anyone is so poor but he can retrench something of his expense". No student ever gathers from a study of the individualist economists that the English proletariat was seething in horror and degradation whilst the riches of the proprietors were increasing by leaps and bounds.

The historical ignorance of the economists did not, however, disable them for the abstract work of scientific political economy. All their most cherished institutions and doctrines succumbed one by one to their analysis of the laws of production and exchange. With one law alone—the law of rent—they destroyed the whole series of assumptions upon which private property is based. The apriorist notion that among free competitors wealth must go to the industrious, and poverty be the just and natural punishment of the lazy and improvident, proved as illusory as the apparent flatness of the earth. Here was a vast mass of wealth called economic rent, increasing with the population, and consisting of the difference between the product of the national industry as it actually was and as it would have been if every acre of land in the country had been no more fertile or favorably situated than the very worst acre from which a bare living could be extracted: all quite incapable of being assigned to this or that individual or class as the return to his or its separate exertions: all purely social or common wealth, for the private appropriation of which no permanently valid and intellectually honest excuse could be made. Ricardo was quite as explicit and far more thorough on the subject than Mr. Henry George. He pointed out—I quote his own words—that "the whole surplus produce of the soil, after deducting from it only such moderate profits as are sufficient to encourage accumulation, must finally rest with the landlord".[4]

It was only by adopting a preposterous theory of value that Ricardo was able to maintain that the laborer, selling himself for wages to the proprietor, would always command his cost of production, i.e., his daily subsistence. Even that slender consolation vanished later on before the renewed investigation of value made by Jevons,[5] who demonstrated that the value of a commodity is a function of the quantity available, and may fall to zero when the supply outruns the demand so far as to make the final increment of the supply useless.[6] A fact which the unemployed had discovered, without the aid of the differential calculus, before Jevons was born. Private property, in fact, left no room for newcomers. Malthus pointed this out, and urged that there should be no newcomers —that the population should remain stationary. But the population took exactly as much notice of this modest demand for stagnation as the incoming tide took of King Canute's ankles. Indeed the demand was the less reasonable since the power of production per head was increasing faster than the population (as it still is), the increase of poverty being produced simply by the increase and private appropriation of rent. After Ricardo had completed the individualist synthesis of production and exchange, a dialectical

[4] "Principles of Political Economy," chap. xxiv., p. 202.
[5] "Theory of Political Economy." By W. Stanley Jevons (London: Macmillan and Co.). See also "The Alphabet of Economic Science" Part I, by Philip H. Wicksteed. (Same publishers.)
[6] See page 22–30 *ante*.

war broke out. Proudhon had only to skim through a Ricardian treatise to understand just enough of it to be able to shew that political economy was a *reductio ad absurdum* of private property instead of a justification of it. Ferdinand Lassalle, with Ricardo in one hand and Hegel in the other, turned all the heavy guns of the philosophers and economists on private property with such effect that no one dared to challenge his characteristic boasts of the irresistible equipment of Social Democracy in point of culture. Karl Marx, without even giving up the Ricardian value theory, seized on the blue books which contained the true history of the leaps and bounds of England's prosperity, and convicted private property of wholesale spoliation, murder and compulsory prostitution; of plague, pestilence, and famine; battle, murder, and sudden death. This was hardly what had been expected from an institution so highly spoken of. Many critics said that the attack was not fair: no one ventured to pretend that the charges were not true. The facts were not only admitted; they had been legislated upon. Social Democracy was working itself out practically as well as academically. Before I recite the steps of the transition, I will, as a matter of form, explain what Social Democracy is, though doubtless nearly all my hearers are already conversant with it.

What the achievement of Socialism involves economically, is the transfer of rent from the class which now appropriates it to the whole people. Rent being that part of the produce which is individually unearned, this is the only equitable method of disposing of it. There is no means of getting rid of economic rent. So long as the fertility of land varies from acre to acre, and the number of persons passing by a shop window per hour varies from street to street, with the result that two farmers or two shopkeepers of exactly equal intelligence and industry will reap unequal returns from their year's work, so long will it be equitable to take from the richer farmer or shopkeeper the excess over his fellow's gain which he owes to the bounty of Nature or the advantage of situation, and divide that excess or rent equally between the two. If the pair of farms or shops be left in the hands of a private landlord, he will take the excess, and, instead of dividing it between his two tenants, live on it himself idly at their expense. The economic object of Socialism is not, of course, to equalize farmers and shopkeepers in couples, but to carry out the principle over the whole community by collecting all rents and throwing them into the national treasury. As the private proprietor has no reason for clinging to his property except the legal power to take the rent and spend it on himself— this legal power being in fact what really constitutes him a proprietor—its abrogation would mean his expropriation. The socialization of rent would mean the socialization of the sources of production by the expropriation of the present private proprietors, and the transfer of their property to the entire nation. This transfer, then, is the subject matter of the transition to Socialism, which began some forty-five years ago, as far as any phase of social evolution can be said to begin at all.

It will be at once seen that the valid objections to Socialism consist wholly of practical difficulties. On the ground of abstract justice, Socialism is not only unobjectionable, but sacredly imperative. I am afraid that in the ordinary middle-class opinion Socialism is flagrantly dishonest, but could be established off-hand to-morrow with the help of a guillotine, if there were no police, and the people were wicked enough. In truth, it is as honest as it is inevitable; but all the mobs and guillotines in the world can no more establish it than police coercion can avert it. The first practical difficulty is raised by the idea of the entire people collectively owning land, capital, or anything else.

Here is the rent arising out of the people's industry: here are the pockets of the private proprietors. The problem is to drop that rent, not into those private pockets, but into the people's pocket. Yes; but where is the people's pocket? Who is the people? what is the people? Tom we know, and Dick: also Harry; but solely and separately as individuals: as a trinity they have no existence. Who is their trustee, their guardian, their man of business, their manager, their secretary, even their stakeholder? The Socialist is stopped dead at the threshold of practical action by this difficulty until he bethinks himself of the State as the representative and trustee of the people. Now if you will just form a hasty picture of the governments which called themselves States in Ricardo's day, consisting of rich proprietors legislating either by divine right or by the exclusive suffrage of the poorer proprietors, and filling the executives with the creatures of their patronage and favoritism; if you look beneath their oratorical parliamentary discussions, conducted with all the splendor and decorum of an expensive sham fight; if you consider their class interests, their shameless corruption, and the waste and mismanagement which disgraced all their bungling attempts at practical business of any kind, you will understand why Ricardo, clearly as he saw the economic consequences of private appropriation of rent, never dreamt of State appropriation as a possible alternative. The Socialist of that time did not greatly care: he was only a benevolent Utopian who planned model communities, and occasionally carried them out, with negatively instructive and positively disastrous results. When his successors learned economics from Ricardo, they saw the difficulty quite as plainly as Ricardo's vulgarizers, the Whig doctrinaires who accepted the incompetence and corruption of States as permanent inherent State qualities, like the acidity of lemons. Not that the Socialists were not doctrinaires too; but outside economics they were pupils of Hegel, whilst the Whigs were pupils of Bentham and Austin. Bentham's was not the school in which men learned to solve problems to which history alone could give the key, or to form conceptions which belonged to the evolutional order. Hegel, on the other hand, expressly taught the conception of the perfect State; and his pupils saw that nothing in the nature of things made it impossible, or even specially difficult, to make the existing State, if not absolutely perfect, at least practically trustworthy. They contemplated the insolent and inefficient government official of their day without rushing to the conclusion that the State uniform had a magic property of extinguishing all business capacity, integrity, and common civility in the wearer. When State officials obtained their posts by favoritism and patronage, efficiency on their part was an accident, and politeness a condescension. When they retained their posts without any effective responsibility to the public, they naturally defrauded the public by making their posts sinecures, and insulted the public when, by personal inquiry, it made itself troublesome. But every successfully conducted private business establishment in the kingdom was an example of the ease with which public ones could be reformed as soon as there was the effective will to find out the way. Make the passing of a sufficient examination an indispensable preliminary to entering the executive; make the executive responsible to the government and the government responsible to the people; and State departments will be provided with all the guarantees for integrity and efficiency that private money-hunting pretends to. Thus the old bugbear of State imbecility did not terrify the Socialist: it only made him a Democrat. But to call himself so simply, would have had the effect of classing him with the ordinary destructive politician who is a Democrat without ulterior views for the sake of formal Democracy—one whose notion of Radicalism

is the pulling up of aristocratic institutions by the roots
—who is, briefly, a sort of Universal Abolitionist. Consequently, we have the distinctive term Social Democrat, indicating the man or woman who desires through
Democracy to gather the whole people into the State,
so that the State may be trusted with the rent of the
country, and finally with the land, the capital, and the
organization of the national industry—with all the
sources of production, in short, which are now abandoned to the cupidity of irresponsible private individuals.

The benefits of such a change as this are so obvious
to all except the existing private proprietors and their
parasites, that it is very necessary to insist on the
impossibility of effecting it suddenly. The young
Socialist is apt to be catastrophic in his views—to plan
the revolutionary programme as an affair of twenty-
four lively hours, with Individualism in full swing
on Monday morning, a tidal wave of the insurgent
proletariat on Monday afternoon, and Socialism in
complete working order on Tuesday. A man who
believes that such a happy despatch is possible, will
naturally think it absurd and even inhuman to stick
at bloodshed in bringing it about. He can prove that
the continuance of the present system for a year costs
more suffering than could be crammed into any Monday afternoon, however sanguinary. This is the phase
of conviction in which are delivered those Socialist
speeches which make what the newspapers call "good
copy", and which are the only ones they as yet report.
Such speeches are encouraged by the hasty opposition
they evoke from thoughtless persons, who begin by
tacitly admitting that a sudden change is feasible, and
go on to protest that it would be wicked. The experienced Social Democrat converts his too ardent follower
by first admitting that if the change could be made
catastrophically it would be well worth making, and
then proceeding to point out that as it would involve

a readjustment of productive industry to meet the
demand created by an entirely new distribution of
purchasing power, it would also involve, in the application of labor and industrial machinery, alterations
which no afternoon's work could effect. You cannot
convince any man that it is impossible to tear down
a government in a day; but everybody is convinced
already that you cannot convert first and third class
carriages into second class; rookeries and palaces
into comfortable dwellings; and jewellers and dress-
makers into bakers and builders, by merely singing
the "Marseillaise". No judicious person, however deeply
persuaded that the work of the court dressmaker has
no true social utility, would greatly care to quarter
her idly on the genuinely productive workers pending
the preparation of a place for her in their ranks.
For though she is to all intents and purposes quartered
on them at present, yet she at least escapes the demor-
alization of idleness. Until her new place is ready, it is
better that her patrons should find dressmaking for
her hands to do, than that Satan should find mischief.
Demolishing a Bastille with seven prisoners in it is
one thing: demolishing one with fourteen million
prisoners is quite another. I need not enlarge on the
point: the necessity for cautious and gradual change
must be obvious to everyone here, and could be made
obvious to everyone elsewhere if only the catastrophists
were courageously and sensibly dealt with in discussion.

What then does a gradual transition to Social Democracy mean specifically? It means the gradual extension
of the franchise; and the transfer of rent and interest
to the State, not in one lump sum, but by instalments.
Looked at in this way, it will at once be seen that we
are already far on the road, and are being urged
further by many politicians who do not dream that
they are touched with Socialism—nay, who would
earnestly repudiate the touch as a taint. Let us see
how far we have gone. In 1832 the political power

passed into the hands of the middle class; and in
1838 Lord John Russell announced finality. Meanwhile, in 1834, the middle class had swept away
the last economic refuge of the workers, the old
Poor Law, and delivered them naked to the furies of
competition.[7] Ten years turmoil and active emigration
followed; and then the thin end of the wedge went
in. The Income Tax was established; and the Factory
Acts were made effective. The Income Tax (1842),
which is on individualist principles an intolerable
spoliative anomaly, is simply a forcible transfer of
rent, interest, and even rent of ability, from private
holders to the State without compensation. It excused
itself to the Whigs on the ground that those who had
most property for the State to protect should pay *ad
valorem* for its protection. The Factory Acts swept
the anarchic theory of the irresponsibility of private
enterprise out of practical politics; made employers
accountable to the State for the well-being of their
employees; and transferred a further instalment of
profits directly to the worker by raising wages. Then
came the gold discoveries in California (1847) and
Austrialia (1851), and the period of leaps and bounds,
supported by the economic rent of England's mineral
fertility, which kindled Mr. Gladstone's retrogressive
instincts to a vain hope of abolishing the Income Tax.
These events relieved the pressure set up by the New
Poor Law. The workers rapidly organized themselves
in Trades Unions, which were denounced then for
their tendency to sap the manly independence which
had formally characterized the British workman,[8] and
which are to-day held up to him as the self-helpful per-

[7] The general impression that the old Poor Law had become an indefensible nuisance is a correct one. All attempts to mitigate Individualism by philanthropy instead
of replacing it by Socialism are foredoomed to confusion.
[8] See Final Report of Royal Commission on Trade Unions,
1869. Vol. I., p. xvii., sec. 46.

fection of that manly independence. Howbeit, self-help flourished, especially at Manchester and Sheffield; State help was voted grandmotherly; wages went up; and the Unions, like the fly on the wheel, thought that they had raised them. They were mistaken; but the value of Trade Unionism in awakening the social conscience of the skilled workers was immense, though to this there was a heavy set-off in its tendency to destroy their artistic conscience by making them aware that it was their duty to one another to discourage rapid and efficient workmanship by every means in their power. An extension of the Franchise, which was really an instalment of Democracy, and not, like the 1832 Reform Bill, only an advance towards it, was gained in 1867; and immediately afterwards came another instalment of Socialism in the shape of a further transfer of rent and interest from private holders to the State for the purpose of educating the people. In the meantime, the extraordinary success of the post office, which, according to the teaching of the Manchester school, should have been a nest of incompetence and jobbery, had not only shewn the perfect efficiency of State enterprise when the officials are made responsible to the class interested in its success, but had also proved the enormous convenience and cheapness of socialistic or collectivist charges over those of private enterprise. For example, the Postmaster General charges a penny for sending a letter weighing an ounce from Kensington to Bayswater. Private enterprise would send half a pound the same distance for a farthing, and make a handsome profit on it. But the Postmaster General also sends an ounce letter from Land's End to John o' Groat's House for a penny. Private enterprise would probably demand at least a shilling, if not five, for such a service; and there are many places in which private enterprise could not on any terms maintain a post office. Therefore a citizen with ten letters to post saves considerably by the uniform socialistic charge, and quite recognizes the necessity for rigidly protecting the Postmaster's monopoly.

After 1875,[9] leaping and bounding prosperity, after a final spurt during which the Income Tax fell to twopence, got out of breath, and has not yet recovered it. Russia and America, among other competitors, began to raise the margin of cultivation at a surprising rate. Education began to intensify the sense of suffering, and to throw light upon its causes in dark places. The capital needed to keep English industry abreast of the growing population began to be attracted by the leaping and bounding of foreign loans and investments,[10] and to bring to England, in payment of interest, imports that were not paid for by exports— a phenomenon inexpressibly disconcerting to the Cobden Club. The old pressure of the eighteen-thirties came back again; and presently, as if Chartism and Fergus O'Connor had risen from the dead, the Democratic Federation and Mr. H. M. Hyndman appeared in the field, highly significant as signs of the times, and looming hideously magnified in the guilty eye of property, if not of great account as direct factors in the course of events. Numbers of young men, pupils of Mill, Spencer, Comte, and Darwin, roused by Mr. Henry George's "Progress and Poverty", left aside evolution and freethought; took to insurrectionary economics; studied Karl Marx; and were so convinced that Socialism had only to be put clearly before the working-classes to concentrate the power of their immense numbers in one irresistible organization, that the Revolution was fixed for 1889—the anniversary of

[9] See Mr. Robert Giffen's address on "The Recent rate of Material Progress in England". Proceedings of the British Association at Manchester in 1887, page 806.
[10] See Mr. Robert Giffen on Import and Export Statistics, "Essays on Finance", Second Series, p. 194. (London: G. Bell and Sons. 1886.)

the French Revolution—at latest. I remember being asked satirically and publicly at that time how long I thought it would take to get Socialism into working order if I had my way. I replied, with a spirited modesty, that a fortnight would be ample for the purpose. When I add that I was frequently complimented on being one of the more reasonable Socialists, you will be able to appreciate the fervor of our conviction, and the extravagant levity of our practical ideas. The opposition we got was uninstructive: it was mainly founded on the assumption that our projects were theoretically unsound but immediately possible, whereas our weak point lay in the case being exactly the reverse. However, the ensuing years sifted and sobered us. "The Socialists", as they were called, have fallen into a line as a Social Democratic party, no more insurrectionary in its policy than any other party. But I shall not present the remainder of the transition to Social Democracy as the work of fully conscious Social Democrats. I prefer to ignore them altogether—to suppose, if you will, that the Government will shortly follow the advice of the *Saturday Review,* and, for the sake of peace and quietness, hang them.

First, then, as to the consummation of Democracy. Since 1885 every man who pays four shillings a week rent can only be hindered from voting by anomalous conditions of registration which are likely to be swept away very shortly. This is all but manhood suffrage; and it will soon complete itself as adult suffrage. However, I may leave adult suffrage out of the question, because the outlawry of women, monstrous as it is, is not a question of class privilege, but of sex privilege. To complete the foundation of the democratic State, then, we need manhood suffrage, abolition of all poverty disqualifications, abolition of the House of Lords, public payment of candidature expenses, public payment of representatives, and annual elections. These changes are now inevitable, however unacceptable

they may appear to those of us who are Conservatives.
They have been for half a century the commonplaces
of Radicalism. We have next to consider that the State
is not merely an abstraction: it is a machine to do
certain work; and if that work be increased and altered
in its character, the machinery must be multiplied
and altered too. Now, the extension of the franchise
does increase and alter the work very considerably;
but it has no direct effect on the machinery. At present the State machine has practically broken down
under the strain of spreading democracy, the work
being mainly local, and the machinery mainly central. Without efficient local machinery the replacing of private enterprise by State enterprise is out
of the question; and we shall presently see that such
replacement is one of the inevitable consequences
of Democracy. A democratic State cannot become a
Social-Democratic State unless it has in every centre
of population a local governing body as thoroughly
democratic in its constitution as the central Parliament.
This matter is also well in train. In 1888 a Government avowedly reactionary passed a Local Government
Bill which effected a distinct advance towards the
democratic municipality.[11] It was furthermore a Bill
with no single aspect of finality anywhere about it.
Local self-Government remains prominent within the
sphere of practical politics. When it is achieved, the
democratic State will have the machinery for Socialism.

And now, how is the raw material of Socialism—
otherwise the Proletarian man—to be brought to the
Democratic State machinery? Here again the path is
easily found. Politicians who have no suspicion that
they are Socialists, are advocating further instalments

[11] This same Government, beginning to realize what it
has unintentionally done for Social Democracy, is already
(1889) doing what it can to render the new County
Councils socialistically impotent by urgently reminding
them of the restrictions which hamper their action.

of Socialism with a recklessness of indirect results
which scandalizes the conscious Social Democrat. The
phenomenon of economic rent has assumed prodigious proportions in our great cities. The injustice
of its private appropriation is glaring, flagrant, almost
ridiculous. In the long suburban roads about London,
where rows of exactly similar houses stretch for miles
countrywards, the rent changes at every few thousand
yards by exactly the amount saved or incurred annually
in travelling to and from the householder's place of
business. The seeker after lodgings, hesitating between Bloomsbury and Tottenham, finds every advantage of situation skimmed off by the landlord with
scientific precision. As lease after lease falls in, houses,
shops, goodwills of businesses which are the fruits of
the labor of lifetimes, fall into the maw of the ground
landlord. Confiscation of capital, spoliation of households, annihilation of incentive, everything that the
most ignorant and credulous fundholder ever charged
against the Socialists, rages openly in London, which
begins to ask itself whether it exists and toils only
for the typical duke and his celebrated jockey and his
famous racehorse. Lord Hobhouse and his unimpeach-
ably respectable committee for the taxation of ground
values are already in the field claiming the value of
the site of London for London collectively; and
their agitation receives additional momentum from
every lease that falls in. Their case is unassailable;
and the evil they attack is one that presses on the
ratepaying and leaseholding classes as well as upon
humbler sufferers. This economic pressure is reinforced
formidably by political opinion in the workmen's
associations. Here the moderate members are content
to demand a progressive Income Tax, which is virtually
Lord Hobhouse's proposal; and the extremists are all
for Land Nationalization, which is again Lord Hobhouse's principle. The cry for such taxation cannot
permanently be resisted. And it is very worthy of

remark that there is a new note in the cry. Formerly taxes were proposed with a specific object—as to pay for a war, for education, or the like. Now the proposal is to tax the landlords in order to get some of *our* money back from them—take it from them first and find a use for it afterwards. Ever since Mr. Henry George's book reached the English Radicals, there has been a growing disposition to impose a tax of twenty shillings in the pound on obviously unearned incomes: that is, to dump four hundred and fifty millions [12] a year down on the Exchequer counter; and then retire with three cheers for the restoration of the land to the people.

The results of such a proceeding, if it actually came off, would considerably take its advocates aback. The streets would presently be filled with starving workers of all grades, domestic servants, coach builders, decorators, jewellers, lacemakers, fashionable professional men, and numberless others whose livelihood is at present gained by ministering to the wants of these and of the proprietary class. "This", they would cry, "is what your theories have brought us to! Back with the good old times, when we received our wages, which were at least better than nothing." Evidently the Chancellor of the Exchequer would have three courses open to him. (1). He could give the money back again to the landlords and capitalists with an apology. (2). He could attempt to start State industries with it for the employment of the people. (3). Or he could simply distribute it among the unemployed. The last is not to be thought of: anything is better than *panem et circenses*. The second (starting State industries) would be far too vast an undertaking to get on foot soon enough to meet the urgent difficulty. The first (the return with an apology) would be a *reductio ad ab-*

[12] The authority for this figure will be found in Fabian Tract, No. 5, "Facts for Socialists".

*surdum* of the whole affair—a confession that the private proprietor, for all his idleness and his voracity, is indeed performing an indispensable economic function—the function of capitalizing, however wastefully and viciously, the wealth which surpasses his necessarily limited power of immediate personal consumption. And here we have checkmate to mere Henry Georgism, or State appropriation of rent without Socialism. It is easy to shew that the State is entitled to the whole income of the Duke of Westminster, and to argue therefrom that he should straightway be taxed twenty shillings in the pound. But in practical earnest the State has no right to take five farthings of capital from the Duke or anybody else until it is ready to invest them in productive enterprise. The consequences of withdrawing capital from private hands merely to lock it up unproductively in the treasury would be so swift and ruinous, that no stateman, however fortified with the destructive resources of abstract economics, could persist in it. It will be found in the future as in the past that governments will raise money only because they want it for specific purposes, and not on *a priori* demonstrations that they have a right to it. But it must be added that when they *do* want it for a specific purpose, then, also in the future as in the past, they will raise it without the slightest regard to *a priori* demonstrations that they have no right to it.

Here then we have got to a deadlock. In spite of democrats and land nationalizers, rent cannot be touched unless some pressure from quite another quarter forces productive enterprise on the State. Such pressure is already forthcoming. The quick starvation of the unemployed, the slow starvation of the employed who have no relatively scarce special skill, the unbearable anxiety or dangerous recklessness of those who are employed to-day and unemployed to-morrow, the rise in urban rents, the screwing down of wages by pauper immigration and home multiplication, the hand-in-hand advance of education and discontent, are all working up to explosion point. It is useless to prove by statistics that most of the people are better off than before, true as that probably is, thanks to instalments of Social Democracy. Yet even that is questionable; for it is idle to claim authority for statistics of things that have never been recorded. Chaos has no statistics: it has only statisticians; and the ablest of them prefaces his remarks on the increased consumption of rice by the admission that "no one can contemplate the present condition of the masses without desiring something like a revolution for the better".[13] The masses themselves are being converted so rapidly to that view of the situation, that we have Pan-Anglican Synods, bewildered by a revival of Christianity, pleading that though Socialism is eminently Christian, yet "the Church must act safely as well as sublimely".[14] During the agitation made by the unemployed last winter (1887-8), the Chief Commissioner of Police in London started at his own shadow, and mistook Mr. John Burns for the French Revolution, to the great delight of that genial and courageous champion of his class.[15] The existence of the pressure is further shewn by the number and variety of safety valves proposed to relieve it—monetization of silver, import duties, "leaseholds enfranchisement", extension of joint stock capitalism masquerading as co-operation,[16] and other irrelevancies. My own sudden promo-

[13] Mr. R. Giffen, "Essays in Finance", Second Series, p. 393.
[14] Proceedings of the Pan-Anglican Synod: Lambeth, 1888. Report of Committee on Socialism.
[15] Finally, the Commissioner was superseded; and Mr. Burns was elected a member of the first London County Council by a large majority.
[16] It is due to the leaders of the Co-operative movement to say here that they are no parties to the substitution of

tion from the street corner to this platform is in its way
a sign of the times. But whilst we are pointing the
moral and adorning the tale according to our various
opinions, an actual struggle is beginning between the
unemployed who demand work and the local authorities appointed to deal with the poor. In the winter, the
unemployed collect round red flags, and listen to
speeches for want of anything else to do. They welcome
Socialism, insurrectionism, currency craze—anything
that passes the time and seems to express the fact that
they are hungry. The local authorities, equally inno-
cent of studied economic views, deny that there is
any misery; send leaders of deputations to the Local
Government Board, who promptly send them back to
the guardians; try bullying; try stoneyards; try
bludgeoning; and finally sit down helplessly and wish
it were summer again or the unemployed at the bottom
of the sea. Meanwhile the charity fund, which is much
less elastic than the wages fund, overflows at the
Mansion House only to run dry at the permanent
institutions. So unstable a state of things cannot last.
The bludgeoning, and the shocking clamor for bloodshed from the anti-popular newspapers, will create
a revulsion among the humane section of the middle
class. The section which is blinded by class prejudice
to all sense of social responsibility, dreads personal
violence from the working class with a superstitious
terror that defies enlightenment or control.[17] Municipal employment must be offered at last. This cannot
be done in one place alone: the rush from other parts

dividend-hunting by petty capitalists for the pursuit of the
ideal of Robert Owen, the Socialist founder of Co-operation; and that they are fully aware that Co-operation must
be a political as well as a commercial movement if it is to
achieve a final solution of the labor question.
[17] Ample material for a study of West End mob panic
may be found in the London newspapers of February
1886, and November 1887.

of the country would swamp an isolated experiment.
Wherever the pressure is, the relief must be given
on the spot. And since public decency, as well as
consideration for its higher officials, will prevent the
County Council from instituting a working day of
sixteen hours at a wage of a penny an hour or less,
it will soon have on its hands not only the unemployed,
but also the white slaves of the sweater, who will
escape from their dens and appeal to the municipality
for work the moment they become aware · that
municipal employment is better than private sweating.
Nay, the sweater himself, a mere slave driver paid
"by the piece", will in many instances be as anxious
as his victims to escape from his hideous trade. But
the municipal organization of the industry of these
people will require capital. Where is the municipality
to get it? Raising the rates is out of the question: the
ordinary tradesmen and householders are already
rated and rented to the limit of endurance: further
burdens would almost bring them into the street
with a red flag. Dreadful dilemma! in which the
County Council, between the devil and the deep sea,
will hear Lord Hobhouse singing a song of deliverance,
telling a golden tale of ground values to be munici-
palized by taxation. The land nationalizers will swell
the chorus: the Radical progressive income taxers singing together, and the ratepaying tenants shouting
for joy. The capital difficulty thus solved—for we need
not seriously anticipate that the landlords will actually
fight, as our President [18] once threatened—the question
of acquiring land will arise. The nationalizers will
declare for its annexation by the municipality without
compensation; but that will be rejected as spoliation,
worthy only of revolutionary Socialists. The no-
compensation cry is indeed a piece of unpractical

[18] Lord Bramwell, President of the Economic Section of
the British Association in 1888.

catastrophic insurrectionism; for whilst compensation would be unnecessary and absurd if every proprietor were expropriated simultaneously, and the proprietary system at once replaced by full blown Socialism, yet when it is necessary to proceed by degrees, the denial of compensation would have the effect of singling out individual proprietors for expropriation whilst the others remained unmolested, and depriving them of their private means long before there was suitable municipal employment ready for them. The land, as it is required, will therefore be honestly purchased; and the purchase money, or the interest thereon, will be procured, like the capital, by taking rent. Of course this will be at bottom an act of expropriation just as much as the collection of Income Tax to-day is an act of expropriation. As such, it will be denounced by the landlords as merely a committing of the newest sin the oldest kind of way. In effect, they will be compelled at each purchase to buy out one of their body and present his land to the municipality, thereby distributing the loss fairly over their whole class, instead of placing it on one man who is no more responsible than the rest. But they will be compelled to do this in a manner that will satisfy the moral sense of the ordinary citizen as effectively as that of the skilled economist.

We now foresee our municipality equipped with land and capital for industrial purposes. At first they will naturally extend the industries they already carry on, road making, gas works, tramways, building, and the like. It is probable that they will for the most part regard their action as a mere device to meet a passing emergency. The Manchester School will urge its Protectionist theories as to the exemption of private enterprise from the competition of public enterprise, in one supreme effort to practise for the last time on popular ignorance of the science which it has consistently striven to debase and stultify. For a while the proprietary party will succeed in hampering and restricting municipal enterprise [19]; in attaching the stigma of pauperism to its service; in keeping the lot of its laborers as nearly as possible down to private competition level in point of hard work and low wages. But its power will be broken by the disappearance of that general necessity for keeping down the rates which now hardens local authority to humane appeals. The luxury of being generous at someone else's expense will be irresistible. The ground landlord will be the municipal milch cow; and the ordinary ratepayers will feel the advantage of sleeping in peace, relieved at once from the fear of increased burdens and of having their windows broken and their premises looted by hungry mobs, nuclei of all the socialism and scoundrelism of the city. They will have just as much remorse in making the landlord pay as the landlord has had in making them pay—just as much and no more. And as the municipality becomes more democratic, it will find landlordism losing power, not only relatively to democracy, but absolutely.

The ordinary ratepayer, however, will not remain unaffected for long. At the very outset of the new extension of municipal industries, the question of wage will arise. A minimum wage must be fixed; and though at first, to avoid an overwhelming rush of applicants for employment, it must be made too small to tempt any decently employed laborer to forsake his place and run to the municipality, still, it will not be the frankly infernal competition wage. It will be, like mediæval wages, fixed with at least some reference to public opinion as to a becoming standard of comfort. Over and above this, the municipality will have to pay to its organizers, managers, and incidentally necessary skilled workers the full market price of their ability, minus only what the superior prestige and

[19] See note 11, above, in this essay.

permanence of public employment may induce them to accept. But whilst these high salaries will make no more disturbance in the labor market than the establishment of a new joint stock company would, the minimum wage for laborers will affect that market perceptibly. The worst sort of sweaters will find that if they are to keep their "hands", they must treat them at least as well as the municipality. The consequent advance in wage will swallow up the sweater's narrow margin of profit. Hence the sweater must raise the price per piece against the shops and wholesale houses for which he sweats. This again will diminish the profits of the wholesale dealers and shopkeepers, who will not be able to recover this loss by raising the price of their wares against the public, since, had any such step been possible, they would have taken it before. But fortunately for them, the market value of their ability as men of business is fixed by the same laws that govern the prices of commodities. Just as the sweater is worth his profit, so they are worth their profit; and just as the sweater will be able to exact from them his old remuneration in spite of the advance in wages, so they will be able to exact their old remuneration in spite of the advance in sweaters' terms. But from whom, it will be asked, if not from the public by raising the price of the wares? Evidently from the landlord upon whose land they are organizing production. In other words, they will demand and obtain a reduction of rent. Thus the organizer of industry, the employer pure and simple, the *entrepreneur,* as he is often called in economic treatises nowadays, will not suffer. In the division of the product his share will remain constant; whilst the industrious wage worker's share will be increased, and the idle proprietor's share diminished. This will not adjust itself without friction and clamor; but such friction is constantly going on under the present system in the opposite direction, *i.e.,* by the raising of the proprietor's share at the expense of the worker's.

The contraction of landlords' incomes will necessarily diminish the revenue from taxation on such incomes. Let us suppose that the municipality, to maintain its revenue, puts on an additional penny in the pound. The effect will be to burn the landlord's candle at both ends—obviously not a process that can be continued to infinity. But long before taxation fails as a source of municipal capital, the municipalities will have begun to save capital out of the product of their own industries. In the market the competition of those industries with the private concerns will be irresistible. Unsaddled with a single idle person, and having, therefore, nothing to provide for after paying their employees except extension of capital, they will be able to offer wages that no business burdened with the unproductive consumption of an idle landlord or shareholder could afford, unless it yielded a heavy rent in consequence of some marked advantage of site. But even rents, when they are town rents, are at the mercy of a municipality in the long run. The masters of the streets and the traffic can nurse one site and neglect another. The rent of a shop depends on the number of persons passing its windows per hour. A skilfully timed series of experiments in paving, a new bridge, a tramway service, a barracks, or a small-pox hospital are only a few of the circumstances of which city rents are the creatures. The power of the municipality to control these circumstances is as obvious as the impotence of competing private individuals. Again, competing private individuals are compelled to sell their produce at a price equivalent to the full cost of production at the margin of cultivation.[20] The

[20] The meaning of these terms will be familiar to readers of the first essay.

municipality could compete against them by reducing prices to the average cost of production over the whole area of municipal cultivation. The more favorably situated private concerns could only meet this by ceasing to pay rent: the less favorably situated would succumb without remedy. It would be either stalemate or checkmate. Private property would either become barren, or it would yield to the actual cultivator of average ability no better an income than could be obtained more securely in municipal employment. To the mere proprietor it would yield nothing. Eventually the land and industry of the whole town would pass by the spontaneous action of economic forces into the hands of the municipality; and, so far, the problem of socializing industry would be solved.

Private property, by cheapening the laborer to the utmost in order to get the greater surplus out of him, lowers the margin of human cultivation, and so raises the "rent of ability". The most important form of that rent is the profit of industrial management. The gains of a great portrait painter or fashionable physician are must less significant, since these depend entirely on the existence of a very rich class of patrons subject to acute vanity and hypochondriasis. But the industrial organizer is independent of patrons; instead of merely attracting a larger share of the product of industry to himself, he increases the product by his management. The market price of such ability depends upon the relation of the supply to the demand: the more there is of it the cheaper it is: the less, the dearer. Any cause that increases the supply lowers the price. Now it is evident that since a manager must be a man of education and address, it is useless to look ordinarily to the laboring class for a supply of managerial skill. Not one laborer in a million succeeds in raising himself on the shoulders of his fellows by extraordinary gifts, or extraordinary luck, or both. The managers must be drawn from the classes which enjoy education and social culture; and their price, rapidly as it is falling with the spread of education and the consequent growth of the "intellectual proletariat", is still high. It is true that a very able and highly trained manager can now be obtained for about £800 a year, provided his post does not compel him to spend two-thirds of his income on what is called "keeping up his position", instead of on his own gratification.[21] Still, when it is considered that laborers receive less than £50 a year, and that the demand for laborers is necessarily vast in proportion to the demand for able managers—nay, that there is an inverse ratio between them, since the manager's talent is valuable in proportion to the quantity of labor he can organize—it will be admitted that £800 a year represents an immense rent of ability. But if the education and culture which are a practically indispensable part of the equipment of competitors for such posts were enjoyed by millions instead of thousands, that rent would fall considerably. Now the tendency of private property is to keep the masses mere beasts of burden. The tendency of Social Democracy is to educate them—to make men of them. Social Democracy would not long be saddled with the rents of ability which have during the last century made our born captains of industry our masters and tyrants instead of our servants and leaders. It is even conceivable that rent of managerial ability might in course of time become negative,[22] astonishing as that may seem to the many persons who are by this time so hope-

[21] See note 8 to the first essay in this volume.
[22] That is, the manager would receive less for his work than the artisan. Cases in which the profits of the employer are smaller than the wages of the employee are by no means uncommon in certain grades of industry where small traders have occasion to employ skilled workmen.

lessly confused amid existing anomalies, that the proposition that "whosoever of you will be the chiefest,
shall be servant of all" strikes them rather as a Utopian
paradox than as the most obvious and inevitable of
social arrangements. The fall in the rent of ability
will, however, benefit not only the municipality, but
also its remaining private competitors. Nevertheless,
as the prestige of the municipality grows, and as men
see more and more clearly that the future is to it,
able organizers will take lower salaries for municipal
than for private employment; whilst those who can
beat even the municipality at organizing, or who, as
professional men, can deal personally with the public
without the intervention of industrial organization,
will pay the rent of their places of business either
directly to the municipality, or to the private landlord
whose income the municipality will absorb by taxation.
Finally, when rents of ability had reached their ir-
reducible natural level, they could be dealt with by a
progressive Income Tax in the very improbable case
of their proving a serious social inconvenience.

It is not necessary to go further into the economic
detail of the process of the extinction of private property. Much of that process as sketched here may be
anticipated by sections of the proprietary class successively capitulating, as the net closes about their
special interests, on such terms as they may be able
to stand out for before their power is entirely broken.[23]

[23] Such capitulations occur already when the Chancellor
of the Exchequer takes advantage of the fall in the current rate of interest (explained on page 35), to reduce
Consols. This he does by simply threatening to pay off the
stockholders with money freshly borrowed at the current
rate. They, knowing that they could not reinvest the money
on any better terms than the reduced ones offered by the
Chancellor, have to submit. There is no reason why the
municipalities should not secure the same advantage for

We may also safely neglect for the moment the
question of the development of the House of Commons
into the central government which will be the organ
for federating the municipalities, and nationalizing
inter-municipal rents by an adjustment of the municipal contributions to imperial taxation: in short, for dis-
charging national as distinct from local business. One
can see that the Local Government Board of the future
will be a tremendous affair; that foreign States will
be deeply affected by the reaction of English progress;
that international trade, always the really dominant
factor in foreign policy, will have to be reconsidered
from a new point of view when profit comes to be calculated in terms of net social welfare instead of individual pecuniary gain; that our present system of imperial
aggression, in which, under pretext of exploration and
colonization, the flag follows the filibuster and trade
follows the flag, with the missionary bringing up the
rear, must collapse when the control of our military
forces passes from the capitalist class to the people; that
the disappearance of a variety of classes with a variety
of what are now ridiculously called "public opinions"
will be accompanied by the welding of society into
one class with a public opinion of inconceivable

---

their constituents. For example, the inhabitants of London
now pay the shareholders of the gas companies a million
and a half annually, or 11 per cent. in the £13,650,000
which the gas works cost. The London County Council
could raise that sum for about £400,000 a year. By threatening to do this and start municipal gas works, it could
obviously compel the shareholders to hand over their
works for £400,000 a year, and sacrifice the extra 8 per
cent. now enjoyed by them. The saving to the citizens
of London would be £1,100,000 a year, sufficient to defray
the net cost of the London School Board. Metropolitan
readers will find a number of cognate instances in Fabian
Tract No. 8. "Facts for Londoners".

weight; that this public opinion will make it for the first time possible effectively to control the population; that the economic independence of women, and the supplanting of the head of the household by the individual as the recognized unit of the State, will materially alter the status of children and the utility of the institution of the family; and that the inevitable reconstitution of the State Church on a democratic basis may, for example, open up the possibility of the election of an avowed Freethinker like Mr. John Morley or Mr. Bradlaugh to the deanery of West-minster. All these things are mentioned only for the sake of a glimpse of the fertile fields of thought and action which await us when the settlement of our bread and butter question leaves us free to use and develop our higher faculties.

This, then, is the humdrum programme of the practical Social Democrat to-day. There is not one new item in it. All are applications of principles already admitted, and extensions of practices already in full activity. All have on them that stamp of the vestry which is so congenial to the British mind. None of them compel the use of the words Socialism or Revolution: at no point do they involve guillotin-ing, declaring the Rights of Man, swearing on the altar of the country, or anything else that is supposed to be essentially un-English. And they are all sure to come—landmarks on our course already visible to far-sighted politicians even of the party which dreads them.

Let me, in conclusion, disavow all admiration for this inevitable, but sordid, slow, reluctant, cowardly path to justice. I venture to claim your respect for those enthusiasts who still refuse to believe that mil-lions of their fellow creatures must be left to sweat and suffer in hopeless toil and degradation, whilst parlia-ments and vestries grudgingly muddle and grope towards paltry instalments of betterment. The right is so clear, the wrong so intolerable, the gospel so convincing, that it seems to them that it *must* be possible to enlist the whole body of workers—soldiers, policemen, and all—under the banner of brotherhood and equality; and at one great stroke to set Justice on her rightful throne. Unfortunately, such an army of light is no more to be gathered from the human product of nineteenth century civilization than grapes are to be gathered from thistles. But if we feel glad of that impossibility; if we feel relieved that the change is to be slow enough to avert personal risk to ourselves; if we feel anything less than acute disappointment and bitter humiliation at the discovery that there is yet between us and the promised land a wilderness in which many must perish miserably of want and despair: then I submit to you that our institutions have corrupted us to the most dastardly degree of selfishness. The Socialists need not be ashamed of beginning as they did by proposing militant organization of the working classes and general insurrection. The proposal proved impracticable; and it has now been abandoned—not without some outspoken regrets—by English Socialists. But it still remains as the only finally possible alternative to the Social Democratic programme which I have sketched to-day.

# 8. THE OUTLOOK

## By Hubert Bland

Mr. Webb's historical review brought us from the "break up of the old synthesis" (his own phrase), a social system founded on a basis of religion, a common belief in a divine order, to the point where perplexed politicians, recognising the futility of the principle of Individualism to keep the industrial machine in working order, with "freedom of contract" upon their lips spent their nights in passing Factory Acts, and devoted their fiscal ingenuity to cutting slice after slice off incomes derived from rent and interest. His paper was an inductive demonstration of the failure of anarchy to meet the needs of real concrete men and women—a proof from history that the world moves from system, through disorder, back again to system.

Mr. Clarke showed us, also by the historic method, that given a few more years of economic progress on present lines, and we shall reach, *via* the Ring and the Trust, that period of "well defined confrontation of rich and poor" upon which German thought has settled as the brief stage of sociological evolution immediately preceding organic change.

The truth of this postulate of Teutonic philosophers and economists no one who has given to it a moment's serious thought is likely to call in question. Nor does anyone who has followed the argument developed in these lectures believe that the transition from

mitigated individualism to full collectivity can be
made until the capitalist system has worked itself out
to its last logical expression. Till then, no political or
social upheaval, however violent, nay, even though
the "physical force revolutionists" should chase the
Guards helter-skelter down Parliament Street and the
Executive Committee of the Fabian Society hold its
meetings in the Council Chamber of Windsor Castle,
will be anything more than one of those "transient
riots", spoken of by Mrs. Besant, which "merely upset
thrones and behead monarchs".[1] All sociologists I
think, all Socialists I am sure, are agreed that until
the economic moment has arrived, although the
hungry or the ignorant may kick up a dust in White-
chapel and make a bloodly puddle in Trafalgar Square,
the Social Revolution is impossible. But I, for my
part, do not believe in the even temporary rout of the
Household Brigade, nor indeed in any popular outbreak not easily suppressible by the Metropolitan
police; and I shall waste no time in discussing that
solution of the social problem of which more was
heard in the salad days of the English Socialist movement—in its pre-Fabian era—than now, *viz.*, physical
force employed by a vigorous few. The physical force
man, like the privileged Tory, has failed to take
note of the flux of things, and to recognise the change
brought about by the ballot. Under a lodger franchise
the barricade is the last resort of a small and desperate
minority, a frank confession of despair, a reduction to
absurdity of the whole Socialist case. Revolutionary
heroics, natural and unblameable enough in exuberant
puerility, are imbecile babblement in muscular adoles-
cence, and in manhood would be criminal folly.

Let us assume then that the present economic
progress will continue on its present lines. That ma-

[1] It is to the half conscious recognition of this generalisa-
tion that the disappearance of militant Republicanism
among the English working classes is owing.

chinery will go on replacing hand labor; that the joint stock company will absorb the private firm, to be, in its turn, swallowed up in the Ring and the Trust. That thus the smaller producers and distributors will gradually, but at a constantly increasing pace, be squeezed out and reduced to the condition of employees of great industrial and trade corporations, managed by highly skilled captains of industry, in the interests of idle shareholders.

In a parliamentarian State like ours, the economic cleavage, which divides the proprietors from the propertyless, ever growing wider and more clearly defined, must have its analogue in the world of politics. The revolution of the last century, which ended in the installation of the Grand Industry, was the last of the great unconscious world changes. It was helped by legislation of course; but the help was only of the negative and destructive sort. "Break our fetters and let us alone", was the cry of the revolutionists to Parliament. The law-makers, not knowing quite what they were doing, responded, and then blithely contracted debts, and voted money for commercial wars. Such a sight will never be seen again. The repeated extension of the suffrage has done more than make the industrial masses articulate, it has given them consciousness; and for the future the echo of the voices of those who suffer from economic changes will be heard clamoring for relief within the walls of St. Stephen's and the urban guildhalls.

Thus the coming struggle between "haves" and "have nots" will be a conflict of parties each perfectly conscious of what it is fighting about and fully alive to the life and death importance of the issues at stake.

I say "will be"; for one has only to read a few speeches of political leaders or attend a discussion at a workman's club to be convinced that at present it is only the keener and more alert minds on either side which are more than semi-conscious of the true nature of the campaign of which the first shots may even now be heard at every bye-election.

But as nothing makes one so entirely aware of one's own existence as a sharp spasm of pain; so it is to the suffering—the hunger, the despair of to-morrow's dinner, the anxiety about the next new pair of trousers —wrought by the increasing economic pressure upon the enfranchised and educated proletariat that we must look to awaken that free self-consciousness which will give the economic changes political expression, and enable the worker to make practical use of the political weapons which are his.

The outlook then from the point of view of this paper is a political one—one in which we should expect to see the world political gradually becoming a reflex of the world economic. That political should be slow in coming into line with economic facts is only in accordance with all that the past history of our country has to teach us. For years and decades the squirearchy retained an influence in the House of Commons out of all proportion to its potency as an economic force; and even at this moment the "landed interest" bears a much larger part in law-making than that to which its real importance entitles it. Therefore we must be neither surprised nor dispirited if, in a cold-blooded envisagement of the condition of English parties, the truth is borne in upon us that the pace of political progress has no proper relation to the rate at which we are travelling towards Socialism in the spheres of thought and industry.

This fact is probably—nay almost certainly—very much more patent to the Socialist and the political student than to the man in the street, or even to him of the first class railway carriage. The noisy jubilation of the Radical press over the victory of a Home Ruler at a bye-election, at a brief and vague reference to the "homes of the people" in a two hours' speech from a Liberal leader, or at the insertion of a "social" plank in a new annual programme, is well and cleverly calculated to beguile the ardent democrat, and strike cold terror to the heart of the timorous Tory. But a perfectly impartial analysis of the present state of parties will convince the most sanguine that the breath of the great economic changes dealt with in Mr. Clarke's paper has as yet scarcely ruffled the surface of the House of Commons.

When the syllabus of this course of lectures was drawn up, those who were responsible for it suggested as the first subheading of this paper, the well worn phrase, "The disappearance of the Whig". It is a happy expression, and one from the contemplation of which much comfort may be derived by an optimistic and unanalytical temperament. Printed are at this disadvantage compared with spoken words, they fail to convey the nicer *nuances* of meaning bestowed by tone and emphasis; and thus the word "disappearance" meets the eye, carrying with it no slightest suggestion of irony. Yet the phrase is pointless, if not "meant surcarstic"; for so far is the Whig from "disappearing", that he is the great political fact of the day. To persons deafened by the daily democratic shouting of the Radical newspapers this assertion may require some confirmation and support. Let us look at the facts then. The first thing which strikes us in connexion with the present Parliament is that it no longer consists of two distinct parties, *i.e.*, of two bodies of men differentiated from each other by the holding of *fundamentally* different principles. Home Rule left out,[2] there remains no

[2] The difference of principle here is more apparent than real. The Gladstonians repudiate any desire for separation, and affirm their intention of maintaining the absolute veto of the imperial Parliament; while the Unionists avow their ultimate intention of giving to Ireland the same powers of self government now enjoyed, or to be enjoyed by England and Scotland.

reason whatever, except the quite minor question
of Disestablishment, why even the simulacrum of
party organisation should be maintained, or why the
structural arrangements of the House of Commons
should not be so altered as to resemble those of a
town hall, in which all the seats face the chair.

But fifty years ago the floor of the House was a
frontier of genuine significance; and the titles "Whig"
and "Tory" were word-symbols of real inward and
spiritual facts. The Tory party was mostly made up of
men who were conscientiously opposed to popular representation, and prepared to stand or fall by their opposition. They held, as a living political creed, that the
government of men was the eternal heritage of the rich,
and especially of those whose riches spelt rent. The
Whigs, on the other hand, believed, or said they believed, in the aphorism "*Vox populi, vox Dei*"; and
they, on the whole, consistently advocated measures
designed to give that voice a distincter and louder
utterance. Here, then, was one of those fundamental
differences in the absence of which party nomencla-
ture is a sham. But there was another. In the first
half of this century the Tories, hidebound in historic
traditions and deaf to the knell of the old *régime*
tolling in the thud, thud, of the piston rods of the
new steam engines, clung pathetically to the old ideas
of the functions of the State and to territorial rights.
The Whigs went for *laisser faire* and the consequent
supremacy of the business man. I am making a perfectly provable proposition when I say that all the
political disputes [3] which arose between the Revolution of 1688 and the enfranchisement of the £10
householder by Disraeli had their common cause in
one of these two root differences. But the battle has
long ago been lost and won. The Whigs have tri-

[3] The battles for Catholic Emancipation and the removal
of the religious disabilities were fought on sectarian rather
than on political grounds.

umphed all along the line. The Tories have not only
been beaten, they have been absorbed. A process has
gone on like that described by Macaulay as following
on the Norman invasion, when men gradually ceased
to call themselves Saxon and Norman and proudly
boasted of being English. The difference in the case
before us is that while the Tories have accepted the
whole of the Whig principles they still abjure the
Whig name.

No so-called Conservative to-day will venture on
opposing an extension of the Franchise on the plain
ground of principle. At most he will but temporise
and plead for delay. No blush of conscious inconsistency suffused Mr. Ritchie's swarthy features when
introducing his "frankly democratic" Local Government Bill. And rightly not; for he was doing no
violence to party principles.

In the matter of the functions of the State the
absorption of the Tory is not quite so obvious, because
there never has been, and, as long as Society lasts,
never can be, a *parti serieux* of logical *laisser faire*.
Even in the thick of the Industrial Revolution the
difference between the two great parties was mainly
one of tendency—of attitude of mind. The Tory had
a certain affection for the State—a natural self-love:
the Whig distrusted it. This distrust is now the sentiment of the whole of our public men. They see, some
of them perhaps more clearly than others, that there
is much the State must do; but they all wish that
much to be as little as possible. Even when, driven
by an irresistible force which they feel but do not
understand (which none but the Socialist does or
can understand), they bring forward measures for
increasing the power of the whole over the part,
their arguments are always suffused in a sickly halo
of apology: their gestures are always those of timorous deprecation and fretful diffidence. They are
always nervously anxious to explain that the proposal

violates no principle of political economy, and with them political economy means, not Professor Sidgwick, but Adam Smith.

The reason why this unanimity of all prominent politicians on great fundamental principles is not manifest to the mind of the average man is that, although there is nothing left to get hot or even moderately warm about, the political temperature is as high as ever. It is not in the dust of the arena, but only in the repose of the auditorium that one is able to realise that men will fight as fiercely and clapper-claw each other as spitefully over a dry bone as over a living principle. One has to stand aside awhile to see that politicians are like the theological controversialists of whom Professor Seeley somewhere says that they never get so angry with each other as when their differences are almost imperceptible, except perhaps when they are quite so.

Both the efficient and the final cause of this unanimity is a sort of unconscious or semi-conscious recognition of the fact that the word "State" has taken to itself new and diverse connotations—that the State idea has changed its content. Whatever State control may have meant fifty years ago it never meant hostility to private property as such. Now, for us, and for as far ahead as we can see, it means that and little else. So long as the State interfered with the private property and powers of one set of proprietors with a view only to increasing those of another, the existence of parties for and against such interference was a necessity of the case. A duty on foreign corn meant the keeping up of incomes drawn from rent [4]: its abolition meant a rise of manufacturers' profits. "Free Trade" swelled the purses of the new *bourgeoisie:*

[4] This is perhaps not, historically, quite true; but the landlords believed that their own prosperity depended upon the exclusion of foreign corn, and that is sufficient for the purpose of my argument.

the Factory Acts depleted them, and gave a sweet revenge to the rent-docked squire. But of this manipulation of the legislative machine for proprietors' purposes we are at, or at least in sight of, the end. The State has grown bigger by an immense aggregation of units, who were once to all intents and purposes separate from it; and now its action generally points not to a readjustment of private property and privileges as between class and class, but to their complete disappearance. So then the instinct which is welding together the propertied politicians is truly self-preservative.

But, it may be asked by the bewildered Radical, by the tremulous Conservative, by the optimistic Socialist, if the political leaders are really opposed to State augmentation, how comes it that every new measure of reform introduced into the House of Commons is more or less colored with Socialism, and that no popular speaker will venture to address a public meeting without making some reference of a socialistic sort to the social problem? Why, for instance, does that extremely well oiled and accurately poised political weathercock, Sir William Harcourt, pointing to the dawn, crow out that "we are all Socialists now"?

To these questions (and I have not invented them) I answer: in the first place because the opposition of the political leaders *is* instinctive, and only, as yet, semi-conscious, even in the most hypocritical; in the second place, that a good deal of the legislative Socialism appears more in words than in deeds; in the third place that the famous flourish of Sir William Harcourt was a rhetorical falsehood; and fourthly, because, fortunately for the progress of mankind, self-preservative instincts are not peculiar to the propertied classes.

For it is largely instinctive and wholly self preservative, this change in the position of the working people towards the State—this change by which, from fearing it as an actual enemy, they have come to look to it as a potential savior. I know that this assertion will be violently denied by many of my Socialist brethren. The fly on the wheel, not unnaturally, feels wounded at being told that he is, after all, not the motive power; and the igniferous orators of the Socialist party are welcome, so far as I am concerned, to all the comfort they can get from imagining that they, and not any great, blind, evolutionary forces are the dynamic of the social revolution. Besides, the metaphor of the fly really does not run on all fours (I forget, for the moment, how many legs a fly has); for the Socialist does at least know in what direction the car is going, even though he is not the driving force. Yet it seems to me that the part being, and to be, played by the Socialist, is notable enough in all conscience; for it is he who is turning instinct into self conscious reason; voicing a dumb demand; and giving intelligent direction to a thought wave of terrific potency.

There is a true cleavage being slowly driven through the body politic; but the wedge is still beneath the surface. The signs of its workings are to be found in the reactionary measures of pseudo reform advocated by many prominent politicians; in the really Socialist proposals of some of the obscurer men; in the growing distaste of the political club man for a purely political pabulum; and in the receptive attitude of a certain portion of the cultivated middle class towards the outpourings of the Fabian Society.

This conscious recognition of the meaning of modern tendencies, this defining of the new line of cleavage, while it is the well-spring of most of the Socialist hopes, is no less the source of some lively fear. At present it is only the acuter and more far seeing of the minds amongst the propertied classes who are at all alive to the real nature of the attack. One has but to listen to the chatter of the average Liberal candidate to note how hopelessly blind the man is to the fact that the existence of private property in the means of production forms any factor at all in the social problem; and what is true of the rank and file is true only in a less degree of the chiefs themselves. Ignorance of economics and inability to shake their minds free of eighteenth century political philosophy [5] at present hinders the leaders of the "party of progress" from taking up a definite position either for or against the advance of the new ideas. The number of English statesmen who, like Prince Bismarck, see in Socialism a swelling tide whose oceanic rush must be broken by timely legislative breakwaters, is still only to be expressed by a minus quantity. But this political myopia is not destined to endure. Every additional vote cast for avowed Socialist candidates at municipal and other elections will help to bring home to the minds of the Liberals that the section of the new democracy which regards the ballot merely as a war-engine with which to attack capitalism is a growing one. At last our Liberal will be face to face with a logical but irritating choice. Either to throw over private capital or to frankly acknowledge that it is a distinction without a difference which separates him from the Conservatives against whom he has for years been fulminating.

At first sight it looks as though this political moment in the history of the Liberal party would be one eminently auspicious for the Socialist cause. But although I have a lively faith in the victory of logic in the long run, I have an equally vivid knowledge that to assure the triumph the run must be a very long one; and above all I have profound respect for the staying powers of politicians, and their ability to play a waiting game. It is one thing to offer a statesman the choice of one of two logical courses: it is another to prevent his seeing a third, and an illogical

[5] *Cf.* The speeches of Mr. John Morley on the eight hours' proposal and the taxation of ground rents. Also the recent writings of Mr. Bradlaugh, *passim.*

one, and going for it. Such prevention in the present
case will be so difficult as to be well nigh impossible;
for the Liberal hand still holds a strong suit—the
cards political.

It is quite certain that the social programme of
our party will become a great fact long before all the
purely political proposals of the Liberals have received
the Royal assent; and the game of the politician will
be to hinder the adoption of the former by noisily
hustling forward the latter. Unfortunately for us it
will be an easy enough game to play. The scent of
the non-Socialist politician for political red herrings
is keen, and his appetite for political Dead Sea fruit
prodigious. The number of "blessed words", the mere
sound of which carries content to his soul, would fill
a whole page. In an age of self-seeking his pathetic
self-abnegation would be refreshing were it not so
desperately silly. The young artizan on five-and-twenty
shillings a week, who with his wife and children
occupies two rooms in "a model", and who is about
as likely to become a Lama as a leaseholder, will shout
himself hoarse over Leaseholds' Enfranchisement, and
sweat great drops of indignation at the plunder of rich
West End tradesmen by rich West End landlords. The
"out of work", whose last shirt is in pawn, will risk
his skull's integrity in Trafalgar Square in defence of
Mr. O'Brien's claim to dress in gaol like a gentleman.

Of course all this is very touching: indeed, to be
quite serious, it indicates a nobility of character and
breadth of human sympathy in which lies our hope
of social salvation. But its infinite potentiality must not
blind us to the fact that in its actuality the dodgy
Liberal will see his chance of the indefinite postpone-
ment of the socializing of politics. Manhood suffrage,
Female suffrage, the woes of deceased wives' sisters,
the social ambition of dissenting ministers, the legal
obstacles to the "free" acquirement of landed property,
home rule for "dear old Scotland" and "neglected little

Wales," extra-ordinary tithes, reform of the House of
Lords: all these and any number of other obstacles
may be successfully thrown in the way of the forward
march of the Socialist army. And the worst of it all
is that in a great part of his obstructive tactics the
Liberal will have us on the hip; for to out-and-out
democratization we are fully pledged, and must needs
back up any attack on hereditary or class privilege,
come it from what quarter it may.

But, to get back to our metaphor of the card table
(a metaphor much more applicable to the games of
political men), the political suit does not exhaust
the Liberal hand. There still remains a card to play—
a veritable trump. Sham Socialism is the name of it,
and Mr. John Morley the man to plank it down.

I have said above that the trend of things to Socialism
is best shewn by the changed attitude of men towards
State interference and control; and this is true. Still
it must not be forgotten that although Socialism involves State control, State control does not imply
Socialism—at least in any modern meaning of the term.
It is not so much to the thing the State does, as to
the end for which it does it that we must look before
we can decide whether it is a Socialist State or not.
Socialism is the common holding of the means of
production and exchange, and *the holding of them for
the equal benefit of all.* In view of the tone now
being adopted by some of us [6] I cannot too strongly
insist upon the importance of this distinction; for the
losing sight of it by friends, and its intentional ob-
scuration by enemies, constitute a big and immediate
danger. To bring forward sixpenny telegrams as an
instance of State Socialism may be a very good method
of scoring a point off an individualist opponent in a

[6] One of the most indefatigable and prolific members of
the Socialist party, in a widely circulated tract, has actually adduced the existence of *hawkers' licenses* as an
instance of the "Progress of Socialism"!

debate before a middle-class audience; but from the
standpoint of the proletariat a piece of State management which spares the pockets only of the commercial
and leisured classes is no more Socialism than were
the *droits de Seigneur* of the middle ages. Yet this
is the sort of sham Socialism which it is as certain
as death will be doled out by the popular party in the
hope that mere State action will be mistaken for really
Socialist legislation. And the object of these givers
of Greek gifts will most infallibly be attained if those
Socialists who know what they want hesitate (from
fear of losing popularity, or from any more amiable
weakness) to clamor their loudest against any and
every proposal whose adoption would prolong the
life of private Capital a single hour.

But leaving sham Socialism altogether out of
account, there are other planks in the Liberal "and
Radical" programme which would make stubborn
barriers in the paths of the destroyers of private
capital. Should, for instance, Church disestablishment
come upon us while the *personnel* of the House of
Commons is at all like what it is at present, few
things are more certain than that a good deal of what
is now essentially collective property will pass into
private hands; that the number of individuals interested in upholding ownership will be increased; and
that the only feelings gratified will be the acquisitive-
ness of these persons and the envy of Little Bethel.

Again, the general state of mind of the Radical on
the land question is hardly such as to make a Socialist
hilarious. It is true your "progressive" will cheer Henry
George, and is sympathetically inclined to nationalization (itself a "blessed word"); but he is not at all
sure that nationalization, free land, and peasant proprietorship, are not three names for one and the
same proposal. And, so far as the effective members
of the Liberal party are concerned, there is no question
at all that the second and third of these "solutions"

find much more favor than the first. In fact, in this matter of the land, the method of dealing with which is of the very propædeutics of Socialism, the Radical who goes for "free sale" or for peasant ownership, is a less potent revolutionary force than the Tory himself; for this latter only seeks to maintain in land the state of things which the Ring and Trust maker is working to bring about in capital [7]—and on the part which *he* is playing in economic evolution we are all agreed.

From such dangers as these the progress of democracy is, by itself, powerless to save us; for although always and everywhere democracy holds Socialism in its womb, the birth may be indefinitely delayed by stupidity on one side and acuteness on the other.

I have gone at some length into an analysis of the possible artificial hindrances to Socialism, because, owing to the amiability and politeness shown us by the Radical left wing during the last twelve months; to the successes which Radical votes have given to some of our candidates at School Board and other elections; and to the friendly patronage bestowed upon us by certain "advanced" journals, some of our brightest, and otherwise most clear-sighted, spirits have begun to base high hopes upon what they call "the permeation" of the Liberal party. These of our brothers have a way of telling us that the transition to Socialism will be so gradual as to be imperceptible, and that there will never come a day when we shall be able to say "now we have a Socialist State". They are fond of likening the simpler among us who disagree with them as to the extreme protraction of the process, to children who having been told that when it rains a cloud falls, look disappointedly out of the window on a wet day, unconscious that the cloud is falling before

[7] It is worth noting that those organs of the press which are devoted more particularly to the landed interest have been the first to hint at the probable desirability of dealing with great *industrial* monopolies by means of legislation.

their eyes in the shape of drops of water. To these cautious souls I reply that although there is much truth in their contention that the process will be gradual, we shall be able to say that we have a Socialist State on the day on which no man or group of men holds, over the means of production, property rights by which the labor of the producers can be subjected to exploitation; and that while their picturesque metaphor is a happy as well as a poetic conceit, it depends upon the political acumen of the present and next generation of Socialist men whether the "cloud" shall fall in refreshing Socialist showers or in a dreary drizzle of Radicalism, bringing with it more smuts than water, fouling everything and cleansing nowhere.

This permeation of the Radical Left, undoubted fact though it is of present day politics, is worth a little further attention; for there are two possible and tenable views as to its final outcome. One is that it will end in the slow absorption of the Socialist in the Liberal party, and that by the action of this sponge-like organism the whole of the Rent and Interest will pass into collective control without there ever having been a party definitely and openly pledged to that end. According to this theory there will come a time, and that shortly, when the avowed Socialists and the much socialized Radicals will be strong enough to hold the balance in many constituencies, and sufficiently powerful in all to drive the advanced candidate many pegs further than his own inclination would take him. Then, either by abstention or by actual support of the reactionary champion at elections, they will be able to threaten the Liberals with certain defeat. The Liberals, being traditionally squeezable folk (like all absorbent bodies), will thus be forced to make concessions and to offer compromises; and will either adopt a certain minimum number of the Socialistic proposals, or allow to Socialists a share in the representation itself. Such concessions and compromises will grow in number and importance with each successive appeal to the electorate, until at last the game is won.

Now it seems to me that these hopefuls allow their desires to distort their reason. The personal equation plays too large a part in the prophecy. They are generally either not yet wholly socialized Radicals or Socialists who have quite recently broken away from mere political Radicalism and are still largely under the influence of party ties and traditions. They find it almost impossible to believe that the party with which they acted so long, so conscientiously, and with so much satisfaction to themselves, is, after all, not the party to which belongs the future. They are in many cases on terms of intimate private friendship with some of the lesser lights of Radicalism, and occasionally bask in the patronizing radiance shed by the larger luminaries. A certain portion of the "advanced" press is open to them for the expression of their views political. Of course none of these considerations are at all to their discredit, or reflect in the very least upon their motives or sincerity; but they do color their judgment and cause them to reckon without their host. They are a little apt to forget that a good deal of the democratic programme has yet (as I have said above) to be carried. Manhood suffrage, the abolition of the Lords, disestablishment, the payment of members: all these may be, and are, quite logically desired by men who cling as pertinaciously to private capital as the doughtiest knight of the Primrose League. Such men regard the vital articles of the Socialist creed as lying altogether outside the concrete world—"the sphere of practical politics". Meanwhile the Socialist votes and voices are well within that sphere; and it is every day becoming more evident that without them the above-mentioned aspirations have a meagre chance of realization. Now, from the eminently business-like Liberal standpoint there is no reason whatever why concessions should not be made to the Socialist at the polling booth so long as none are asked for in the House of Commons. And even when they are demanded, what easier than to make some burning political question play the part which Home Rule is playing now? Thus an endless vista of office opens before the glowing eyes of the practical politician—those short-sighted eyes which see so little beyond the nose, and which, at that distance only, enable their owner to hit the white.

The Radical is right as usual in counting on the Socialist alliance up to a certain point. For us the complete democratization of institutions is a political necessity. But long before that complete democratization has been brought about we shall have lost our patience and the Radicals their temper.

For as Mr. Hyndman tells the world with damnable (but most veracious) iteration, we are "a growing party." We recruit by driblets; but we do recruit; and those who come to us come, like all the new American newspapers, "to stay." Our *faith*, our reason, our knowledge, tell us that the great evolutionary forces are with us; and every addition to our ranks causes us, in geometrical proportion, to be less and less tolerant of political prevarication. Directly we feel ourselves strong enough to have the slightest chance of winning off our own bat we shall be compelled both by principle and inclination to send an eleven to the wickets. They will have to face the opposition, united or disunited, of both the orthodox parties, as did the defeated Socialist candidates at the School Board election in November, 1888. And whether our success be great or small, or even non-existent, we shall be denounced by the Radical wire-pullers and the now so complaisant and courteous Radical press. The alliance will be at an end.

There is yet another way in which we may win the ill-will of our temporary allies and, at present, very good friends. I have spoken above of certain reactionary items of a possible Radical programme, which, although they have a grotesque resemblance to Socialism, are worlds away from being the thing itself. These proposals we not only cannot support, but must and shall actively and fiercely oppose. At the first signs of such opposition to whoever may be the Liberal shepherd of the moment the whole flock of party sheep will be in full cry upon our track. The ferocity of the *mouton enragé* is proverbial; and we shall be treated to the same rancour, spleen, and bile which is now so plenteously meted out to the Liberal Unionists.

The immediate result of this inevitable split will be the formation of a definitely Socialist party, *i.e.*, a party pledged to the communalization of all the means of production and exchange, and prepared to subordinate every other consideration to that one end. Then the House of Commons will begin dimly to reflect the real condition of the nation outside; and in it we shall see as in a glass, darkly, or smudgedly, something of that "well defined confrontation of rich and poor", of which all who attend Socialist lectures hear so much, and to which, *ex hypothesi*, the world, day by day, draws nearer. Then, also, will begin that process which, I submit, is more likely than either the absorption of the Socialist or the prolonged permeation of the Radical: namely, the absorption of the Radical himself into the definitely pro-private capital party on the one side, and the definitely anti-private capital party on the other.

A really homogeneous Socialist party once formed, the world political reflects the world economic, and there is no longer any room for the Radical, as we know the wonder. Each fresh Socialist victory, each outpost driven in, each entrenchment carried, will be followed by a warren-like scuttle of alarmed and well-to-do Radicals across the floor of the House of Commons, which will once more become a true frontier; and, finally, the political battle array will consist of a small opposition, fronting a great and powerful majority, made up of all those whose real or fancied interests would suffer from expropriation.

Thus far the outlook has been clear and focusable enough; and it has needed no extra-human illumination to see the details. All that has been wanted has been normal vision and a mind fairly free of the idols of the cave. But here the prospect becomes dim and uncertain; and little purpose would be served by trying to pierce the mist which enshrouds the distant future.

Much, very much, will depend upon the courage, the magnanimity, the steadfastness, the tact, the foresight, and above all upon the incorruptibility of those whose high mission it will be to frame the policy and direct the strategy of the Socialist party in those early days of its parliamentary life. It will have sore need of a leader as able as, and more conscientious than, any of the great parliamentary figures of the past. The eye expectant searches in vain for such a man now among the younger broods of the new democracy. He is probably at this moment in his cradle or equitably sharing out toys or lollipops to his comrades of the nursery. And this is well; for he must be a man quit of all recollections of these days of *Sturm und Drang*, of petty jealousies, constant errors, and failing faith. He must bring to his task a record free from failure and without suspicion of stain.

But whatever may be the difficulties in store for us who name the name of Socialism, of one thing at least they who have followed this course of lectures may make quite sure. That, however long and wearisome the struggle, each day brings us nearer victory. Those who resist Socialism fight against principalities and powers in economic places. Every new industrial development will add point to our arguments and soldiers to our ranks. The continuous perfectioning of the organisation of labour will hourly quicken in the worker the consciousness that his is a collective, not an individual life. The proletariat is even now the only real class: its units are the only human beings who have nothing to hope for save from the levelling up of the aggregate of which they form a part. The intensifying of the struggle for existence, while it sets *bourgeois* at the throat of *bourgeois,* is forcing union and solidarity upon the workers. And the *bourgeois* ranks themselves are dwindling. The keenness of competition, making it every year more obviously impossible for those who are born without capital ever to achieve it, will deprive the capitalist class of the support it now receives from educated and cultivated but impecunious young men whose material interest must finally triumph over their class sympathies; and from that section of workmen whose sole aspiration is to struggle out of the crowd. The rising generation of wage workers, instead of as now being befogged and bedevilled by the dust and smoke of mere faction fight, will be able at a glance to distinguish the uniforms of friend and foe. Despair will take sides with Hope in doing battle for the Socialist cause.

These lectures have made it plain enough to those who have hearing ears and understanding brains that mere material self-interest alone will furnish a motive strong enough to shatter monopoly; and after monopoly comes Socialism or—chaos. But the interest of the smaller self is not the only force which aids us in the present, or will guide us in the future. The angels are on our side. The constant presence of a vast mass of human misery is generating in the educated classes a deep discontent, a spiritual unrest, which drives the lower types to pessimism, the higher to enquiry. Pessimism paralyses the arms and unnerves the hearts of those who would be against us. Enquiry proves that Socialism is founded upon a triple rock, historical, ethical, and economic. It gives, to those who make it, a great hope—a hope which, once it finds entrance into the heart of man, stays to soften life and sweeten death. By the light of the Socialist Ideal he sees the evil—yet sees it pass. Then and now he begins to live in the cleaner, braver, holier life of the future; and he marches forward, steeled and stimulated, with resolute step, with steadfast eye, with equal pulse.

It is just when the storm winds blow and the clouds lour and the horizon is at its blackest that the ideal of the Socialist shines with divinest radiance, bidding him trust the inspiration of the poet rather than heed the mutterings of the perplexed politician, bidding him believe that

> "For a' that, for a' that,
> It's coming yet for a' that,
> That man to man the world o'er
> Shall brothers be for a' that."

# INDEX

Absentee Proprietors, 41
Abstinence, Reward of, 35
Abstract method in Economics, 40
Administrative Errors, 60
"Administrative Nihilism," 61
Adulteration Acts, 65
Aged, Treatment of the, 204
Agriculture and Machinery, 92
Aladdin's uncle outdone, 25
Aliens, Necessity under Socialism for a law of, 172
Althorp, Lord, 100
America (See United States)
American Independence, Declaration of, 89
Anarchists, Modern, 216
Anarchy preferred to corrupt State regulation by progressive thinkers, 215
Andrews, E. Benjamin, on Trusts, 120
Angels, constitution and status of, 150
    Condition of their imitation on earth, 152
Argyle, Duke of, 174
Aristotle, 217
Arkwright's inventions, 54, 88
Aristocratic employments, 151
Ashley, Lord (See Lord Shaftesbury)
Associated Capitals, Competitive force of, 195
Associations, Legal position under Socialism of voluntary, 171
Austin, John, 62, 166, 223
Autobiography of John Stuart Mill, 76, 80
Aveling, Rev. F. W., 80

Balfour, Rt. Hon. A. J., 147
Barbarous Countries, Exploitation of, 106-7
Bastille, Fall of the, 55-6, 89
Bebel, August, 165
Bedford, Duke of, 174
Bellamy, E. (author of "Looking Backwards"), 198
Benefit Association, Sheep and Lamb Butchers' Mutual, 125
Benevolence and Omnipotence, The dilemma between, 43
Bentham, Jeremy, 51, 62, 63, 81, 223
Bequest, 168
Berkeley, Bishop, 63
Besant, Annie, 187
    Walter: His belated chivalry, 150
Bimetallism suggested as a solution of the social problem, 234

Birmingham, 71
    Compared with Warwick, 170
Bismarck, Socialism and Prince, 257
Blanc, Louis, His Definition of Communism, 180
Bland, Hubert, 77, 247
Bloodshed: How to argue with its advocates, 244-5
Bonanza farms, 92
Bourgeoisie, The Factory Acts and the, 254
    Free Trade and the, 254
Bradford, 71
Bradlaugh, Charles, 244
Bramwell, Lord, 49, 236
Bright, John, 101, 113
Brittany, Standard of comfort in, 170
    Peasants of, 183
British Association, 213
    Mind, The Vestry stamp upon the, 247
Bryce, James, 112
Brook Farm, 48
Browning, Robert, 43
Burns, John, 234
Bunyan, John, 185

Cade, Jack, 217
Cairnes, J. E., on the idle rich, 111
Canada, Conquest of, 89, 102
Canals, Socialization of, 191
Cant. Its source, 20, 144
Capital: Is not machinery, 33-4
    Is the result of saving, 33-4
    Is spare subsistence, 33-4
    Cannot be safely taken by the State except for immediate employment as capital, 231
    Source of municipal capital, 235
    Provision for municipal accumulation, 239
"Capital" (Karl Marx's work), 42, 58
"Capital and Land" (Fabian Tract), 67
Capitals, Competitive force of associated, 194-5
    Unscrupulousness of, 100
    Its idea self-destructive, 152
    Morals of, 100, 147, 152
    Characteristic effects of, 153
    Its origin in piracy and slave-trading, 214
Capitalist: Separation of his function from those of the *entrepreneur*, 110
    Regulation of the, 67
    Type of the, 146

Capitalist combinations and State action, 128
Capitulations by proprietary classes, 243
Career open to the talented, 22
Carlyle, Thomas, 51, 64
Cartwright, Rev. Edmund, Inventions of, 87
Caste (See Class)
Castlereagh, Viscount, 56
Catastrophic Socialism, 187, 224, 245, 248
Catechism, Misquotation of the Church, 152
Catholic Church, Socialism of the, 157
Catholic Emancipation, 56, 252
Centralization of State industries, 194, 243
Chalmers, Rev. Thomas, 62
Charity, 36, 225, 235
"Charter, The People's," 73
Chartism, 73, 228
Cheque Bank: Suggestions as to Communal currency, 204
Children: In Communes, 204
  Effect of Socialism on the status of, 244
"Christian Socialism," 112, 113
Church Catechism, The, 152
Church, The Catholic, 157
Church of England: A mere appanage of the landed gentry, 52
  Effect of property holding on the Democratization of the, 244
"Church Reformer, The," 62
Churches, 20
Churchgoing, Hypocrisies of, 20
Church, Declaration of the Pan-Anglican Synod concerning Socialism and the, 234
Civilization and Societies, 39
Civil Servants: Their reputation for unconscientiousness, 148, 224
"Claims of Labor, The," 59
Clanricarde, Lord, 81
Clarke, William, 48, 84, 187, 247
Class Feeling and Morality, 36, 143, 146, 147, 149-52
Classes, Separation of, 36
Cleavage, Economic, 248
Clive, Robert, 88, 102
Coal mining, Application of machinery to, 199
Coal monopoly in the United States, 112
Cobden Club disconcerted by the appearance of Imports not paid for by Exports, 228
Cobden, Richard, 106, 112
Colonization, Modern, 40, 244

Coleridge, S. T., 63
Combination, 32
  Benefits of, 125-6
Commercial policy of England under Capitalism, 102
Commodities: Exchange of, 24
  Process by which their value is reduced to the cost of production of the most costly unit of the supply, 29, 239
Common Sense, 133, 161
Commune: Its establishment in England already accomplished, 189
Communes, 16
Communism defined, 180
Communities, Savings of, 170
  Debts of, 176
Compensation for expropriated proprietors, 235
Competition: Theory of, 216
  Decline of, 115
  Effect on wages, 236
Comte, Auguste, 47, 48, 51, 228
Comte de Paris, 48
"Condition of the Working Classes" (F. Engel's work), 58
Conduct and Principle, Incompatability set up by Private Property between, 20
Conscience, Social, 188
Conservatives, Present attitude of, 253
Consols: Nature of the operation called "reducing," 243
Consumption, Associated, 166, 181
Contracts restricted in England, 178
Contradictions apparently besetting the investigation of value, 26
Conventions as to Morality, 138-9
Cooking, Public and private, 191
Co-operative Movement: 63, 115, 171, 196
  Socialist origin of the, 112, 234
  Aims of the leaders, 234
Co-operative Experiments, 178
Co-ordination, Social, 81
Copper, The "corner" in, 118
Copyright, 166, 181-2
Corners, 32
Cost of Production: What it means, 29
  Reduction of value to, 29
  On inferior soils, 17
Cotton Manufacture, Progress of the, 96
Cotton-seed Oil Trusts, 124
County Councils, The new, 57, 170, 176, 189, 230, 243

County Council, The London,
243
County Family, Origin of the, 20
County Farms, Organization of,
190
County Government Act (See
County Councils)
Covent Garden Market and the
Duke of Bedford, 174
Crime: Its relativity, 146
Criminal Class: Its formation,
36, 154
Crompton, Samuel, Inventions of,
54
Cultivation of the Earth:, 15
Its beginning, 17
Its "margin," 84
Effect of exploration on the
progress of, 15
Discrepancies between its ac-
tual progress and that de-
duced from abstract econom-
ics, 15
Culture, Effect on profits of in-
dustrial management of the
spread of, 240-1
Currency, Suggestion as to
communal, 204
Cynicism of our time, 20
Routed by Socialism, 44

Dante, 24
Darwin, Charles, 64, 120, 228
"Darwinism and Politics," 77
Darwinian theory appealed by
monopolists, 120
By Socialists, 77
Day, The working, 193
Debt, The National, 176
Debts, Law as to, 172
Of Communities, 174
Decentralization, Necessity for,
229
Definitions of economic rent, 17
Demand, Effective, 37
Supply and, 23
Democracy: Import of, 51, 52,
57, 81, 82, 260
Instability of, 82
Postulated by Socialism, 223
Further steps necessary to
consummate, 229
Democrat, Distinction between
the ordinary and the Social,
223
Democratic Federation (See
S.D.F.)
De Quincey, Thomas, 63
Desire as a social motor, 134,
142
Detailed suggestions for social
organization of unemployed
labor, 190-1
De Tocqueville, A. C. H. C., 49

Devil worship, 43
Diocesan Councils, Central
Conference of, 82
Dirty Work, 198
Discipline in socialized industries,
195
Discovery of new countries, 39
Disestablishment of the Church,
252
Dishonesty a product of
Capitalism, 153
Disingenuousness of class Econo-
mists, 31, 37, 39
Dismal Science now the Hopeful,
44
Dismissal, Power of, 196
Dissolution of the Old Synthesis,
52
Division of labor, 17
Drainage Acts, 64
Drinking Fountains, Communism
exemplified in, 183
Drone and Worker, 18

Earnings distinguished from the
revenue of Private Property,
40
Ecclesiastical intolerance, Reac-
tion against medieval, 216
Economics (See Political
Economy)
Economists (See Political Econo-
mists)
Education: Reform of, 75
Moral, 142
A necessity for morality, 153
Socialist ideal of, 158, 183
Effect on profits of industrial
management, 241
Tendency of Social Democracy
to encourage, 241
Eight Hours, Working day of,
193
Electors, Number of, 57
Elizabethan merchant
adventurers, 215
Emigration, 225
Employer: Differentiated from
Capitalist, 110
And laborer, 188
Not harmed by Socialism, 239
Engels, F., 59
England: Her social policy to-
day, 37
In 1750, 52
Her foreign policy dictated by
Capitalism, 106-7
Her mineral fertility, 225
"English Factory Legislation"
(See also Factory Legisla-
tion), 58
Entrepreneur (See Employer)
Episcopal Conference, 83
Equality of remuneration, 201-3

Index:

Errors (See Mistakes exposed by Socialism)
Ethics: Metaphysic of, 132
  Positive science of, 132
Evolution, Effect of hypothesis of, 43, 77
Exchange of Commodities, 24
  Mechanism of, 26
Exchange Value (See Value), 26
Exploitation, 35

Factories before the Factory Act, 57, 97
Factory Legislation, 58, 64, 100, 172, 225
Factory System: Introduction to the, 53, 86
"Facts for Londoners," 243
"Fair Trade," 129
Family: Effect of Socialism on the, 244
  Isolation of the, 168, 182
  Origin of the County, 20
Farms: Organization of County, 191
  Bonanza, 194
Fawcett, Henry, 18
Federation of Municipalities, 243
Feudalism: Survival of, 52
  Reaction against its domineering, 216
  Feudal dues, 60
Fielden, John, 101
Filibuster, The colonizing, 244
Final Utility, Theory of, 27, 29
Flag, Trade following the, 244
Flats, Living in, 167
Fly-Shuttle, Invention of the, 87
Foreign Investments, Interest on, 228
Foreign Markets, The fight for, 106, 243
Foreign Policy, Effect of Capitalism upon, 103
  Effect of Socialism upon, 243
Foreign Trade following the flag, 243
Forestalling, 31
Fourier, F. C. M., 167
Fox, Charles James, 55
Foxwell, Professor H. S., 59
Free Ferry, The London, 70
"Free Land" and the Radical party, 76, 260
Free Trade Movement, 105-6
  Foreign investments left out of the account by the, 228
  The bourgeoisie and the, 254
Freethinker, Possible election to the Deanery of Westminster of an avowed, 244
French Revolution, 54, 88, 234

Friction caused by introduction of Municipal Socialism, 239
Furse, Canon, 82

Gambling, 16
Gasworks, Socialization of, 69, 190, 243
George III, 103
George, Henry, 133, 174, 218, 228, 231, 233
Georgism, Checkmate to, 233
Giffen, Robert, 228, 234
Gladstone, Right Hon. W. E., 72
  Retrogressive instincts of, 225-6
Glasgow, 70
  Growth of, 54
Godin and Leclaire, Experiments of, 206
Godwin, William, 62
Gold: As money, 26
  Effect of discoveries in California and Australia, 225
Goschen, Right Hon. G. J., 35
Gould, Jay, 100
Government: In 1750, 53
  Industries carried on by, 66
  "Government Organization of Labor," 72
Gradual Socialization, 52
  Compensation a condition of, 236
Greek Republics, 172, 201, 216
Greenock, 70
Gronlund, Laurence, 165, 167, 171
Grote, George, 62
Ground values, Municipalization of, 235
Growth of Towns, 54
Guild of St. Matthew, 62
Guillotining, 244

Habits: Moral, 136
  Automatic, 137
Harbors, Nationalization of, 204
Harcourt, Rt. Hon. Sir W. V.:
  On the teetotal stump, 147
  "We are all Socialists now," 254
Hargreaves, James, The inventions of, 54, 87
Harrison, Frederic, 81
Hastings, Warren, 102
Haves and Have-nots, 249
Head Rents, Relative insignificance of, 23
Hegel, G. W. F., 219, 223
High Church party, 62
Historical: Method in Economics, 39
  Development of Private Property, 39
  Basis of Socialism, 46

Historical *(Continued)*
  "Historical Basis of Socialism"
    (Hyndman's work), 47
"History": "Of Agriculture and
    Prices," 53
  "Of the 18th Century," 54
  "Of Private Bill Legislation,"
    60
  "Of the Reform Bill," 52
Hobbes, Thomas, 216
Hobhouse, Lord, 231, 235
Hobhouse, Sir John Cam, 98
Homestead Law, 173
Hospital, The, 36
House of Commons, 243
  Lords, Abolition of, 229
Household Suffrage, 55
Huddersfield, 70
Human Life, Disregard of
    Capital for, 199
Hume, David, 60, 218
Huxley, Professor, 81
Hyndman, H. M., 47, 228
Hypocrisy, 20, 215

Ibsen, Henrik, 183
Icaria, 48
Idleness, Association of prosperity
    with, 20
Idlers: their fate under Socialism,
    205
Illth, 37
Illusions, Economic, 218
Immigration, Pauper, 171-2
Improvements in Production, 22
  Effect of unforeseen, 24
Incentive to Labor: Under
    Socialism, 205
  Under Leasehold system, 230
Income Tax, 178, 204, 225
  An instrument of expropriation,
    236
  "Rent of ability" recoverable
    by, 243
Independent Weavers, Transfor-
    mation of the, 86
India, Conquest of, under Clive
    and Warren Hastings, 88,
    102
Indifference, Law of, 27
Individualism: Outbreak of, 59
  Abandonment of, 81
  The Change of Socialism
    from, 188
  Confusedly opposed to Social-
    ism, 134
  Its moralization, 136, 142
  Anti-Social manifestation, 144
  Protestant form of, 157
  Abolished in production, 159
Industrial Organization, Centrali-
    zation of, 199-200, 243
Industrial Remuneration Confer-
    ence, 81

Industrial Revolution, 53-5, 64,
    84, 187, 215
  Attitudes of parties during, 253
Industrialism, Evil effects of, 97
Industry, Under Socialism, 187
  Nationalization of, 67
  As virtue or vice, 147-9
  Disgraceful for women, 149
  *La grande industrie,* 249
Inequality, 16
  Mischief of, 38
  Sense of it lost in contempla-
    tion of equality before God,
    43
Inferior soils, Resort to, 16
Ingram, J. K., 113
Injustices produced by private
    appropriation of land, 20
Insanity, Definition of, 136, 139
Inspection of Industry, 67
Institutions, History of, 143
Insurance, National, 42
  Municipal, 70
Insurrectionism, 224, 236
Intellectual Revolt, The, 248
Interest:, 35
  Fall in the current rate often
    mistaken for a tendency in
    Interest to disappear, 35
  Mr. Goschen's operation for se-
    curing to the community
    the advantage of the fall in
    the current rate, 35
  A tribute, 146, 158
Interest, Class, 143
International morality in the
    Middle Ages, 214
International Trade the dominant
    factor in foreign policy, 103,
    243
Invention, Consequences of, 199
Inventor, The first, 22
Iron Industry, 88

Jevons, W. Stanley, 219
Joint Stock Companies:
  Development of, 67, 111
  Not objects of public sympathy,
    188
Joseph the Second, 51

Kaye of Bury, 87
Kingsley, Charles, 62, 64, 112
Kitchens: Separate, 168
  Public, 183
Kropotkin, Peter, 91, 216

Labor: Mouth honor to, 20
  In the market as a commodity,
    24
  Displaced by machinery, 92
  Fruits of, 144
  Municipal organization of, 190,
    235

Labor (*Continued*)
  Labor colonies, 200
  Beginning of State organization
    of, 235
Laborer and Employee (See
    also Proletarian), 188
*Laisser-faire*, 58, 60, 62, 63, 77,
    98, 216
Lancashire, Old, 85
  Expansion of, 95
  Weavers' grievances, 105
Land, Rent of, 17–8
  Point at which it becomes a
    close monopoly, 22
  Powers of the County Councils
    to hold, 189
  Nationalization of, 73, 228
Landlord, what he costs, 31
Landed Interest, Its policy,
    249
Lassalle, Ferdinand, 85, 219
Law of Indifference, 27–8
Rent (See also Rent), 17, 81,
    218
"Leaseholds Enfranchisement,"
    76, 234
Leaseholds: Origin of, 23
  Confiscation at expiry of, 230
Lecky, W. J., 55, 102, 105
Leclaire and Godin, Experiments
    of, 206
Leeds, 54, 60, 70
Legislation: Breakdown of
    medieval, 216
  (See also Factory Legislation)
Levelling-down action of Private
    Property, 29
Levi, Leone, 81
Liberal and Radical Union in
    favor of County Councils
    holding land, 72, 189
Libraries, Public, 183
Liberal Party, Its Policy on
    Socialism, 254–7
Liberty and Equality, 80, 214
Liberty and Property Defence
    League, 72
Lincoln, Abraham: The moral of
    his assassination, 108
Liverpool, Growth of, 54
Lloyd, Henry D., on "Lords of
    Industry," 117
Local: Improvement Acts, 64
  Self-Government, 229
  Government Boards dealings
    with the unemployed, 234
  Government Board of the
    future, 243
Lodging Houses, Municipal, 73
London: Facts concerning, 243
  The County Council, 243
  Extraordinary proportions
    reached by Economic Rent
    in, 230

Liberal and Radical Union, 72,
    189
London and South Western
    Railway Shareholders, 111
"Looking Backwards," 198
Louis XVI, 84
Lying, As vice or virtue, 148

Machinery: Shoemaking by, 85
  Agriculture by, 92
  Displacement of hand labor by,
    92
  Progress of, 189, 199
  Substitution for hand labor in
    disagreeable employments,
    198
  Chimney sweeping by, 199
Maine, Sir Henry, 49, 82
Malthus, Rev. T. R., 53, 188, 219
Man as producer and exchanger,
    28
"Man *versus* the State," 72
Management, Profits of industrial,
    239
Managers, Qualifications and
    present value of industrial,
    239-43
Manchester, 54, 60, 70
Manchester School, 106, 226
  Its Advocacy of Protection,
    236
Manners, Lady Janette on "Are
    Rich Landowners Idle?",
    151
Manorial Rights, 53, 60
Manors, 16, 53, 60
Marginal Utility (See Final
    Utility)
Margin of Cultivation, 17, 20
  Obligation of private com-
    petitors to charge the full
    cost of production at, 239-41
Markets: Effect on rent of
    proximity to, 17
  The fight for foreign, 106, 243
Marriage, Contract of, 178
Marshall, Alfred: Definition of
    rent, 18
Marx, Karl, 58, 219, 228
Matthew, Guild of St., 62
Maurice, F. Denison, 62, 64, 112
Meliorism, 43
Men, Traffic in, 24
Mercantile System, 60
Method of criticism on Moral
    Basis, 133
Metoeci in Athens, 172
Middle Ages, Social organization
    in the, 213
Middle Class: Its callousness, 105
  Its moral ideas, 149-52
  Its misunderstandings of
    Socialism, 220
  Its dread of mob violence, 235

Militant organization of the working class forcible revolution, 244, 248
Militarism and immigration, 172
Military Service, 180
Empires of the Continent, 172
Mill, James, 49, 62
Mill, John Stuart, 18, 52, 62, 64, 76, 79, 80, 228
Mills, 60
Milk Exchange of New York, 124
Milton, John, Proposal as to schools, 183
Mines: Their horrors before legislation initiated by Lord Ashley, 97
Nationalization of, 204
Mines Regulation Acts, 64
Minor poetry, Socialist provision for the publication of, 196
Mirabeau, 88
Missionaries, 244
Mistakes exposed by Socialism:
That Society is no more than the sum of its units, 17, 77
That Private Property encourages industry, 21
That Private Property establishes healthy incentive, 21
That Private Property distributes wealth according to exertion, 21
That Rent does not enter into price, 31
That Exchange Value is a measure of true wealth, 37
That "the poor ye shall have always with you," 44
That riots, regicide, and bloodshed make Revolutions, 84, 224
Mob Violence, middle-class dread of, 235
Molesworth, W. N., 52
Money, Function of, 26
Monopolies, 32
And Democracy, 125
Necessity for protecting the Postmaster's, 226
Moral Basis of Socialism, 131
Habits and their origin, 137
Education of the Individual, 142
And of Society, 158
Moralists, Foolish, 21
Morality, 132
Relativity of, 134
Recognizable on in Society, 136
Conventional, 137, 139, 146, 149
Natural, 141, 151
Practical, 143

Class, 20, 44, 149, 151, 152, 215
Elementary conditions of, 148
Developed conditions of, 158-9
Socialist, 159
Medieval, 213-4
Elizabethan, 214
"Morals and Health Act," (1802), 64
More, Sir Thomas, 216
Morley, Right Hon. John, 72, 244, 257, 258
Motors, Influence of new, 54
Municipal: Corporations Act, 55
Action, 70
Socialism, 72, 234
Debt, 70
Development, 75
Prestige of municipal employment, 238
Municipalities, Growth of, 54, 55, 68, 69, 70, 72
(See also County Councils)

Nabob, The appearance in English social life of the, 54
Napoleon: "The career is open to the talented," 22
"A nation of shopkeepers," 102
Nasmyth, James, invents the steam-hammer, 88
National Insurance, 42
National Liberal Federation, 72
"National Review, The," 151
Nationalization of Rent:, 42, 72
Its results if unaccompanied by Socialist organization of labor, 224
Inter-municipal rent, 243
Rent of ability, 240-1
(See also Progress and Poverty.)
Nature: Caprices of, 16-21
"Red in tooth and claw," 43
Unmorality of, 44
Newcommen, Thomas, 54
Newspapers under Socialism, 196
New Harmony, 167
New Motors, Influence of, 54
New River Company, 171
New York Legislature—Committee on Trusts, 58
Nexus, The social, 51, 53, 77

Oastler, Richard, 100
O'Connor, Fergus, 228
Oldest Families—Tradition of their superiority, 20
Oldham, 70
Olivier, Sydney, 131
Omnipotence and Benevolence, The dilemma of, 43
Optimism: rebuked by Science, 43

Optimism (*Continued*)
  The individualist economist
    and their, 218
Organism, The Social, 77
Outlook, The political, 247
Over-population, 36
Owen, Robert, 63, 112, 167, 234

Painters, Gains of fashionable,
    240
Paley, Rev. William, 62
Palmerston, Chinese policy of
    Lord, 106
*Panem et Circenses*, 231
Parasitism, Economic, 147
Parliaments, Annual, 229
Parks, Public, 167
Parties, State and fundamental
    differences of, 252-3
Patent Rights, 166, 181
Patronage in the public service,
    223
  Effect of appointment by, 224
Pauper Labor, How to deal with,
    191
Payment of representatives, 229
Peasant Proprietorship, 76
Period of Anarchy, 57
Perpetual pension, Privately ap-
    propriated Rent is of the
    nature of a, 17
Pessimism, 43, 266
Peterloo, 55
Philanthropy, Futility of, 225
"Philosophic Radicalism," 63
Physical force, 187, 224, 247
  Advocated by Lord Bramwell,
    235
Physicians, Gains of fashionable,
    240
Piracy and the Slave Trade in the
    16th century, 214
Pitt, William, His motives, 103
Plato, 153
Plener, E. von, 100
Plebeians in ancient Rome, 172
Police: Conduct of Socialists
    charged upon by the, 139
  Recent action of the ex-Chief
    Commissioner of, 234
Political: Tendencies, 73, 248
  Reform, 76, 255
  "Political Science Quarterly,"
    48, 112
  Economy (See Political
    Economy)
Political Economy:, 16
  Basis of Socialism in, 15
  Definition of Rent in treatises,
    17
  Theory apparently contradicted
    by history, 39
  Untrustworthiness of abstract,
    39

Its guns turned against Private
  Property, 44
Old school and new, 44
Rise of modern, 63, 216
Perceived to be a *reductio
  ad absurdum* of Private
  Property, 219
Present political parties and,
  253, 254
Poor Law: A Socialist institution
  degraded, 157
  Reform, 75
  The old and the new, 225
Population: Increase and its
  effects, 20, 32, 219
  Its control by public opinion,
    233
  (See also Overpopulation)
Post Office: A Socialistic institu-
  tion, 180
  Socialization of the postal sys-
    tem, 190
  Economy of collectivist
    charges exemplified by, 226
Press: Its liberty after the social-
  ization of printing, 196
  Clamor for bloodshed from the
    newspapers of the proprie-
    tary class, 235
Preston, 177
Prices cannot be raised to com-
  pensate diminished profits,
    238
Printing, Socialization of, 196
Private Property: Beginning of,
  16
  Its levelling-down action, 31
  Injustice of, 38
  Not now practicable in its
    integrity, 38
  Its abrogation conceived as an
    attempt to empower every-
    one to rob everyone else,
    42
  Its revenue distinguished from
    earnings, 42
  Composition of incomes
    derived from, 42
  Institution of, 144
  Conditions of its possibility,
    144
  Effect on sex relations, 152
  Idea of, 152
  Rights of, 188
  Cheapens the laborer, 240
  Tends to make the majority
    mere beasts of burden,
    241
  Process of extinction of,
    243
  The State and, 254
  (See also Property)
Private Enterprise compared
  with Public, 226

Produce: Unjust division resulting from private appropriation of land, 20
Production: Improvements in, 22
  Effect of unforeseen improvements in, 23
  Conditions of production and exchange, 28
  Associated, 167, 182
Profit:, 22, 29
  Sweater's, 238
  Most important form of "Rent of Ability," 240
  Effect of calculating it in net social welfare instead of individual pecuniary gain, 243
  "Profit Sharing," 205
Programme of Social Democracy, 244
Progress: Conditions of, 132
  Rate of in politics, industry, and thought, 249
"Progress and Poverty," 174, 218, 228, 231, 260
"Progress of Socialism," 66
Proletarian: The first, 21
  Predicament of landless, 23
  End of his absorption by the as tenant, 24
  Sold into bondage, 24
  Operation of the law of value on his position as a vendor of labor, 32
  How the Democratic State will deal with him, 230
  (See also Proletariat)
Proletariat: Origin of the, 21
  Exploitation of, 36
  Physical degradation of, 97
  Type of, 146
  Morals of, 153-4
  So-called "intellectual," 241
  (See also Proletarian)
Property: Under Socialism, 165
  Definition and economic analysis of, 166
  (See also Private Property)
Prosperity, Association of idleness with, 20
Prostitutes, their making, 154
Protection: Decay of, 105
  In the Middle Ages, 214
  Advocated by the Manchester School, 236
Proudhon, P. J., 219
Public Health Acts, 64
  Opinion, 244
Purchasing Power—Pernicious effect of its unequal distribution, 39

Quit Rents, 23

Radicalism: Philosophic, 63
  The modern Radical Programme, 73
  Ordinary destructive variety, 223
  Permeation of Socialism, 261
  Absorption of, 265
  The land question and, 261
Railways: Requisites for making them under Capitalism, 33
  Development of, 107
  Socialization of, 190
Raphael's pictures, 173
Ratepayer, How Socialism will first affect the, 238
Rates, Growth of, 70
Reactionary Legislation, Danger of, 129
Reform Bills, 55-7, 225-6
Regicide: Its victims, 108
  Its futility, 187
Registration, Anomalous conditions of voters, 229
Regulation of Industry:
  Mediaeval, 59, 213-4
  Modern (See Factory Legislation)
Rent: Recognized and paid by worker to drone, 17
  Definitions of economic rent by standard economists, 17-8
  Point at which rent ceases to be strictly "economic rent," 23
  Enters into price of all commodities except those produced at margin of cultivation, 31
  Relation to cost of production, 31
  Nationalization of, 42, 72, 230
  Is common wealth, not individually earned, 42
  Moral aspects of, 144-52, 157
  Case of Birmingham and Warwick, 170
  Law of, 218
  Illustration of economic rent, 220
  Urban, 230
  Effect of municipal Socialism on, 239
  How County Councils can manipulate, 240
  Nationalization intermunicipal, 243
  Effect of Free Trade on agriculture, 254
  Rent of Ability, 22, 238
  Industrial profit the most important form of, 240
  Raised by Private Property, 240

Rent (*Continued*)
  May become negative, 241
Republicanism: Disappearance of
  militant Republicanism in
  England, 248
Residuum: Genesis of the, 154-6
  Its appearance of public hos-
  pitality, 157
Respectability, Falsehood of cur-
  rent, 44
Reward of Abstinence, 35
  Of effort in the cause of
  Socialism, 184
Revolt, The Intellectual, 63
Revolution: Middle class notions
  of, 84
  Socialist attempt to organize
  militant, 244
Ricardo, David, 18, 62, 219
Riches are not Wealth, 37
Rights of Man, Declaring the,
  244
Rings, Growth of capitalist, 32,
  116, 174, 247
Ritchie, Right Hon. C. T., 190
Ritchie, D. G., 77
Rochdale Pioneers, 112, 171
Roebuck, J. A., 62
Rogers, Professor Thorold E., 53
Rousseau, J. J., 62
Rural economy in 1750, 53
Ruskin, John, 64
Russell, Lord John, announces
  finality, 225
Russia's industrial competition in
  the world market, 228
Rutland, Duchess of, on the hard
  work of country gentlemen,
  151
Ryot, Suppression of Indian, 156

S. D. F. (Social Democratic
  Federation), 228
Sadler, Michael Thomas, 100
Salisbury, Rt. Hon. the Marquess
  of, 177
Satan, His moral activity, 147
  Rehabilitation of, 157
"Saul": Optimism as expressed
  in Robert Browning's poem,
  43
Saving: Capital the result of,
  33-5
  Savings of communities and of
  individuals, 170
Schools as they should be, 182
Scott, Sir Walter, Political types
  in "Rob Roy," 102
Secretan, Eugene, 118
Seeley, J. R., 253
Self, Extension of, 141-2
Self-defence, Origin of the Noble
  Art, 139
"Self-help," 38, 226

Seligman, E. R. A., 112
Servants, Domestic, 153, 231
Servantgalism an Effect of
  Capitalism, 153
Services, Property in, 178
Settlement, Law of, 53
Seven Years' War, The, 88
Sewer Cleaning under Socialism,
  198
Shaftesbury, Lord, 100
Shaftesbury Avenue, Land near,
  171
Shakespere, Suggested Duke of,
  181
Shaw, G. Bernard, 15, 213
Shelley, P. B., 139
Shoemaking by hand, 86
  By machinery, 90
Shopkeeping, Joint-Stock, 111
Sidgwick, Henry, 18, 80, 178
Sidmouth, Lord, 55
Six Acts, The, 55
"Six Centuries of Work and
  Wages," 53
Slave Trade, The, 214
Slavery, The White, 58
Slaves Released when not worth
  keeping, 32
Smiles, Samuel, 22
Smith, Adam, 53, 60
Societies: Failure of previous
  attempts to establish true,
  38
  Societies and Civilizations, 39
  (See also Society)
Society: Hypothesis that it is no
  more than the sum of its
  unit, 17, 77
  The Matrix of Morality, 136
  Evolution of Primitive, 136,
  138, 141-3, 154-6
  Industrial, 144
  Parasitic, 147-9
  Fashionable, 149
Soils, Resort to Inferior, 17
Somers, Robert, 113
Social: Utility Divorced from
  Exchange value, 37
  Character of Social Change,
  51-2
  Evolution, 52, 68, 79
  "Social Statics," 58, 81
  Health, 77
  Organization, 79, 187
  Instinct, 141, 151
  Social Democratic Federation,
  228
Socialism, 16, 40, 180, 220, 224,
  244, 254, 258-60
  Economic basis of, 15
  Bearing of Economic Analysis
  of Individualism on, 40
  Substitutes Meliorism for
  Pessimism, 43, 266

Historic Aspect, 46
"Socialism in England," 47
Change in, 47, 165
Early Utopian, 47, 51, 165, 187, 216, 221
Industrial Aspect, 84
The Capitalist and, 126, 128
Moral Aspect, 131
Its Genesis, 134
New Conception of, 165
Property under, 165
Definition of pure, 180
Industry under, 187
Change from Individualism to, 188, 213
Local machinery of, 189, 229
Dirty work under, 198
Transition to, 213
Practical difficulties of, 220
Honesty of, 221
Must be introduced gradually, 224
Solution of the Compensation difficulty, 235-6
Effect on Rent, 239
Friction caused by introduction of, 239
Outlook toward, 247
Prince Bismarck's view of, 257
The Liberal Party and, 257
True and False, 258-9
Two views of the future of, 260
Practical politicians and, 263
(See also the Index Generally)
Socialist Politics, 72
Programme, 73
Formation of party, 264
Socialist and the police, 139
Early (See Utopian Socialism)
The mot d'ordre for, 190
Social Democrats fall into line as a political party, 229
The Radical Press and, 260
Parliament and, 263
Future leader for, 265
Spencer, Herbert, 58, 64, 72, 86, 133, 216, 228
St. Matthew, Guild of, 62
Standard Oil Trust, 121
"Star, The," 73
State: Social Democratic, 16
Functions under Socialism, 204
Corruption of the, 221
Whig conception of the, 221
Conception of the perfect, 223
Decentralization in the Social Democratic, 229
Private Property and the, 253
Attitude of parties toward the, 253
Idea and content of the, 254
The working-class and the, 254
Statistics and Statisticians, 234

Steam applied to cotton spinning, 87
Stuart, Professor James, 73
Subletting of Tenant Right, 20
Subsistence Wages, Rationale of, 33
Sunday: Hypocrisis of church-going, 20
The English, 182
Sunderland, 70
Supply and Demand: Action of, 23, 240
Value decreases with Supply, 26
Final effect on wage-labor, 33, 36
Sweating, How to defeat, 235
Sweeping Chimneys: Replacing of boy labor by machinery in, 199
Syndicate of Copper Corners, 119
Synthesis: The old, 52, 215
The new, 76

Talent, Career open to, 22
Taxation: Reform, 73
Of ground values, 230
Novel character of recent demands for, 231
Telegraphs, Socialization of, 190
Ten Hours' Bill, The, 100
Tenant Rights: Perpetual, 17, 20, 21
Replaced by finite leases, 23
Tennyson, Alfred, 98
Test and Corporation Acts repealed, 55
Theatres, Communal, 184
Tocqueville, A. C. H. C. de, 49
Tonquin, French policy in, 107
Tory of fifty years ago, 252-3
Absorption of the party, 253
"Total Utility," 28
Toynbee, Arnold, 54
Trade: Secrets of, 32
Discredit and rehabilitation of as a pursuit for the nobility and gentry, 149
Trade Unions, 73, 181, 226
Wages in, 193
Royal Commission (1869), 226
Trafalgar Square: The police in, 139, 235
The Fountains in, 148
Traffic in Men, 24
Tramways, Socialization of, 69, 189
Transition to Social Democracy, 213
Truck Acts, 64
Trusts, 32, 189, 194, 247
Tucker, Benjamin R., 216

Turgot, A. R. J., 218
Two-man power more than
    double One-man power, 17

Unemployed: Their existence a
    proof that the labor they
    could replace has no ex-
    change value, 189
    Social pressure created by the,
    231
United States: Results of
    Individualism plus political
    liberty in the, 40
    Declaration of Independence,
    88
    Growth of monopoly in the,
    111
    Extent to which monopoly has
    gone in the, 116-7
Unskilled Labor, Fate of, 154
Unsocialism, 16
Utilitarian questioning and
    scientific answering, 43
    The Utilitarians, 62
Utility: Its relation to Value, 26
    "Total Utility," "Marginal,"
    or "Final Utility," 27-8
    Divorced from Exchange Value,
    37
Utopian Socialism, 47, 51, 165,
    187, 216, 221

Valjean, Jean, 139
Value in Exchange, 26
    Not explained by the money
    mechanism, 26
    Man's control over it consists in
    his power of regulating
    supply, 31
    Divorced from social utility, 37
    Theory of, 218-9
Vestrydom congenial to British
    mind, 244
Villiers, C. P., 62
Virtues conditioned by social
    evolution, 138, 139-47
Voluntary Associations: Their
    legal position under
    Socialism, 171
Von Plener, E., 58

Wages, 32
    Subsistence level, 33
    Adjustment, 201

Rise after 1840, 226
Apparently raised by Trade
    Unions, 226
Competitions wages, 236
Socialistic wages, 200, 236-8
Walford's Insurance Cyclopædia;
    70
Walker, F. A., 18
Wallas, Graham, 165
Walpole, Sir Robert, 103
Warren, Sir Charles, 234
Wars for foreign markets, 106,
    243-4
Warwick compared with
    Birmingham, 170
Waterloo Bridge, Socialization of,
    182
Waterworks, Socialization of, 70,
    190
Watt, James, 54
Watts, Isaac, on the cotton
    manufacture, 96
Wealth: Divorced from Exchange
    Value, 37
    Distinguished from "Illth," 37
    "Wealth of Nations," 53
Weaver, extirpation of the
    handloom, 87, 103-5
Webb, Sidney, 46, 47, 138, 247
Westminster, Duke of, 233
Whig Philosophy, 221
    Economics, 221
    Disappearance of the, 250
    The Whig of fifty years ago,
    250-52
White Slavery, 58, 64
"White Terror, The," 55
Whitman, Walt, 130
Wicksteed, P. H., 219
William the Silent, Assassination
    of, 108
Women: Effect of Property
    System on, 149-52
    Outlawry of, 229
    Economic independence of,
    244
Worker and Drone, 18
Working class: Militant
    organization of, 245
    The State and the, 254
    Political superstition of the,
    258

Zeitgeist, Effect of the, 68